Praise for
Blaze of Light

"The Medal of Honor Society is comprised of a highly elite group of American heroes. What Gary Beikirch did to receive his medal is unforgettable—and the story of what he overcame afterward is as big and moving as they come."

—GARY SINISE, Oscar®-nominated actor

"From the windblast of landing choppers to the sensory assault of close-quarters battle, *Blaze of Light* put me right in the middle of the steaming jungles of Vietnam. Gary Beikirch was grievously wounded and facing a ruthless enemy, and his selfless choices made him the rarest of war heroes—one whose valor is measured not in lives taken but in lives saved."

—LYNN VINCENT, *New York Times* best-selling author of *Indianapolis*

"You will be blessed by this story of amazing courage and selflessness. What happened on April 1, 1970, at Camp Dak Seang in the Kontum Province of South Vietnam forever changed the life of Gary Beikirch. He is a true American hero—a man of humility, faith, and servant leadership. This story is so powerful it could change your life."

—COLONEL JIM COY (RET.), 3rd SFG, Persian Gulf War

"Those who have experienced battle say time expands. Seconds feel like minutes, and minutes and hours stretch into virtual time warps. Marcus Brotherton successfully illustrates such perception of time in his telling of Gary Beikirch's harrowing story. Marcus propelled me into the darkness of impending doom with speed and precision while casting light on the humanity and bravery of the characters who inhabit the pages I blew through. This book left me thoroughly inspired and honored to have 'met' yet another hero who earned the Medal of Honor."

—ERIC BLEHM, *New York Times* best-selling author of *Fearless, Legend,* and *The Only Thing Worth Dying For*

"I was on the Nixon White House staff while Gary Beikirch was serving in Vietnam's jungles. As the White House looked at the mega-issues of the war, we too easily lost sight of the incredible micro-moments of heroism displayed by Gary and others, which are so skillfully described by Marcus Brotherton. Marcus shows not only the intensity of the war in the compound where Gary fought but also the pathos in the soul of the warrior. This book sheds needed light in an age when many are trapped in the darkness of PTSD."

—WALLACE HENLEY, former White House and congressional aide and coauthor of *God and Churchill,* with Sir Winston Churchill's great-grandson Jonathan Sandys

BLAZE
of LIGHT

COURAGE FOR BATTLE, FAITH FOR CRISIS

BLAZE
of LIGHT

THE INSPIRING TRUE STORY OF GREEN BERET MEDIC
GARY BEIKIRCH, MEDAL OF HONOR RECIPIENT

MARCUS
BROTHERTON

WATERBROOK

Hardcover ISBN 978-0-525-65378-3
eBook ISBN 978-0-525-65379-0

Copyright © 2020 by Marcus Brotherton

Cover design by Kristopher K. Orr; cover photography by Getty Images, Picavet (sunset), Alamy, Aviation Visuals (helicopter)

Published in the United States by WaterBrook, an imprint of Random House, a division of Penguin Random House LLC.

WATERBROOK® and its deer colophon are registered trademarks of Penguin Random House LLC.

Library of Congress Cataloging-in-Publication Data
Names: Brotherton, Marcus, author.
Title: Blaze of light : the inspiring true story of Green Beret medic Gary Beikirch, Medal of Honor recipient / by Marcus Brotherton.
Description: First edition. | Colorado Springs : WaterBrook, an imprint of Random House, 2020.
Identifiers: LCCN 2019027340 | ISBN 9780525653783 (hardcover) | ISBN 9780525653790 (ebook)
Subjects: LCSH: Beikirch, Gary B. (Gary Burnell), 1947- | United States. Army. Special Forces—Biography. | Medal of Honor—Biography. | Medical personnel—United States—Biography. | Vietnam War, 1961-1975—Medical care—United States. | Christian biography—United States.
Classification: LCC U53.B378 A3 2020 | DDC 959.704/37 [B]—dc23
LC record available at https://lccn.loc.gov/2019027340

Printed in the United States of America
2020—First Edition

10 9 8 7 6 5 4 3 2 1

SPECIAL SALES
Most WaterBrook books are available at special quantity discounts when purchased in bulk by corporations, organizations, and special-interest groups. Custom imprinting or excerpting can also be done to fit special needs. For information, please email specialmarketscms@penguinrandomhouse.com.

For anyone who's ever fought through a battle
or sheltered in a cave

Contents

Contents

PART I

The War

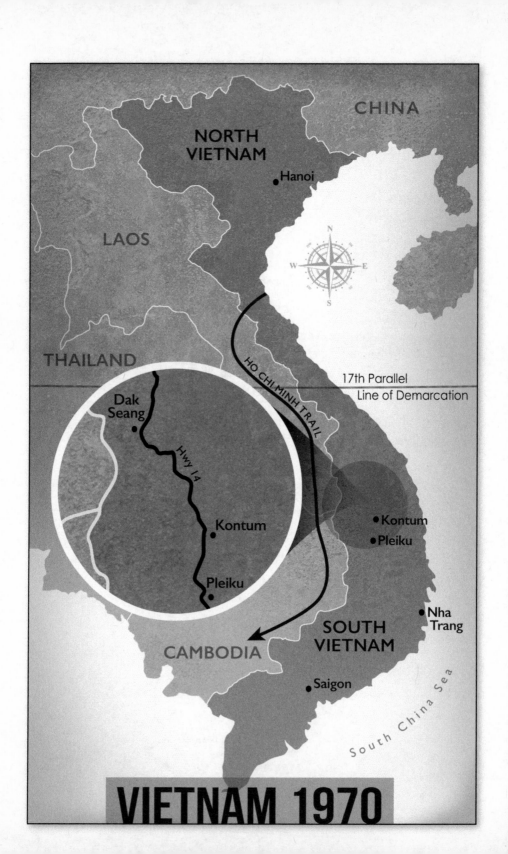

CHINA

NORTH
VIETNAM

• Hanoi

LAOS

THAILAND

HO CHI MINH TRAIL

17th Parallel
Line of Demarcation

Dak
Seang

Hwy 14

Kontum

Pleiku

Kontum
Pleiku

Nha
Trang

CAMBODIA

SOUTH
VIETNAM

Saigon

South China Sea

VIETNAM 1970

Prologue

In the haze before sunset, on the first day of the siege, an enemy rocket destroyed the last building still standing in the village of Dak Seang. He saw it explode in a chaos of splinters and nails while bullets whizzed overhead and mortars from the North Vietnamese Army (NVA) shook the ground. The smell of sulfur and burning bodies filled the air. Still, he knew the assault wasn't over yet.

It was April 1, 1970. Army Green Beret medic Gary Beikirch, age twenty-two, lay in a two-foot-deep bomb crater on a stretcher, paralyzed from the waist down, watching the battle continue to rage while he drifted in and out of consciousness. Blood seeped from three wounds in his stomach and back. He'd done all he could to help, even after being paralyzed. He'd cared for the wounded until he collapsed. In one hand he still clutched a short CAR-15 snub-nose assault rifle, a protector of the innocent lives in his charge. But now even the strength to keep his eyes open was nearly gone.

Breathing hard next to him, dressed in baggy jungle fatigues, a T-shirt, and unlaced boots, lay a young Montagnard medical assistant named Tot. He held an old Korean-era M2 carbine, but with his bandolier of ammo spent, the only bullets left were in his magazine. This was his village, located in the Central

Highlands region of Vietnam, about twelve kilometers from the Ho Chi Minh Trail.

To Gary's other side lay another Green Beret—one of the best-trained specialists in the military. Short, muscular, chewing the stump of an unlit cigar, Dizzine was his last name. Everybody called him Dizzy. He had his communications radio pressed against his ear so he could discern the commands through the static. He was nearly out of ammo too.

The three men saw silhouettes in the distance. NVA troops were already inside the wire. Running. Shooting. The murk of smoke and gunpowder in the air made visibility tricky. Two soldiers emerged, sprinting toward the crater. At first, it was hard to tell whose side they were on. They charged closer. Gary guessed what Dizzy and Tot were thinking: *Make sure of your target. Be accurate. Don't go crazy.* They spotted black and green pajamas. Pith helmets. Tot took down the first. Dizzy fired a short burst from his M16 and leveled the second.

"Chopper's coming," Dizzy said. "Get him ready."

Tot glanced at Gary. "*Bac Si* [the Vietnamese word for "doctor"], you must go now."

Gary raised his hand in protest, then gave a slight nod.

American fighter jets streaked overhead and unleashed rockets and bombs. Gunships—aircraft that provide support for ground troops—rained machine-gun fire. As a last resort to prevent the Special Forces camp from being overrun, the Green Berets had directed air support to fire directly onto their position. But the plan to combat the assault wasn't working.

Earlier in secret, at dawn on the same day, some ten thousand NVA soldiers had encircled the camp. The enemy barrage had begun in darkness. Hours of incessant shelling had destroyed every big gun that protected Dak Seang, knocked out the Special Forces observation tower and antennae, ruined the generator houses, and now hit and flattened every building above ground. After five hours NVA had started infiltrating the camp from hidden underground tunnels. Simultaneously, above ground, multiple groups of enemy soldiers led charge after charge. Tied together two by two at the wrist, each pair of soldiers advanced side by side. They were drugged up and glassy eyed, and when they reached the protective concertina wire surrounding the camp, they detonated explosives strapped to their bodies. Suicide runs. This enabled other NVA soldiers to run over the corpses and up inside the wire.

Gary scanned the skies. Choppers were usually a welcome sight at the camp. They brought in mail and supplies. Medicine. Word from home. But the skies this evening exploded like a hellish version of the Fourth of July.

"There it is." Tot motioned with his chin. "You will make it, Bac Si."

Gary heard the *whoomp, whoomp, whoomp* of a medevac helicopter. He tensed. Because of the heavy enemy fire, the evacuation could last only seconds. Dizzy and Tot grabbed the ends of Gary's stretcher and poised, waiting. The chopper hovered and descended. Gary lifted his head and spotted the faces of the door gunner and pilot. Three more crewmen were inside. He laid down his head and braced himself, anticipating the sprint over rough ground. He heard a *pop, pop, pop* and raised his head again.

The chopper was smoking, leaking fuel, its side riddled with bullet holes. The pilot reversed course and lifted the craft up and out of harm's way, limping toward safety at the next camp a few miles away.

"Don't worry," Dizzy said. "Another will get here."

Gary lifted his free hand from his side. It dripped blood. Although he'd done it earlier, again he took stock of his wounds: Shrapnel in his spine. Small-arms fire through his back and right hip. Either shrapnel or small-arms fire in his abdomen—hard to tell which. Under the makeshift bandage on his belly, his internal organs lay exposed and hung to one side. He closed his eyes. Maybe he drifted into unconsciousness. Maybe not. Half an hour passed. Maybe an hour. He heard shouts. Screams. Explosions. Dizzy firing his rifle. Then Tot's voice again:

"This one's yours, Bac Si. Get ready."

Again Gary heard a *whoomp, whoomp, whoomp*. Again he tensed. Again he lifted his head and spotted the faces of the door gunner and pilot. He lowered his head and braced himself. Then he heard a distinct hiss, felt the thud of two small explosions. Then one huge explosion. His body jolted. Gary lifted his head to look. Flames engulfed the chopper. It plunged to the ground like a rock.

A low groan escaped his lips. All his remaining strength melted away. All reserves of will. He'd lost too much blood. The fighting had proved too desperate. As much as Gary longed for rescue, he didn't want a third chopper even to try. Why risk the lives of another five men?

Two more silhouettes charged through the dusk toward the crater. At thirty meters, one cocked his arm to throw a hand grenade. Frenzied eyes. Sweaty brow. Dizzy aimed and brought him down. Tot wasn't far behind in taking out the second. But their ammo couldn't hold out much longer.

Dizzy's radio crackled. "Support the north wall. Now! Move!" Another breach of defense. More enemy soldiers were overrunning the village. Gary sensed unconsciousness overtaking him again. As the cacophony around him faded, Gary found himself staring far off at the blackened jungle. He wanted to live, but he didn't sense anger anymore. Nor did he feel fear. Death was inevitable. He knew that now. He sensed only sadness, the lament a warrior feels when unable to return to battle. Death beckoned all lives. All Green Berets. All allied Montagnard fighters. All villagers. The defenders' situation was hopeless . . .

And Gary knew he could do nothing more to help.

Heart of a Warrior

Gary Burnell Beikirch (pronounced bye-kirk) didn't realize what a dangerous world he'd been born into on August 29, 1947, particularly when, at just eighteen months of age, he toddled up the stairs of the old Victorian duplex in Rochester, New York, spotted an open window, and leaned out against the screen.

He and his parents lived upstairs, while his aunt and uncle lived downstairs. Mealtimes were often a shared experience, and on this evening, while the grown-ups were engrossed in conversation, Gary had toddled off.

The child stood alone. The wind blew off the shore of nearby Lake Ontario, ruffling his hair. For a moment, the screen held fast while the toddler fingered the clasp that held the screen shut. Directly out the window, more than twenty feet below, lay the marble-hard surface of a blacktopped driveway.

Years later, Gary would wake in the middle of the night, breathless, shocked awake by repeated dreams of falling. In his dreams he fell and fell but never hit the ground. Fears soaked into his dreams like sweat soaked into his sheets. He feared breaking his head open. He feared the look on his parents' faces—anxious, desperate—as they peered over him in a hospital bed, where he lay in critical condition.

The latch opened.

Gary tumbled out the window. The toddler hit the pavement headfirst with a massive thud. He was rushed to the emergency room at Strong Memorial Hospital, where X-rays showed his skull plates cracked in multiple places. The doctors, after closing the gashes in his scalp with more than one hundred stitches, weren't sure he would survive the night. A priest came to administer last rites.

Gary hovered between life and death. Time slowed for Gary's parents, George and Norma, as they hoped and waited, wondering whether Gary would ever heal or be the same. An article in the Rochester *Democrat and Chronicle* (May 5, 1949) moralized, "Like too many youngsters before him, little Gary's curiosity led him to the catch on the screen."

The Beikirchs were a middle-class family. George built carburetors at Rochester Products, a division of General Motors, the plant where most of the town worked. After Gary's fall, George could barely concentrate on his job. On the side he played Triple-A baseball with the Rochester Red Wings, and all the players came by the hospital to sign a baseball for the boy. Norma worked as a homemaker. She spent her days and nights at the hospital, watching over her struggling son.

The parents had little to lean on except the love and support of their extended family and friends. That—and they knew their son had the heart of a fighter. They'd even named him with a future battle in mind, choosing Gary, a Germanic name meaning "spear," sometimes translated as "loyal warrior." They knew their son would be tough.

Another factor came into play during the crisis, although it remained hidden to the family until years later. Gary's mother and father were not churchgoers or part of any faith tradition. Yet every evening, on the other side of Rochester, a ten-year-old girl knelt beside her bed and begged God to spare his life. Gary's cousin Janet had been told the toddler would most likely die, but with all the faith of a child, she vowed to pray for his recovery for however long it took.

Gary's days in the hospital stretched into weeks. Surgery followed surgery. Stitches followed stitches. The doctors were concerned that even if Gary pulled through, he might experience long-term brain damage. Janet kept praying.

The hospital-stay grew expensive and strained the family. To help, Norma went to work on the same carburetor line as her husband. Tragically, her hand caught in a machine and was crushed. There were no disability payments then. Her hand never fully recovered, so when she could work again, she found another job at a clothing store to make ends meet.

Slowly, steadily, against the odds . . . Gary fought his way back to full health. Doctors and therapists examined him and pronounced him cured. Gary's mental astuteness was deemed above average. His motor coordination was found to be excellent.

The pediatricians didn't know exactly what had occurred, why the fractured pieces of Gary's skull had not pierced his brain or caused any lasting damage. They knew only that factors beyond the here and now had played in the boy's recovery.

His parents chalked up this outcome to things that can't be fully explained.

———

Gary's first memory of his father is warm—playing catch together in the backyard. By then the family had moved from the duplex into a home of their own. George didn't want his son playing in the front yard, where a boy might follow a ball into the busy street. So the backyard, with its clipped grass and leafy willow tree, became an idyllic place for Gary to romp with Flash, the family's pet boxer. Here Gary and his dad threw a baseball back and forth, with George stopping every so often to show Gary how to place his fingers on the ball to throw curves and fastballs. George predicted that Gary would become a pitcher one day, and Gary dreamed of the major leagues.

But not every memory is warm. Gary remembers spinning around and around on a high stool at a bar. George had bought Gary a Coke that came with a paper straw in a tall glass of ice. As Gary drank his Coke, he spun the stool. The bartender knew George well and they joked together. At the front of the bar sat an old bowling machine. George handed Gary a stack of nickels and told him to play the machine. Gary slid a heavily weighted disk down the lane at the pins, which disappeared when the disk smashed into them.

When his nickels ran out, Gary went back for more and was surprised to find a woman with long eyelashes sitting next to his dad. George dropped more nickels into the boy's hand and brushed him aside, and Gary went back to the game. But when that stack of nickels ran out, his father and the woman weren't at the bar anymore. The bartender handed Gary more nickels. Gary played for hours until his dad showed up.

The next Saturday they went back to the bar, and a similar string of events occurred. Another tall glass of Coke. Another spinning barstool. Another stack of nickels. Another woman.

When Gary was six, he came home from first grade in the late afternoon as always, but that evening his father didn't come home for supper. At the dinner table, Gary's mom told him they needed to move because Gary's father had sold their house. Gary felt confused. He loved that house, and they'd just finished his upstairs room in knotty pine boards—he loved the smell of that wood.

His father wasn't home the next night either. Or the next. Gary and his mom soon moved in with a friend from work named Helen. The holiday season came, and a family Christmas party was held at the home of Gary's aunt and uncle. His mother had three sisters and one brother, and they and their spouses all gathered for the party, along with Gary's twelve cousins. Gary, playing in a room with all the cousins, was jumping on a pogo stick he'd received as a present. Suddenly, the clatter from the grown-ups' room hushed. Gary's mom appeared in the doorway and told Gary that his father was here and wanted to see him.

Gary followed her into the grown-ups' room. His dad was wearing a suit with a long trench coat. He took off his fedora, picked Gary up, and carried him to a more private room, where he set his son on his knee.

"I need to leave," the father said. "I probably won't see you anymore. But always know that I love you."

He set Gary on his feet, stood, then knelt at the boy's level and gave him a hug. His father led Gary by the hand out to where his cousins played, and then let go of his hand. One of the younger uncles was bouncing on the pogo stick, so Gary's attention was diverted. He doesn't remember his father leaving the party.

Later, the uncle, under the influence of too many drinks, hopped back on the pogo stick in an impromptu contest to see who could jump the farthest. The pogo stick broke. The uncle toppled off and Gary cried.

He tried to gather himself, but he found that his hold over himself had become very slack. The tears flowed far harder than they would have if he'd been merely a boy with a broken Christmas present.

———

For some time, little stability existed in young Gary's life. He and his mother moved constantly, staying for a season here and there with relatives and friends.

When Gary turned eight, his mother asked if he'd like to go to the nearby Seabreeze Amusement Park. His mother's friend Helen planned to drive, and she owned a sporty convertible that Gary always enjoyed riding in. Usually Gary sat alone in the back seat, but that day a man named George Schwartz sat with him. The man seemed kind enough and made an effort to know Gary. Together they went on rides at Seabreeze, threw darts at balloons, and knocked over milk bottles with a ball.

Not long afterward, Gary's mom said that she and Mr. Schwartz were getting married and asked whether Gary would like to have his last name changed to Schwartz. He didn't want to change his name, and he doesn't remember much about his mother's wedding ceremony, only that his cousins found it strange that a boy would attend the wedding of his parent—not many children were doing so in that *Happy Days* era.

Gary developed a liking for George Schwartz as a stepfather. A picture of George and Gary sitting by a hotel pool shows George with his arm around Gary just as if he were his own son. One day Gary's mom asked him if he'd prefer to call his stepfather "Dad." Gary said sure, he could call him "Dad" as easily as he'd been calling him "George." A week or so later, Gary's mom told him that he was going to have a little brother or sister and asked if Gary would like to choose the name. Gary had a buddy from school named Larry, so he chose that name when his new baby brother was born.

The new family—George and Norma Schwartz, Gary, and Larry—soon moved into an apartment in Rochester. Gary started fourth grade and, after a rough game of dodgeball, got into his first fistfight with the local bully. Gary tasted victory, and the bully never bothered him again. The spear was proving fierce.

George Schwartz enlisted in the naval reserve that same year to bring in extra money for the family. He'd served in the Pacific with the navy during World War II and had a photo album that contained pictures of the aftermath of battles on the Pacific islands. Gary pored over the album, horrified. He saw burnt and decapitated bodies, blood, guts—his introduction to the realities of war.

Not long after signing up for the reserve, George left for his annual two-week training. At the airport during boarding, the ramp separated from the plane, and George stepped into the gap, fell forward, and broke his femur. Part of the broken femur rammed upward and pierced his abdomen. He stayed in the hospital a long time and was never right physically after that, always in pain. Even then he worked three jobs—the first as a machinist for Delco, the second at a smaller machine shop, the third at a discount store, where he unloaded trucks. The family hardly ever saw him.

At the start of sixth grade, Gary's family moved again to Rochester's Tenth Ward, which had a reputation as a rough area. They lived in a duplex, part of a subsidized-housing project for veterans. Gary was a good student in sixth and seventh grades, making straight As and throwing himself into school. He took music lessons and played trumpet and French horn. He joined the Cub Scouts. He played baseball, football, and soccer. He was chosen standard bearer for his school, an honor that meant he raised the flag at school each morning and held the flag for assemblies while students recited the Pledge of Allegiance.

Each Wednesday afternoon within the Rochester public school system, students were given the option of leaving school to attend religious education classes at nearby churches. Gary stayed behind in the classroom a few times but discovered that most students went, including many of his friends, who were mostly from Lutheran families. These students weren't particularly religious either, yet most had figured out that the classes meant an easy way out of school for the afternoon. Gary had never been to church. He decided he'd rather get out of school than sit in a nearly empty classroom.

Twenty kids attended his religious education class, and all the students were energetic. Some more than others. After three rowdy classes were held, the religious education teacher decided to kick the rowdiest students out of the group. An elderly woman named Anne Koch offered to help with the rowdy boys so they wouldn't be sent back to school. Gary was in this group, along with four other boys. Mrs. Koch led Gary's group across the street to a house owned by a school family who'd allowed use of their living room. Her hair was beautiful and silvery, her voice peaceful and calm—an educator unlike anyone Gary had ever encountered.

Each Wednesday, Mrs. Koch served the boys snacks—Coke and chips, or milk and cookies—then they simply talked. She allowed them to talk about anything that interested them, no matter the topic. Gary began to look forward to Wednesday afternoons. The other boys must have been as mesmerized because no one ever was disrespectful toward the elderly woman. Her pedagogical method was to win the boys' attention not by lecturing but by listening. Some of the boys started to share deeper things with the group—about their cares and concerns, about arguments their parents or siblings were having, about challenges they faced at school. Mrs. Koch just listened.

One afternoon, when the boys were sitting on the stairs with Mrs. Koch, she spoke to them about a historical figure who could help them see a new way forward in life. She read to them from a little book—a New Testament, she called it—about how God loved the world so much that he allowed this man to die to take away the sins of the world. Fortunately, if anyone believed, the person

13

would have eternal life. She described how God had sent his Son not to judge the world but to save the world. She asked the boys if they wanted to pray.

A few of the boys prayed with Mrs. Koch, and while Gary did not pray, he bowed his head and closed his eyes out of respect. Somehow he sensed it was important.

———

Before he reached ninth grade, Gary had moved eleven times and attended eight schools. Ever a good athlete, he made the varsity soccer team as a freshman and made the all-county team. But he let his grades slip and started acting out, feeling the strain of the constant moves, the family's lack of money, and the grief he still experienced over his biological parents' divorce.

Gary's feelings and rebellious acts escalated. At school, Gary and a friend named Chuck grew angry with a teacher and shoved him. Both boys were expelled. Chuck was sent to military school, but Gary's mother went to the principal to advocate for her son's readmission under the condition that his behavior improve. Gary was allowed back in, and he did shape up, although during nonschool hours he continued to make risky choices.

Gary and his pals hot-wired cars and went for joyrides. They broke into the school and other buildings after hours to explore and goof off, simply because they could. Once, he was arrested and taken back to the house in handcuffs. His parents prepared to move again, but Gary refused, and when they left, he lived with some cousins for the remainder of high school.

Gary wonders today if he always had a bit of a problem with authority since he never wanted to conform to the expectations of others or follow rules. That mind-set didn't help much in school, but it would make him a perfect candidate for Special Forces, where being a strong-willed, determined, out-of-the-box thinker was an asset.

He threw himself into his remaining years of high school. He joined the wrestling and gymnastics clubs. He joined a high school service fraternity and eventually became president. He continued playing varsity soccer. He became president of the varsity club, which was composed of all the varsity athletes in the school.

A cheerleader at Greece Olympia High School caught Gary's eye. She was vibrant and had short-cropped auburn hair. They dated seriously for two years, and Gary thought his future was settled. Other friends their age were marrying right out of high school. The cheerleader was headed to Brockport for college, about half an hour west of town, and Gary decided to go there too. She planned to major in physical education, and Gary figured he'd join the same program.

In September 1965, they entered the university, along with more than nine hundred other freshmen. During an orientation session, the president said to the class of incoming freshmen, "Look to your right. Now look to your left. In six months, one of the three of you will be gone."

That statement made Gary shiver because the draft was underway. If you were eighteen or older and enrolled in university, your status was 2S—meaning you were exempt from the draft. But if you were the same age and not a student, then your status was 1A—eligible for immediate military service. After high school a few of Gary's classmates had enlisted, but Gary felt no inclination toward the military. To him, Vietnam seemed like a faraway place he'd heard about only on TV.

At Thanksgiving, the girlfriend told Gary she wanted to end the relationship. She'd met a guy over the summer at the post office and was interested in dating him. Dazed, Gary wandered downtown to the Stoneridge theater and queued up to see a movie. Friends spotted him, realized something was off, and led him to a nearby restaurant, where he poured out his heart. Although he had encountered challenges in the past, nothing had hit him as hard as this breakup. His goals, his motivation, even his reasons for looking forward to the future had been wiped away. He no longer felt as if he had any reason to be enrolled in university. Except to avoid the draft.

Gary's grades plummeted. He started drinking and cutting classes. Friends dropped in at the bar to make sure he got back to his dorm safely. He finished his freshman year somehow, but his grade point average was dismal. Over the summer he continued drinking and partying.

The following September he returned to the university and felt slightly more invested. He played soccer and mostly managed to stay out of bars. Fall semester finished and spring semester began. Gary and a dormmate named Tom made a bet with some other guys to see which pair of friends could hitchhike the fastest from the university down to Daytona Beach, Florida. Gary and Tom dressed in shorts and T-shirts, walked to the highway early the first morning of spring break, and stuck out their thumbs. The guys hadn't calculated how far away Daytona Beach was (one way is more than eleven hundred miles), but they were determined to win the bet.

Their first hitch went smoothly, and they made it as far as Pennsylvania. On the second ride some Pennsylvania mountain folk took them to the middle of the Poconos. It was nighttime and snow was falling. Gary and Tom shivered along the freeway in their shorts and T-shirts, still holding a cardboard sign that read "Daytona Beach!" Fortunately, two college guys in a Pontiac GTO—also headed to the party at Daytona Beach—picked them up and drove them the remainder of the way.

On the beach, Tom began to violently vomit blood. He was rushed to a hospital emergency room, diagnosed with a perforated ulcer, and informed that a full recovery would take place only with several weeks of complete rest and a change in diet. Gary and Tom vowed to stop drinking so much beer, and Tom dropped out of college so he could recuperate. Gary stayed with him in Florida and quit college too. After a few weeks Tom recovered. They pooled their money, bought a 1955 Chevy hot rod, and cruised home to New York.

Gary knew that beach bums were soon drafted. Now that he was home, he needed a plan. A good friend named Don Jacques had just been dumped by his girlfriend, too, and since Don's family had a legacy with the Marine Corps, he told Gary he was enlisting. Don wanted Gary to join the Marines with him, but Gary thought that all marines were crazy.

"Well, then, what are you going to do?" Don asked Gary one afternoon while sitting at a bar.

Gary thought a moment. He'd recently read a book by Robin Moore titled *The Green Berets,* which would soon be turned into a movie starring John Wayne. Gary had a history of making quick decisions, and to him those Green Berets seemed like a noteworthy bunch of guys. In the book they looked to be doing challenging and adventurous work in the jungles of Vietnam.

"I'm gonna become a Green Beret," Gary said.

He spoke on impulse yet with commitment. Plus, he couldn't wait to wear the uniform. He envisioned walking onto the Brockport campus, strutting his stuff, showing his ex-girlfriend what she'd given up.

Don wished Gary luck. They said their goodbyes and promised to keep in touch. Don was a close friend. Maybe Gary's best friend. A few weeks later, on August 31, 1967, Gary was on a bus headed to Buffalo, ready to make the pledge to join the military.

Don made good on his vow and joined the Marines. He was one of the youngest men ever to graduate from Officer Candidate School and be commissioned in the Marine Corps. Everybody liked Don. He was a good athlete with a stocky build and chiseled good looks. He was soon sent to Vietnam, and in his letters home, he talked about missing his mom and dad, and about genuine friendships with the men he commanded.

In February 1968, Gary received a letter and newspaper clipping from a high school friend. When Gary recalls this today, many decades later, a faraway look still comes across his face and he chokes up. Don had been killed at Khe Sanh.

When Don died, Gary was still working toward becoming a Green Beret. His experiences in Vietnam still lay ahead, and the thought of going to the war in this wild country raised goosebumps. Fighting as a Green Beret in the mountains of Vietnam was for men of renown, Gary thought. Surely not for him. It was for crack troops skilled in the techniques of unconventional warfare. For the soldiers of the Special Forces. No, he didn't want to go to Vietnam. He'd try to get sent somewhere else, even as a Green Beret. Vietnam was only for men of legends.

Vietnam was only for John Wayne.

Death or a Better Man

Gary Beikirch's decision to quit college and enlist in the military might have seemed spontaneous or even rash, yet his breakup with his girlfriend had merely greased the emotional skids, while the conversation with Don Jacques at the bar had simply pushed him to take the plunge. Actually, Gary had thought a lot about the decision in the preceding months.

The seeds had been sown initially when he interacted with demonstrators. College campuses were hotbeds of political activism in the late 1960s, and Gary attended rallies and protests on the campuses of SUNY Brockport and the University of Rochester to talk with the participants, although he seldom came away with any concrete conclusions. He would often ask individual protesters two questions: "How do you know this to be true?" and "Have you been there?" and was continually surprised when protestors stared at him with blank faces and ended the dialogue abruptly. Gary decided that too many folks were merely regurgitating rhetoric they'd heard from others. He wanted to understand the larger picture.

The seeds took root because of the influence of the resident director in Gary's dorm, Ed Matthews, a military man who seemed to possess wisdom that others didn't have or appreciate. A quiet guy, Ed was twenty-six and enrolled in graduate school at Brockport. He never advertised his military service, and Gary knew about it only because one day as he passed Ed's room, the door was open and Gary saw a picture of Ed in uniform. Gary stopped and asked if he could talk for a minute.

"Sure," Ed said. "Come on in."

Ed set aside the book he'd been reading and asked Gary about his plans, his beliefs, and what he considered important in life. As they conversed, Gary noticed that Ed gave him his full attention, never broke eye contact, nodded when appropriate, and encouraged further dialogue. Gary had a lot of questions, and Ed never told him what to do. Gary soon wished he could talk with Ed more often about deeper matters, instead of talking with the bartender at the local tavern as usual.

Ed's final statement burrowed deep into Gary's brain: "The military will either kill you or make you a better man. You have to decide." Ed picked up his book again and began to read, and Gary understood the conversation was over. But for a long time to come, he reflected on the implications of Ed's words.

———

When Gary discussed his plans to enlist with family and friends, the reactions were mixed. After graduation from high school in Rochester, many local youths attended college or worked for Kodak or Rochester Products; this pattern even had a name—"the Rochester rut."

An uncle was surprised that Gary didn't want to find a job, get married, and settle down. Gary said he was searching for what was important in life but didn't think Rochester was the place to find the answer.

Friends furrowed their brows and spoke about the immorality of war, the allegedly unclear reasons America was involved in Vietnam, and the dangers of imperialism and unrestrained capitalism. They tried to debate these issues with Gary, but he steered clear of arguments. He told them that he was joining the military to discover the truth and that they could talk more when he got out. And Gary wasn't interested in fighting in Vietnam—his initial goal simply was to become a Green Beret. He figured he'd serve someplace else anyway, an idea that was not unfounded: at the time, the Special Forces groups were the First Special Forces Group, which operated in Okinawa, the Third Special Forces Group stationed at Fort Bragg, North Carolina, but responsible for actions in Africa, the Fifth Special Forces Group in Vietnam, the Sixth Special Forces Group in the Middle East, the Seventh Special Forces Group at Fort Bragg, which could be sent anywhere needed, the Eighth Special Forces Group in Panama, and the Tenth Special Forces Group in Germany.

Political and socioeconomic opinions weren't big on Gary's list of reasons for enlisting either—at least not any opinions he had formed yet. He understood that since the Truman administration, America had committed its resources to helping non-Communist people become free. Eisenhower and Kennedy and Johnson had agreed with this policy, even though the war in Vietnam had become complicated, with participants and interests sometimes unclear. The motto of the Army Special Forces is the Latin phrase *De oppresso liber,* which means "To free the oppressed." This was part of the reason Gary wanted to be a Green Beret—to provide freedom for anybody who wanted to be free.

Though many of his friends did not agree with his decision to enlist, they threw an awesome going-away party for him.

Downtown at the recruiting station on the corner of Church and Fitzhugh Streets, Gary told the recruiter he wanted to join the Green Berets. The recruiter looked surprised and skeptical and explained that a person could not enlist to become a Green Beret but had to complete a long and arduous journey. First, Gary would need to go through basic training, followed by infantry training. Then Airborne School. Then—and only then—Gary could volunteer for Special Forces.

"It's a difficult process, son," the recruiter said. "Do you think you're good enough?"

Gary responded immediately: "Where do I sign?"

On August 31, 1967, Gary and other recruits boarded a bus for the hour-long ride to Buffalo. After they arrived at the induction center, they were ushered into a room with desks. While waiting, the guys exchanged names and a few details about who they were, why they were there, and what they wanted to do in the military. Some were going into the army, while others had chosen the navy, air force, or marine corps. A few had been drafted. Others had dropped out of college. Some had just graduated from high school. After a couple of hours, an officer came in, ordered the recruits to stand in rows, raise their right hands, and repeat the following oath:

> I, _____, do solemnly swear (or affirm) that I will support and defend
> the Constitution of the United States against all enemies, foreign and
> domestic; that I will bear true faith and allegiance to the same; and that
> I will obey the orders of the President of the United States and the
> orders of the officers appointed over me, according to regulations and
> the Uniform Code of Military Justice. So help me God.

Gary felt staggered by the weight of the commitment. He also felt relieved: at least he wouldn't need to make any more major decisions for the next three years.

At 8:00 p.m., the recruits were loaded onto buses and driven to the airport. A plane flew the army recruits to McGuire Air Force Base in New Jersey. Off the plane, they waited, then were bused to Fort Dix, where they were met immediately by drill instructors (DIs), the men who for the next eight weeks would be their fathers, mothers, teachers, protectors, harassers, and gods.

It was now midnight, but no one dared to close his eyes because of a blur of yelling and barked orders from the DIs. The recruits were herded into Supply to get new army clothing, bedding, and gear; then sent to the barbers to say goodbye to their hair; then routed to the dispensary for a quick physical; then doubletimed to the barracks, where the men stood outside in formation.

"Fall out!" a DI shouted. "Go inside and find a bunk with a footlocker! Make your bed! Put your stuff into the footlocker! Then go to bed!" Every other word was linked to an expletive.

The floors in the barracks were called "bays," and each contained twenty bunkbeds along the walls and down the middle. Gary found an empty bunk on the second bay. It was already 3:30 a.m.

Gary fell into a deep sleep. Not much later, shrill whistles blasted. *Am I dreaming?* Gary wondered. Sticks drummed water buckets. Men were shouting and cursing. Bunks were being tipped over and hitting the floor with a crash. It was 4:30 a.m., and the first night of sleep in the army was officially over.

A few moments later, the recruits were outside, running. *What did I get myself into?* Gary thought. This was his new life for the next eight weeks. Whistles and curses blurred with shouts and sweat. One day turned into the next. Each morning, before entering the mess hall at 5:00 a.m., the recruits needed to climb hand over hand across a horizontal ladder suspended eight feet in the air. When they finished, they ran the gauntlet of other soldiers who pushed, shoved, and tripped them as they ran into the mess hall.

A basic trainee was generally assigned KP (kitchen patrol) once during boot camp. KP lasted an entire day and involved washing dishes, scrubbing pots and pans, cracking dozens of eggs, peeling bags of potatoes, or separating paper trash from edible garbage, which local farmers collected for livestock. During his first week Gary mumbled a complaint under his breath one morning, so his DI decided he needed more character development and assigned Gary an extra day of KP.

His second week, Gary reported to formation with an unpolished belt buckle and was given another day on KP. The third week his boots weren't spit shined enough—the DI couldn't see his reflection. Another day on KP. On and on it went. For the eight weeks he was in basic, Gary was assigned KP nine times.

Whenever he wasn't in the kitchen, Gary was learning how to march, fire a weapon, and polish boots and brass. He ran and climbed and grunted and studied military protocol and fighting tactics. He and his platoon of thirty-nine other soldiers learned to think and act as a team.

As the weeks wore on, they found themselves welded together as a unit, filled with a new sense of pride and accomplishment, and devoted to a cause greater than any one person. They lived out the values of duty, service, and sacrifice.

The young men in his unit didn't seem like the warriors he'd imagined. They were all good guys— earnest, compassionate, and dedicated. One of them, Jim Petersen from Rochester, became a friend. Jim was shorter and muscular, and when other guys dropped out, Jim would rally the rest to press on. Jim and Gary ended up going all the way through Special Forces training together.

Gary also met a guy named Bill Tastle, a tall and studious soldier who wanted to become a medic. Bill wore big glasses with a black plastic frame attached to his head with a band. Years later, Bill would earn his PhD and become a professor at Ithaca College.

There was Bob Link, an inspiring and dedicated recruit who would also become a medic. Later, when the soldiers were sent to Fort Sam Houston, had a day off, and wanted to party, Bob would shake his head, grab the guys and their books, and herd them to a park to study.

Gary's closest friend in basic was Larry Beaver, an American Indian of the Seneca Nation from the Tonawanda, New York, area. Physically fit and ever affable, Larry constantly encouraged his fellow troops. It might be 2:00 a.m. and raining, with all the guys in a field trying to stay warm under half a poncho liner, and Larry would laugh and say, "No problem. Right now I'm tapping into the Indian spirit." If another guy piped up and asked, "Hey, how can I tap into that spirit too?" Larry would shrug and say with a smile, "Sorry. Only for Indians."

Graduation from basic training felt like a big accomplishment to Gary, but he was only getting started in his military journey. As soon as he finished boot camp, he began advanced infantry training (AIT), which ran for another eight weeks at Fort Dix. Each day, for eight to ten hours, the soldiers trained to become experts at using weapons—the M14 rifle, the M60 machine gun, the M79 grenade launcher, the .50 caliber machine gun, the .45 pistol, and more. The men also became skilled at patrolling, ambushes, and defensive maneuvers. They became hardened emotionally and mentally as their bodies were shaped into fighting machines. The early shock that Gary experienced as he learned what a particular weapon could do gradually became simple acceptance, even as his shaking muscles filled out and steadied. Gary had been a physical education major at college and had considered himself in good shape before he began basic. But now he admitted that army training pushed him to a new level of athleticism.

During AIT he befriended Emil Cirone, an Italian with wiry hair who could grow a full beard in a day and a half. Emil came from Buffalo but talked with a New York City accent, almost like a mobster. It was now winter, and they were training outside on field exercises and often sleeping in the woods, where they learned to snap together ponchos to make a shelter half.

One night Emil, Jim Petersen, and Gary shared a shelter on a defensive perimeter. It was too cold to sleep, and from 11:00 p.m. until 4:00 a.m., Emil, Gary, and Jim talked Triple-A baseball—drilling one another in friendly jest about which city had the best players, best pizza, and most snow. Gary noted that Emil interspersed stories about his family, how close they were, how fond he was of them. Despite being transformed into toughened soldiers, the young men held on to their softer sides too.

When AIT finished, the men were sent to jump school at Fort Benning, Georgia. Jump school was unusual because all ranks were together—an officer might be learning to jump alongside a buck private. To the trainers (called Black Hats), everybody was "lower than whale [feces] at the bottom of the ocean"—a colorful description Gary often heard during training.

In jump school, Gary was pushed to even greater physical fitness as he learned the impact of determination and strength of human spirit. The first week was solely a physical training regime that pushed the soldiers to new levels of perseverance. Each morning started with a five-mile run, followed by three hours of physical training: endless chin-ups, sit-ups, push-ups, squats, and the dreaded "dying cockroach" drill, where you lay on your back and slowly extended your legs upward, gradually bringing your hands forward until you grabbed your legs. Then you had to hold this position until the Black Hats let you quit. Doing the dying cockroach meant joints and sinews were pulled in new directions, limbs trembled, and abdominal muscles ached.

More than once Gary felt he simply could not do one more repetition of an exercise. His body was ready to quit. But at those moments he learned to say, *Don't quit. All you need to do is one more.* So he would do one more push-up and then repeat the same mantra: *Don't quit. All you need to do is one more.* Then one more push-up. Repeat the mantra. On and on, all the way to the end.

In the second week of jump school, the vigorous physical training continued. Each morning brought a five-mile run, followed by endless calisthenics. The rest of the time was spent learning the basics of jumping out of an airplane. Hours were spent exiting a mock airplane door on the ground to ensure the soldiers learned the right body position. Without the correct form, the shock of the prop blast upon exiting a plane could spin them around and tangle the parachute suspension lines. Tangled lines often meant a chute wouldn't open properly and could cause a crash.

Additional hours were spent suspended eight feet in the air on a device called the Swing Lander Trainer. Men were swung backward, forward, and side to side, then without warning were dropped to the ground. This way they would learn how to safely land, regardless of which way the wind was blowing.

After mastering the eight-foot trainer, the men were escorted to a thirty-two-foot tower to learn how to overcome the fear of exiting from a greater height. Thirty-two feet didn't sound like much of a height to Gary, but he noticed that many a man, when faced with the prospect of jumping from that height, decided he would rather be part of the ground troops.

Next came jumps from a 250-foot tower. Men were harnessed into riggings and hoisted into the air. Once they were released, a parachute would slow their fall, and the men learned how to steer by pulling on their suspension lines. A number of soldiers washed out at this phase too.

In the third week, the men faced an actual jump. Gary donned his chute and the rest of his gear, cinched tight every strap, lumbered to an old Korean

Conflict–era C-119 aircraft, and waddled aboard. Men sat in rows of canvas seats on both sides of the cabin. The aircraft taxied down the runway, took off, and slowly rose to 1,250 feet. The door of the plane remained open, and wind whooshed by.

Sitting in anticipation was the hardest part as the guts of the old plane shook and rattled. Gary noticed the soldier across from him. The soldier's eyes widened, and he sucked in quick, short breaths. Gary attempted to reassure the man with a smile, but when the soldier met Gary's gaze, he quickly averted his eyes. You jumped as a team, but each man needed to overcome his own fears.

After what seemed like hours, the jumpmaster shouted over the wind, "Get ready!" The command indicated the plane was about ten minutes from the drop zone. Responding to that command, in addition to all the commands that followed, had been practiced over and over again.

"Outboard personnel, stand up!" The men in the row across from the open door stood up.

"Inboard personnel, stand up!" The men in the row on the same side as the door stood up.

"Hook up!" Gary fastened his static line to the anchor cable. The static line deployed a man's chute.

"Check static lines!" Gary double-checked to make sure the static line was connected to the cable.

"Check equipment!" Gary checked all his equipment one last time, as well as the equipment of the guy ahead of him.

"Sound off for equipment check!" The man in the farthest position from the door started the count, and each man ahead of him lowered the number. "Ten okay!" "Nine okay!" "Eight okay!" As each man shouted "Okay!" he slapped the butt of the guy ahead.

"Stand in the door!" This was the moment everybody had been waiting for. The noise of the wind was deafening. Gary's body screamed to release the tension.

"Go!"

The man closest to the door exited the aircraft. "Go!" The next man jumped. "Go! Go! Go!" The line of men tumbled out of the plane.

Gary jumped. The rush of speed felt enormous. In a flash the roar of the propellers and airplane engines vanished. He counted "One one-thousand, two one-thousand, three one-thousand." After four seconds he felt a powerful jolt as the static line reached its end and yanked the parachute out of its sack. The parachute snapped open. He felt as if someone had grabbed him from behind. A beautiful silence filled his ears. He looked up to make sure that his canopy had fully opened and that no suspension lines were wrapped around the canopy. If his suspension lines were tangled, that was called a "streamer," and he would need to pull his reserve chute immediately. Fortunately, all lines looked okay.

Gary focused on the sky and view before and underneath him, views only birds see. The colors impressed him the most and became the clues to his reality. He saw blue sky, white clouds, manicured green fields, then brown. The brown was the drop zone. Plowed earth. Gary pulled on his risers and steered toward the brown, checking the area around the zone for trees, power lines, and water hazards. Mentally he rehearsed the three-point landing: balls of feet, side of calf and thigh, side of butt. Closer . . . closer. The ground was here. His feet skimmed the earth. He touched three body points, then rolled, bringing his feet over his head and landing on the opposite side of his body. A perfect landing. He jumped to his feet, gathered his chute, and ran—euphoric—toward the rally point.

Over the next three days, Gary made four more jumps, the last in full combat gear. He finished jump school and earned the distinction of becoming Airborne, a paratrooper. Now, finally, he could try to become a Green Beret.

———

Fifteen soldiers in Gary's outfit hoped to become Green Berets. First, a team of Green Berets came from Fort Bragg to interview and test the men for three days. Gary felt awed when he saw them. They wore starched fatigues, and their bodies and faces looked as if they had been chiseled out of granite. Quiet humility accompanied the Green Berets' appearance. Their mere presence declared that they knew who they were, were confident in what they could accomplish, and found no need to convince others.

The initial screening consisted of physical fitness tests, as well as a number of perceptual and situational incidents to evaluate decision-making skills. At the end of three days, ten men were sent packing. The remaining five men—Gary among them—passed and were sent to Fort Bragg.

Phase 1 of Special Forces training involved ten weeks of military tactics, land navigation, psychological and guerrilla warfare training, more weapons training, and unbelievable torment—all designed to test a man's limits, to take him past his breaking point. Most of the instructors were Green Berets who had already been to Vietnam or who had years of out-of-the-box thinking and combat experience in Korea. The instructors said their job was to make the recruits "feel comfortable with the uncomfortable." Mornings came early, sometimes at 2:00 a.m., and often were accompanied by yelling, screaming, rage, and orders.

More than once the trainees were told their position had been compromised —they needed to hustle and find a new safe place immediately. Many days a cold rain fell, leaving the men muddy, wet, chilled, or freezing. They hiked, climbed, ran, jumped, and crawled. The men were doused with water. They were kicked in the gut. Their faces were shoved into the mud. Repeatedly the instructors shouted, "You don't have to be here! You can quit anytime!" They were testing the men's resolve, even trying to break them. Gary learned to endure hell, and during the worst of times, he felt as if his spirit separated from his body. He felt like a plastic bubble floating in the ocean. The waves could toss him about, yet all he needed to do was go with the flow.

During their final field training exercise, Gary and his group parachuted into the forest, high up in the Uwharrie Mountains of northwest North Carolina. Once on the ground, they connected with a group of former Green Berets and others who role-played indigenous populations. For the next two weeks, Gary and his group organized the role players and trained them to conduct ambushes and other operations against troops from the 82nd Airborne, who were also training in the mountains.

To add to the realism, the men were told that, every once in a while, they might encounter real-life mountain folk intent on protecting illegal moonshine stills. Sure enough, far out in the woods, Gary spotted a shack guarded by six armed mountain men. He knew that they might think he was a federal agent and open fire. Carefully, Gary crept out of the area unnoticed.

At the end of the phase 1 training, the men returned to Fort Bragg and were awarded their green berets. The ceremony took place outside the John F. Kennedy Memorial Chapel on the post. About thirty men graduated with Gary. He felt joy, satisfaction, elation, but he knew more training lay ahead. Even though the actual beret had been awarded, no one could yet call himself a Green Beret. They needed to go through their military occupational specialty (MOS) training, as well as another ten weeks of phase 2 training, before they would officially graduate and be assigned to a Special Forces group.

Gary and the others interviewed with Special Forces personnel to determine their MOS: weapons, demolitions, communications, medical, or operations and intelligence (open only to senior enlisted personnel). Since Gary had already been trained as a light weapons specialist, he was advised to enter the advanced weapons program.

Gary had liked his weapons training and appreciated that every Green Beret must be combat ready, but he had a different desire. Ever since reading about the Green Berets, he had wanted to become a medical specialist, which at the time was considered the most difficult course in the military. So Gary pressed to become a medic, and an officer made Gary a deal: he would approve the request, but if Gary received worse than a B in any part of the coursework, he would be removed from the program and shipped off to a conventional army unit. Gary accepted the challenge and pressed forward. He had no doctors in his family and no previous medical training, but he liked the idea of helping people medically.

Gary realized that this desire had always been a core motivation for his joining the military. He'd never wanted to hurt people; he wanted to help them.

3

The Thousand-Yard Stare

Routine would be short lived, but the first phase of the medical program was routine for every army combat medic: Special Forces Basic Aidman's Course (MOS 91A). The intensive eight-week course trained every medic how to treat any basic emergency medical situation encountered in combat: stop bleeding, maintain an airway, administer morphine, start an IV.

After completing this basic course, Gary was sent for phase 2 at Fort Sam Houston in San Antonio. Fort Sam housed the medical training center for the military as well as the finest burn center in the country. This phase lasted for ten weeks, and the instructors were military medical doctors, dentists, and veterinarians. The doctors taught the trainees surgical procedures, pharmacology, hematology, diagnostics, and treatment of diseases. The dentists taught the Green Berets how to fill, restore, and pull teeth. Veterinarians instructed the trainees how to treat various diseases found in animals. To gain expertise in these skills, the students worked on goats.

The training at Fort Sam was a challenge not only because of the difficult subject matter but also because each class felt a mandate to outperform the previous class. This mind-set was common among special units and often called for a prank or physical challenge. Back in jump school, for instance, a team of Navy SEALs had gone through the training with Gary and his outfit. If they were all on a five-mile run and the final half-mile marker was passed, their leader would order the SEALs to break formation and sprint the rest of the way. When the rest of the class got to the finish line, the SEALs would be standing at attention in formation. The Black Hats would order the SEALs to give them twenty push-ups, and their response would always be "One hand or two hands, Sergeant?" On the morning of their final day at the 250-foot tower, one of the SEALs climbed the tower and suspended a huge inflatable frog.

At Fort Sam, a cannon was fired each morning. As a prank, one class filled the cannon with golf balls, breaking almost every window in the officers' quarters.

San Antonio has a zoo where Green Berets would often go to study on weekends. Once, four Special Forces students sneaked into the zoo on a Saturday night, kidnapped an alligator, took him back to the base, and tied him to the commanding officer's porch. The officer and his family received quite a surprise the next morning when they headed for church. (To this day, Gary won't admit which pranks he was involved in!)

Phase 2 of medical training felt like college to Gary because of the competition and academic pressure. Many students entering the program already knew something about medicine or first aid—including one classmate who already had obtained his bachelor's in biology and premed before entering the military (he ended up finishing first in the phase 2 class). Although Gary spent his fair share of time drinking at the Bavarian beer garden and dancing to the music of German tuba players at the world's fair in San Antonio, he still buckled down hard enough to finish third in his class.

Crazy things sometimes happened after Gary drank too much, particularly when he was out with his army buddies, so he chose to spend more time by himself on weekends to avoid getting in trouble.

One sunny weekend afternoon, Gary was downtown by himself and decided to go to a movie at the Majestic, the main downtown theater. He bought his ticket, some popcorn, and a soda and headed inside, knowing only the title of the movie—*The Restless Ones*. Gary liked westerns and action movies, and the title drew him in. He sat near the front and in an aisle seat—this was because of Special Forces training, in case he needed to make a quick getaway.

The movie was about a teenager and some of his trials. *Kind of a strange movie,* Gary thought, but he found himself identifying with the main character's angst and how he overcame his trouble. At the end of the movie, the lights went on and Gary thought, *Hmmm. I'll really need to think about things.* Oddly, three men walked to the front of the theater and started talking about God. They asked if anyone would like to come forward and pray. Gary was surprised—this had never happened to him in a movie theater. Some moviegoers walked down to the front, but without hesitation Gary stood and walked out. He certainly wasn't going to go forward and pray!

On the way out he noticed a wall poster for the movie that mentioned it was presented by Billy Graham. Gary wasn't sure who that was, although he made a mental note to ask someone later.

———

After completing phase 2 medical, Green Berets could choose which military hospital they wanted for their ten weeks of on-the-job training. Gary chose Darnall Army Hospital in Fort Hood, Texas, a short bus ride from San Antonio. He'd heard that Darnall provided strong experience in emergency room trauma incidents, an area that intrigued him.

Darnall did not disappoint. There, Gary was trained in surgery, pediatrics, obstetrics and gynecology, and emergency medicine. He also worked in the lab, pharmacy, psych ward, and morgue. The students were exposed to every kind of medical situation imaginable because the trainers knew that Green Berets would be sent to places without doctors, where they would need to administer every kind of medical care. At Darnall, Gary treated a patient who had attempted suicide. He helped deliver babies. He also developed deeper empathy for those suffering.

While Gary worked in the morgue, he observed his first autopsies. He learned how to detach from the reality in front of him, to view each body objectively, and to assist the doctors with little emotional reaction.

One day a six-month-old baby boy was brought into the morgue. Under supervision, Gary took a scalpel and cut through the flesh of the skull until he hit bone. Then the physician took over. With a small rotary handsaw, he cut through the bone of the skull, then used a small chrome hammer and chisel around the top of the skull and gently removed the cap of bone. Gary was not comfortable, finding it difficult to detach emotionally. He wondered what would happen when he was sent overseas. When he was all alone. Would he be able to do what he needed to do?

Each day's shift at Darnall lasted twelve to fourteen hours. On weekends, to unwind from the stress, Gary and his pals would go to town and drink or go to the zoo or a park. A buddy had a Triumph Spitfire sports car, and one weekend night a bunch of guys piled into the two-seater and headed to the desert to drink beer. They drank until soused, then Bob, an English lit major from Syracuse University, leaned back against the warm sand and recited *Beowulf*—at least, Gary *thought* it was *Beowulf*. Bob was so gifted that he could both quote from memory and make up stuff as he went along.

Gary didn't care about the accuracy. Their worlds were unfolding in incredible ways. They were soldiers. They had beer and the desert. Bob's words shimmered in the midnight air.

———

After finishing up at Darnall, Gary returned to Fort Bragg for what became the most unique and challenging phase of his medical training. The students referred to the next eight weeks simply as "dog lab." The pressure was on here too. If the students didn't perform as needed, they still could be washed out of the program.

When the students were learning how to administer IVs or catheters or to insert NG tubes down the throat and into the stomach, they performed the procedures on each other. This was part of their empathy training. Their instructors wanted the students to know what these procedures felt like, but some things could not be practiced on medical students. Thus the purpose of dog lab.

The idea was straightforward: in order to learn what they needed to know about life and death, the students worked on live patients in situations where death was possible—and, in some cases, inevitable. Over the years dogs had proved the most realistic subjects. The students were taken to the pound, and each selected his dog. This made the connection more real. Emotions were involved now, and the trainers wanted the experience to be difficult. Some students informally gave their dogs names, even though from then on they were allowed to refer to their dogs only as "patients," not even as "canine patients." Gary selected a mongrel with long white-and-gray hair. He did not name his dog—he knew it was going to be hard enough.

Students were assigned to teams and rotated through the following roles: surgeon, assistant surgeon, inside circulator, outside circulator, and anesthesiologist. Each position was critical to every operation's success. Each posed unique challenges.

When the lab began, each patient was given a thorough physical. Then the students were ordered to take the dogs out to a secluded area where each patient was shot with a .22 caliber bullet in the hindquarters to simulate combat trauma. The race to save the life was on. The patient was quickly evacuated to the operating room, where the students performed emergency medical procedures. An IV was inserted. Fluids were administered. Sedatives were given. The wound was debrided and damage was repaired.

Once surgery was over, each team needed to nurse its patient back to health using only dressing changes and sterile techniques. They could not use antibiotics because they could not be guaranteed access to such things in the field.

After the initial wound healed, each student performed two more surgical procedures—a tracheotomy and an amputation. After completion of these procedures and when the patient had healed, the patient's life often was terminated with an intracardiac injection of sodium thiopental or a similar chemical. Some students received permission to keep their patients, the result being a lot of three-legged dogs around Fort Bragg.

The pressure was always on during dog lab. If a dog died during surgery, then the students would be either washed out of the program or recycled to the next class, depending on the cause of death and whether the surgeon was negligent. Once, while Gary worked as assistant surgeon, the anesthesiologist yelled that the patient's blood pressure was dropping. The dog's heart was failing and within seconds stopped beating. Gary immediately opened the patient's chest. He and the surgeon performed cardiac massage and other lifesaving procedures to try to restore the patient's vitals. To Gary's relief, the heart began to beat again on its own.

After completing dog lab, the students faced the final obstacle before completing the medical training phase. For up to forty-five minutes, a board of doctors grilled each candidate with questions from any area of medical, surgical, dental, and veterinary care. If a candidate made it through this barrage of questioning, he then reached into a jar and drew a card that described a situation he might encounter in the field. The candidate received a few minutes to select other students for role play; then they acted out the situation. The doctors scrutinized each action and decision, and the candidate had to explain at each stage what he was doing, why he was doing it, and what he hoped to accomplish.

The final ten weeks of Special Forces training were referred to as phase 2. For eight weeks students were instructed in small unit tactics, ambush situations, critical incidents, guerrilla warfare, psychological operations, and anything else an instructor might dream up. Torment returned. During the final two weeks, students were dropped off in the Uwharrie Mountains for fourteen days of straight hell. Something about it was so unspeakable that even now Gary has blocked the specifics from his memory. He will say only that his resolve and desire were tested greatly and, over and over again, he simply told himself not to quit.

When he finally returned from the woods, he was told he had made it. He was ready to graduate and receive his flash (insignia) that's worn on the front of

It didn't take long for the sergeant major to come around. Gary probably needed the occasional attitude adjustment, but as an elite Special Forces soldier, he knew his stuff. Eventually, the sergeant major became so impressed that he assigned Gary to a Special Forces demonstrations team, a group of selected specialists who traveled the country doing public relations to educate about and promote interest in Special Forces. The team appeared at state fairs, conventions, and schools. They demonstrated hand-to-hand combat, use of specialized weapons, emergency medical procedures, and rappelling from helicopters.

Gary's team was often asked to train National Guard and Army Reserve units during their required annual training. The Special Forces team would make a dramatic entrance by parachute, then put the troops through their paces. Gary enjoyed the work, as it helped him both stay sharp and hone his teaching skills. One of the Green Berets' main missions is to teach indigenous personnel to become a fighting force.

But when their duties were over, Gary and his team were sent back to Fort Bragg. Back to KP, guard duty, and cleaning the headquarters building. Gary was bored. He wanted to do something more meaningful with his time. He felt edgy. Ornery. Even angry. His days off were often spent drinking, partying, and bar-fighting in nearby Fayetteville. The guys affectionately referred to it as "Fayette-Nam." Run-ins with military police were common—not just for Gary but for many of the rough-around-the-edges Special Forces troops. Most guys had concluded there wasn't much to do in town except drink.

Once, Gary pulled all-night guard duty, then had a day off. He drove to Fayetteville early in the morning, stopped at the first open bar, and started drinking. He wasn't a steady drinker, and hours-long binges never sat well in his gut. The last thing he remembered was staggering out of the bar and putting another coin in the parking meter.

The next memory was a painful one. He woke up and tried to move but hurt all over. His eyes were swollen—he could hardly see. He was lying on a bed of some sort. Then he looked up and saw his team sergeant behind bars.

"Hey, Top," Gary called. "What are you doing in jail?"

"I'm not in jail." He shook his head. "You are."

The sergeant filled Gary in on the rest of the story. According to the police report, after Gary put the coin in the meter, he climbed into his car and started driving. Fully sloshed, he veered too close to the side of the road, hit a parked car, bounced the other direction and hit another, and kept driving. A Fayette-ville police officer saw his erratic driving and hit the lights and siren. Gary glanced behind him, shrugged, and accelerated. He sped out of town and hit the interstate.

One police car after him led to two cars, and two cars led to three. The third was a state trooper. Gary was soon in a full-on high-speed chase. The cops finally ran Gary off the road, but he emerged from his car brandishing a billy club, which he always carried under the seat for emergencies. The cops surrounded him, took him to the ground, and beat him into submission.

Rumor had it around Fayetteville that anyone who couldn't make it into the Special Forces was washed out and became a policeman. This rumor angered police officers—especially when they encountered an unruly Special Forces soldier.

Gary was bruised all over. Several ribs were broken. The police didn't even take a mug shot—his face was too bashed up to be recognizable.

The sergeant told Gary his charges: driving while intoxicated (DWI), hit and run, assault with a deadly weapon, resisting arrest. (Those are the ones Gary remembers today, although he's sure there were more.) If convicted, he would face both civilian and military consequences.

"What should I do?" Gary asked.

"Get a lawyer," the sergeant answered.

Gary was released from jail. The sergeant took him back to the barracks, where Gary lay on his bunk, wondering how he could ever get out of this jam. He called a lawyer. A day later at their initial meeting, the lawyer listened for a few minutes, then pushed his chair away from his desk, shuffled some papers, and said, "I've heard the same story from more than one soldier. How soon are you leaving the country?"

"I don't know, sir," Gary said. "Our team's on alert and may be going to Mali, Africa, in a couple of months."

"Not good enough." The lawyer shook his head. "Can you do anything to make it so you'd leave right away? You gotta get sent to Vietnam. That's the only hope you've got, buster."

Gary shrugged. "I guess I could reenlist."

He returned to base and requested assignment to the Fifth Special Forces Group in Vietnam. The decision came with a pleasant surprise—a $600 bonus and a promotion to specialist (E-4), which meant a pay raise. The military also accommodated Gary's request to leave the country soon—in thirty days, if possible. His orders quickly came through.

"Congratulations," his lawyer said over the phone. "But you still need to report to court. Here's my advice: don't say anything until I tell you, and even then, only say 'Guilty, Your Honor,' and then keep your mouth shut."

The day of Gary's court appearance, he showed up in his dress uniform, his hands clammy, his chest tight. Person after person ahead of him faced the judge. Soldiers with far fewer charges were sentenced to serious jail time. When Gary's name was called, he went forward and sat next to his lawyer. The judge and the lawyer exchanged a barrage of legal-sounding words, few of which Gary understood, although he recognized two pleas from his lawyer: "Vietnam" and "mercy." The judge started to speak to Gary. His lawyer nudged him to stand.

"How do you plead?" the judge boomed.

"Guilty, Your Honor," Gary said. His voice sounded dutiful. Repentant. Quiet.

"I find you guilty of reckless driving and fine you one hundred dollars."

The gavel banged. It took Gary a while to realize that the lawyer had copped a sentencing deal with the district attorney. Gary was on his way to Vietnam.

"Good luck," the lawyer said as they left the courthouse. "Oh, by the way, my fee is five hundred dollars."

Gary shook his head. *So long, reenlistment bonus.*

The army gave him two weeks' leave. Gary went home and said goodbye to his family and friends. There was no farewell party this time since he'd vowed to quit drinking.

A couple of days before he left, Gary received a phone call. His cousin Jan, the same cousin who'd prayed when he fell out the window as a baby, had grown up and married a guy named Buck. He'd been a sailor in the navy, then had come home and earned a master's degree in education, although he seldom worked as a teacher. Mostly he did carpentry, remodeling, and odd jobs. He owned a scuba-diving shop and often took off work to head overseas on service trips, to speak at conferences, or to lead Bible studies for his church. Buck and Jan said they wanted to come see Gary before he left for Vietnam.

Gary was intrigued—and also puzzled. He hadn't seen Jan for years, and he'd never met Buck. They lived in Lone Pine, California. Why would anyone come all the way across the country to see someone they barely knew, even if he was a cousin?

Both were smiling when they arrived. Buck had big bushy sideburns; Jan's hair was cut short. Gary found them sincere and genuinely interested in him. Gary had always seen Jan as a religious person, and Buck was very attached to Jesus—at least, he sure talked about him a lot. Both said they were praying for Gary.

They talked to him about their Jesus stuff, but Gary said thanks, he didn't need whatever they were sharing. Gary tried to explain that Green Berets were self-sufficient, resourceful. They didn't need anything in life other than themselves and their teammates.

Buck nodded. Jan smiled. Each gave him a hug. That was it. Buck and Jan packed up and returned to California. A few days later, Gary boarded a plane headed for Fort Lewis, Washington, set to leave from there on his deployment.

A high school buddy had enlisted in the army and was now married and stationed at Fort Lewis. When Gary arrived, his friend suggested they go out for a drink. One beer turned into many, and one day turned into seven. So much for the vow to quit drinking. Gary missed reporting for duty by five days but figured, *What's the worst they can do—send me to Vietnam?*

When he finally reported, he saw troops from the Ninth Infantry getting off the plane. They'd just returned from their tour in Vietnam. Gary stared at them, and they stared back with a look he'd never seen.

Retired marine Sergeant Major Joe Houle, talking about his first day in Vietnam, described the squad he joined this way: "The look in their eyes was like the life was sucked out of them." The condition even had a name, which Gary soon became familiar with: the thousand-yard stare.

4

In-Country Chaos

Heat. Heat rose from the tarmac. Heat blasted, as if from a huge furnace, and wind and dust blew against Gary's face and the back of his neck. Heat induced sweat, and the resulting dampness spread across his chest and the backs of his knees and settled into his armpits and crotch.

It was June 1969, South Vietnam, and already he felt tense.

Gary had left Fort Lewis for Asia with a ragtag group of replacements. From the mainland United States, they flew to Hawaii. Then Guam. Then Cam Ranh Bay, where an American air force base lay on a small inlet on the southeastern coast of Vietnam. It was a huge military installation where a multitude of troops and tons of supplies entered the country. The landscape was flat, with sand and dirt, paved runways, and numerous tents. The air smelled of diesel fuel. Metal buildings and airplane hangars populated the area. The roar of airplane engines filled Gary's ears along with the constant rumble of deuce-and-a-halves (two-and-a-half-ton trucks) driving troops and supplies this way and that.

After Gary stepped off the plane, he glanced at the guys he was with. Several shrugged. Nobody knew what to do. He looked around for someone—anyone—to tell them where they needed to go.

The base was a huge place with chaos as a background. Nervousness mixed with the sweat and heat and dust and grime. Then a jeep pulled up, and a thick-looking sergeant first class barked orders. For a moment Gary felt that his group had been rescued from their bizarre and chaotic introduction to Vietnam. But the bizarre and chaotic had only just begun.

Since he had come to the country on a different set of orders from the original ones and because he was only a spec 4, Gary was assigned to a replacement company at Cam Ranh Base and immediately ordered on to latrine detail until someone could figure out what to do with him. Latrine detail was at the far end of the spectrum of unpleasant. On base, soldiers defecated into fifty-five-gallon drums that had been cut in half. Gary's first job as a Green Beret in Vietnam was to douse the waste with diesel fuel, light it, then stir it vigorously as it smoldered into dank ashes. This was his job the whole first day. Then the second day—minute after minute, hour after hour—heat from the drums billowed up with foul black smoke and a nauseating stench. He shook his head and thought, *Welcome to Vietnam, soldier.*

As the sun set the second day, Gary's eyes caught a striking figure walking by. The man wore a green beret and jungle fatigues and had sergeant major stripes. The figure stopped walking. He stared at Gary, his eyes widened, and he shouted, "Hey, Beret! What *exactly* are you doing?"

"Exactly what it looks like, Sergeant Major!" Gary called back.

The sergeant major walked closer. "What's your MOS?"

"I'm a medic."

"You want to stay here?"

Gary almost laughed. "Not at all."

The sergeant major grabbed Gary by the arm and escorted him away from the smoldering latrines, straight over to a stocky C-7A Caribou propeller plane. The sergeant major was from II Corps and worked with a special operations group up in the city of Kontum (often spelled Kon Tum), located inland in Vietnam's Central Highlands region, near the Laotian and Cambodian borders. He motioned to the pilot, introduced him to Gary, and told Gary to climb aboard.

"But I don't have any orders," Gary said. "No paperwork. I don't have any-thing yet."

"Don't worry about any of that," the sergeant major said. "This guy will take you right to Nha Trang."

The pilot nodded and grinned. Gary shrugged and scrambled aboard.

A coastal city, Nha Trang was the location of the Fifth Special Forces head-quarters. Gary learned that every Green Beret newly in country was supposed to spend a couple of weeks in Nha Trang while going through specialized training to acclimatize to the weather and conditions in Vietnam. The training included being barged out to Hon Tre Island, where each morning for five days Gary and about thirty other men placed seventy-five-pound sandbags in their packs and marched up and down the island's mountain. On his first march up, Gary was surprised to see that at the top Special Forces had set up a shack with an ice cream maker, their very own improvised Dairy Queen. He grinned. He'd heard that Special Forces guys would do anything to simulate the comforts of home.

Even on Hon Tre Island, the danger of being in a war zone was very real. Hon Tre was classified as a "free-fire area," which meant that Vietcong (VC) troops (Communist guerrilla forces who joined the North Vietnamese Army in fighting against South Vietnam, the US, and allies) roamed the island and were hostile to American troops, who were authorized to fire at the enemy without needing any coordination with headquarters. Gary and the other soldiers didn't encounter any Vietcong while he was there, but after their mountain climbs, they went on patrols, shot from the hip at pop-up practice targets (called the "quick kill" technique), and called in practice artillery and air strikes.

When the training at Nha Trang concluded, Gary was soon on a chopper headed north for the city of Pleiku in the Central Highlands, the headquarters for B Company. Pleiku was considered even more dangerous, closer to the heart of the war. He was set to do a short rotation in a Special Forces hospital manned by Vietnam's Civilian Irregular Defense Group (CIDG). The CIDG program had been developed by the Central Intelligence Agency (CIA) in the early 1960s and included anti-Communist South Vietnamese military units not formally associated with the country's national armed forces. Gary was surprised at the level of sophistication in the hospital, which existed in the middle of a war zone.

Baptism by fire came swiftly. His first night, the hospital was drilled in an intense rocket attack. The incoming shells didn't create any large-scale destruction but created enough noise and disorder to make Gary's hair stand on end. The next morning, Gary began his first shift. A call came that a medevac chopper was bringing in a critically wounded soldier. Gary and two Vietnamese medics rushed out to the helipad, where they heard the *whoomp, whoomp, whoomp* of the chopper. As the helicopter approached, they turned their heads away to protect themselves from the wind gusts created by the whirling rotors.

The chopper touched down, and the medical team sprinted to the open door, where the soldier lay bleeding. Gary could see he was wounded in his head, chest, arms, and legs. The most serious wound appeared to be to the head, where a bandage had been hastily wrapped in an attempt to stop the bleeding. As they rushed him into the emergency room, the head bandage slipped off. Gary choked, but he kept working on the man, even while on the run. He saw that the bandage hadn't been applied to stop the bleeding—it was holding the soldier's head together, as most of the back of his head had been blown off. He didn't stand a chance. Although the soldier was still alive when the helicopter brought him in, he died before the medics could do anything to try to save him.

Later, while scrubbing the soldier's blood off his hands, Gary reminded himself that he had seen trauma before. During his training at Darnall Army Hospital, he had watched people in pain. He'd even held people as they died. But something about this soldier's death felt different. This death came from trauma created by war, and it felt more horrible than anything Gary had experienced.

Back home in the States, the aura surrounding 1967's summer of love was still palpable. Woodstock was right around the corner. Six hundred million people around the world watched their TVs as Neil Armstrong became the first man to walk on the moon. But Vietnam certainly wasn't experiencing a season of love or scientific progress.

Gary couldn't fathom the emotion of the man who had fired the gunshot or mortar round that caused the soldier's head wound. Was it anger? Was it rage? Was it jealousy, greed, or indifference? Gary had a hard time grasping why one human being would do this to another human being. This wound of war—the first he'd seen as a medic—felt devastating beyond comprehension.

———

The days working at the CIDG hospital passed swiftly, and a connection made there would prove significant to Gary's future in Vietnam. Over the next two months, Gary diagnosed and treated diseases endemic to Vietnam, including cholera, malaria, and parasitic illnesses. He practiced his lab work and surgical procedures and participated in skin grafts and amputations.

During this time Gary met the Montagnard people, an ethnic minority that inhabited the jungles of the Central Highlands. In French, *Montagnard* means "mountain dweller" or, more colloquially, "mountain man." As a group, the Montagnards were friendly with Americans and allied with the South Vietnamese, even though the Vietnamese generally considered the Montagnards a lower class and seldom had much to do with them. Gary soon developed deep respect for the Montagnard people and an appreciation for the magnitude of the task they faced—fighting for their survival. He wondered how he might work more closely with them.

One of the senior noncommissioned officers (NCOs) at the hospital was Master Sergeant Dan "Mac" McGinley. A veteran of World War II and the Korean Conflict, Mac was already on his fourth tour in Vietnam. He was well past the age of being deployed, but he had been granted a special dispensation from President Lyndon Johnson. Mac was gruff, short, stocky, bald, and raspy voiced—yet with a heart that fully occupied his barrel chest. A Green Beret himself, Mac took Gary under his wing and taught him everything he knew about combat medicine and living with indigenous tribes. He became a mentor and guide.

Mac explained that some four and a half years earlier, in 1965, a tremendous slaughter of Montagnards had occurred in a Central Highlands camp called Dak Sut. Thousands of villagers had been gunned down by the North Vietnamese Army and Vietcong. Not long afterward, in 1966, a team of Green Berets had returned to that region of the jungle, made contact with Montagnards from the Sedang tribe, and built some new fortifications about twenty-five miles from Dak Sut. Mac had been the original medic in this new camp that he described as "the Shangri-la of Vietnam." In military terms the new camp was known simply as A-245 because of its place on a grid. It was approximately ten kilometers from the Laotian border.

Situated in a small valley along the Dak Poko River, the new camp was filled with beautiful and steadfast people, "friendly yet fierce," Mac added. They were no friends of the Communists and had vowed to fight alongside anyone who would help defend their homes and region. Mac convinced Gary that his medical skills would be wasted if he stayed in a hospital and that he would gain valuable experience at an A camp as a team medic.

Two companies of Montagnard reactionary forces had already been assigned to protect this new camp—about four hundred soldiers total. The rest of the camp's 2,300 people were women and children—mostly spouses and off-spring of the Montagnard soldiers. A team of twelve Green Berets helped defend the village against the North Vietnamese Army (NVA) and the Vietcong, although that far north they fought mostly against the NVA. One of the specific reasons for the Special Forces to be there was to monitor movement along the nearby Ho Chi Minh Trail, the main north-south route of the Communists. Whenever movement was detected along the trail, the Green Berets and Montagnard fighters would set up ambushes or call in air or artillery strikes to disrupt the flow. Sometimes the camp was used as a base for cross-border operations into Laos to monitor known North Vietnamese strongholds.

Before long, Mac asked Gary, "Would you like to go live and work in Camp A-245?"

Gary liked the sound of working with an indigenous people group. Already he felt drawn to the Montagnard people's pluck and resolve. Hospital staff members were impressed with Gary's work skills, and he soon went before a hastily created promotions board and was promoted to buck sergeant (E-5).

The hospital chief asked him to stay on in Pleiku, but Gary declined, saying he was committed to going out into the field. As chief medic at Camp A-245, his job would be to live there for a year, treating the Montagnards' sicknesses, learning from their culture, and helping them any way he could.

The camp's Montagnard name foreshadowed the future of the place. It was remote and vulnerable, and it would take a while before Gary discovered what the other name of Camp A-245 meant. The locals called the village Dak Seang.

It meant "river of blood."

———

Before heading to Dak Seang, Gary needed to report to his B Team located in Kontum. By Vietnamese standards Kontum was considered a city, but it wasn't as big as Pleiku or cities such as Saigon (with a population of about two million during the war). Being in the highlands, Kontum was populated by some Vietnamese but mostly by Montagnards who had left the jungle and transitioned to city life. Both Pleiku and Kontum were inhabited by Montagnards who belonged to the Jarai or Bahnar tribe. Although they had kept many of their traditions and cultural ways, they also had become westernized, enjoying many of the conveniences that city life provided.

The structure of Army Special Forces was based on a "C Team, B Team, A Team" concept. C Teams were headquarters-type organizations located in each of the corps areas that had operational responsibilities for two to three B Teams. In turn, each B Team supported four to five A Teams. Gary's B Team, B-24, was located in Kontum, where he often would fly for supplies over the next months. Or at times he would borrow a jeep to make the hour-long and sometimes-dangerous journey from Dak Seang down Highway 14 to his C Team in Pleiku.

Initially Gary didn't stay in Kontum long. It was late August 1969, and on the morning when Gary boarded the chopper for his first trip to Dak Seang, he felt strong emotions, although he couldn't sort out exactly which emotions they were. He thought, *Wow, this is it. This is real. All I've trained for. All I've endured. All I've been working toward begins today.*

The chopper lifted off and headed toward the jungle. Gary felt the rush of wind in his face. He heard the crackle of the radio as the pilot communicated with others in the aircraft.

"Sit back!" the closest door gunner yelled. "We might encounter ground fire."

Gary sat back in the canvas seat in the rear of the helicopter, but he couldn't help inching forward to peer out the open side door. The concrete and steel of Kontum gave way to jungle, a sea of green.

The jungle looked beautiful, but it also prompted fear. Gary had learned that the foliage was called "triple-canopy jungle" and was composed of three layers of vegetation, starting with the small brush and vines that grew as tall as a man and strangled soldiers as they hiked. Next came medium-sized trees—ten to twenty feet tall. Snipers loved hiding in those trees. Finally, the third layer— monstrous jungle trees up to a hundred feet tall that were home only to birds, monkeys, and other wildlife that could climb that high. The third layer also hid the movement of North Vietnamese troops and supplies passing through the jungle. This was the vegetation that had prompted the US to use a controversial chemical called Agent Orange to destroy wide swathes of foliage so enemy movement could be detected.

The chopper Gary was riding in was a Bell UH-1 Iroquois, nicknamed the Huey, the iconic flying workhorse of the Vietnam War. With skids on the bottom, the chopper had a split-windshield glass front, big side doors that slid back and forth, and an M60 machine gun mounted on each side. Normally an entire squad of twelve men could ride in the chopper, but today the Huey was on a resupply mission to Dak Seang, so inside sat only the crew chief, two door gunners, two pilots, and Gary. The door gunners sat on the floor with their legs hanging outside, their feet on the skids.

Gary sat back again and tried to collect his thoughts amid the roar of the rotors. His mind flashed back to the first casualty he'd seen at the CIDG hospital—the soldier with the fatal head wound. Surely he'd soon see more of those types of casualties. Gary's insides twisted and he rubbed the back of his neck. He took deep breaths in an effort to calm himself. He wondered whether the camp would be quiet when he arrived or whether automatic rifle and rocket fire would greet him. If he would be one of the guys immediately hit or one of the lucky ones.

"Almost there!" a door gunner yelled. He swatted Gary on the knee. Gary leaned forward and glanced out the door. Below him the mountains gave way to a green valley, and at the bottom of the valley, the foliage had been trimmed and a clearing carved out of the jungle. He could make out a large square about four football fields big, the size of a small college campus. Around the compound the ground was green, but inside, the ground looked dirt brown. Silver rooftops dotted the compound. As anxious as Gary felt, he was able to notice the land below was gorgeous. Except for the scraped landscape of the camp, the entire region looked lush. Rich with color. Humid, hot, and wet.

The chopper circled the area twice, then descended. At the far end of the square was a jagged paved airstrip. Then a smaller area with a big letter *H*. The chopper headed down toward the *H*—the helicopter's landing spot. Gary spotted trenches and concertina wire that bordered the square and acted as the camp's first line of defense. Inside the wire he could see the roofs of maybe fifty buildings along the perimeter of the square, built almost like another wall around the site. Then inside the compound he counted another thirty roofs or so—mostly small buildings, although there were a few larger ones, too, maybe one thousand square feet each. Gary would find out later that one of the larger buildings was a school for children.

Just before the chopper landed, Gary saw a jeep with two men speeding down a dirt road toward the helicopter pad. The men looked friendly enough. This would be Gary's home for the next year and would become a place that would change his life forever—in some ways for good, in many ways for harm.

The chopper touched the dirt. Welcome to Dak Seang.

Jungle Shangri-La

As the chopper's rotors spun to a stop, the door gunners and crew chief readied themselves to unload supplies. The jeep with the two men pulled up with a screech of brakes. Gary climbed out of the chopper with his M16 rifle and rucksack. He yanked his duffel bag out and tossed it on the ground, wondering what he should do next.

"Y'all bring the movie?" one of the guys from the jeep yelled in a Kentucky drawl. "I sure hope y'all brought it!"

Gary didn't know anything about a movie, but the guy who yelled soon came closer, shook his hand, and introduced himself as Staff Sergeant Nelson. He was a Green Beret, about five feet, ten inches tall with a wiry build and a thin face, probably in his early thirties. From Nelson, Gary learned that movies were rare and cherished possessions in A camps. The troops would pull a deuce-and-a-half into the center of the camp, drape a white sheet over the side, and fire up a projector. The Montagnards loved American movies, particularly westerns. Everyone would gather around to watch.

The other guy in the jeep stepped out and introduced himself as Pat Dizzine, a Green Beret communications specialist in his early twenties who went by the nickname Dizzy. He was short and muscular and was chewing the stump of an unlit cigar. Dizzy asked Gary to clarify the pronunciation of his last name, then asked, "You got a nickname?"

Gary shook his head.

"Well, don't worry," Dizzy said with a laugh. "We'll find one for you soon."

The three Green Berets jumped into the jeep. Nelson drove them away on the dirt road as the chopper's engines revved up and the bird lifted off. As the chopper flew farther and farther away, Gary felt viscerally how the eerie silence of the jungle replaced the whir of the rotors. It was hard to explain the stillness. Even over the roar of the jeep, Gary could "hear" the jungle's silence, feel it in his gut. He concluded it was the sound of *remoteness*. Of being far away from civilization.

The laughter of Gary's two new teammates snapped him back to reality. The three of them chatted about home and family and guys they'd all trained with, although the conversation was herky-jerky as Nelson constantly swerved to avoid holes, ruts, and boulders in the dirt road that led to the camp.

From the ground perspective, Gary could see and understand more of the camp's protective makeup. It wasn't just one row of concertina wire surrounding the perimeter, as he'd guessed from the air. They drove by multiple rows of the razor-sharp wire, along with rows of other barbed wire and bamboo stakes sharpened at the top and planted in the ground, aimed in the direction an enemy would charge.

Fifty-five-gallon drums also dotted the camp's perimeter. Dizzy explained that each drum was filled with gasoline and rigged with explosives—all set to blow at a moment's notice. After about seventy-five yards, the jeep came to the main walls of the camp—sandbags piled on sandbags and reinforced with concrete and timbers. Dak Seang was a formidable fortress. On each side of the road into the camp sat guard towers manned by Montagnard fighters holding machine guns.

Once inside the outer wall, they drove through the main part of camp and entered the inner part through another secured, sandbagged area. Here lay the

Jungle Shangri-La

Green Berets' barracks—called a "team house"—along with a communications bunker, generators, and a medical dispensary. Most of the buildings had been built essentially underground, so only the roofs and door openings showed. Nelson parked the jeep by the team house, and Gary headed inside with Nelson and Dizzy to meet the other team members.

A plaque above the door read,

To really live, you must almost die.
To those who fight for it, life has a meaning
the protected will never know.

Gary paused after he read the sign, letting the words filter through his mind, absorbing the meaning of the saying. More than a motto, it was an invitation to live in a new way, with a core of noble values. Although he didn't understand all the nuances of the motto, he felt the words were nudging him, even sweeping him into a new bold and selfless way of life, centered on what really matters.

Captain Paul Landers was the team leader. A quiet guy with close-cropped hair, he impressed Gary as someone who knew his stuff—not like some of the other team leaders Gary had met along the way who only barked orders. Captain Landers was from Florida and quickly proved himself a good listener who inspired others to follow his lead. Gary would learn that Captain Landers' leadership style was first to wait to see how things were run, then to make changes. Immediately he struck Gary as wise.

Lieutenant Ed Eck looked like a burly wrestler with a tight, squat frame. From Maryland, he was the team's executive officer, second in command. All the men were munching on a meal, and Lieutenant Eck kept up a constant conversation. After a few months he would rotate out and be replaced by First Lieutenant Ed Christensen, a tall and muscular officer with a blond brush cut who became known for his easygoing manner and conceptual thinking.

Along with Dizzy, Chris Pollard was a communications specialist. He was a technical thinker who kept up the conversation with Lieutenant Eck and constantly cracked jokes.

Their weapons specialist was Staff Sergeant Gordy "The Rock" Wiley, a tall, large-framed guy. Every time he spoke, he drew a laugh. Gary learned that the Montagnards loved The Rock, and later, when he stood outside, Gary saw how The Rock towered over the small Montagnards. He quickly proved a good guy to be around and mentored Gary regarding the critical details of the camp.

Sergeant Franklin John Rock was the name of a fictional World War II veteran in a series of comic books from that era, and the series featured a supporting character named "The Kid." Wiley soon bestowed that nickname on Gary. Together they were The Rock and The Kid. Dizzy approved of Gary's nickname.

Their demolitions specialists were Eric Pekkala and Rick Colvin. Both had engineering backgrounds and analytical minds—they were studious and businesslike. They shook hands with Gary and welcomed him aboard.

Operations and intel were handled by Master Sergeant Weeks, the top NCO on the team. His job was to keep the officers in line and alive, and Gary sensed that a larger separation existed between him and the rest of the team, even compared with the other officers and the team. Weeks was a lifer, and the men seemed to be in awe of him. Plus, he was large framed—huge.

Other men would come and go in the months that Gary was in Dak Seang and, as strange as it might seem today given the iconic closeness that often develops between combat soldiers, some five decades later it's difficult for Gary to remember everyone who served on the team, particularly because new team members came regularly to replace those who got sick or wounded or left for some R & R. Officers especially would circulate through the camp for a short time, mostly if they were interested in getting fired at by the enemy, then written up for a Combat Infantry Badge or another award. It wasn't a respected practice, but it did occur.

The introductions over, Gary was shown to his bunk to stow his gear, then led by Doc Nelson to the dispensary. There was a lot to learn, and Gary needed to get up to speed right away. His first few days in camp were spent mostly with Nelson, the camp's head medic who was leaving in two weeks, when Gary would run the dispensary by himself.

They began by meeting the Montagnard medics and becoming familiar with the underground medical bunker, which housed all the medical supplies and records, along with an emergency operating room. Gary was familiarized with alert procedures, security details, emergency escape and evasion routes, procedures for communicating with other camps, and many other details necessary for the camp's survival.

Nelson introduced Gary to the Montagnard head medic, a married man in his late twenties named Thung (pronounced *tung*). Thung was well groomed, spoke good English, and always wore a freshly pressed shirt with a pair of green fatigue pants. Even though Thung had no formal medical training, he had learned a lot from Nelson, and he was constantly eager to learn more.

Each day, Thung's wife brought him his lunch at the dispensary—soup and shrimp or snails and rice. Some Montagnards had darker features, with jet-black hair and dark black skin. But other Montagnards showed more of a mixed French heritage, with slender faces and a lighter, almost almond skin color. Thung's wife looked French. She had long auburn hair, a slender face, and stunning eyes. It was easy for Gary to see that she and Thung enjoyed an easy and close relationship. They were always smiling and laughing gently with each other, gracious in their interactions. She often helped out at the dispensary by taking temperatures and blood pressures. Her dream was to become a nurse, although education wasn't readily accessible to her. She reminded Gary a bit of the older students he'd met back home at the university in Brockport.

A strange wistfulness filled the eyes of Thung's wife, too, as if she sensed that life might be too short. Gary wondered if the opportunities she dreamed of would ever come her way.

———

Each morning, Doc Nelson and Gary held a sick call in the dispensary, a practice that soon became Gary's responsibility, although Thung oversaw much of it. People queued up outside the dispensary. Montagnard villagers brought in kids with coughs, colds, and fevers. People came in with various aches and pains. One of the other Montagnard medics would help examine each person, write down the complaint, and lead the person through a tunnel into the bunker.

Thung often spoke to the Montagnards in a type of Sedang slang, which Gary never understood a word of, although he soon learned a few words of regular Sedang. If Thung suspected a goldbrick, someone wanting to get out of that day's work, he simply said a few words in Sedang slang, and the person would hang his head, turn around, and walk away. But Thung was savvy and gracious in diagnosing actual sicknesses. He sent people into the treatment room for Gary to take a closer look at, or he helped cleanse wounds or prescribe medicine. Gary performed many operations using local anesthesia, and Thung assisted. More serious surgeries requiring general anesthesia were sent back to Pleiku. The medical bunker was well stocked with medicines, bandages, microscopes, a table for operating, and an autoclave for sterilizing instruments. Engineers had strung wires that connected to the generator, so the bunker had electric lights.

After sick call was finished, Gary would meet with the medics and give training to improve their skills or help them advance to different jobs in the dispensary. Additionally, Gary would train Montagnard soldiers to serve as medics in the field during combat operations. He was continually impressed with the intelligence and quickness he witnessed in the other medics. Looking back today, Gary is in awe of the responsibility handed to him as a twenty-two-year-old kid. He was responsible for the health not only of the Green Berets and Montagnard troops but also of every other person in the camp—the troops' children and wives and other relatives too.

One of his first jobs was to complete, along with Thung, a medical folder for each person in the camp. Gary and Thung performed exams and did blood work. Meeting the people at the dispensary and completing the folder on each person helped Gary come to know the people and learn who they truly were.

As the days turned into weeks and months, Gary learned firsthand that every age of person—and every condition imaginable—was treated in the dispensary. He even delivered babies. When it came to a camp doctor, he was it.

One day Gary noticed that the children had hardly anything to play with. A group of boys, maybe six or seven years old, were playing in the dirt. He walked over and bent down to see what they were doing and was surprised to find that they had hooked together the links from belts of expended M60 machine gun rounds and made tiny toy "machines." The boys moved the machines through the piles of dirt as if they were building roads. He asked a boy what he liked best.

"Trucks!" the boy said. *Of course!*

Gary sent $400 home to his mother, and she mailed back a hefty supply of Matchbox trucks and cars. The kids jumped up and down in their excitement over their new toys. Gary noticed that they never seemed saddened by what they lacked. The children seemed content with living simply, and when they did get treats such as the Matchbox toys—they were overjoyed.

Some days Gary felt like a camp counselor. He took the children on hikes and to the nearby Dak Poko River, where the Americans had spaded out a swimming hole for the kids.

True to Nelson's word, the Green Berets hung up sheets and showed movies every week. The villagers really liked their westerns. Roy Rogers and his palomino horse, Trigger, always drew smiles. John Wayne was a favorite.

Even in the jungle, life can quickly develop into a routine. Gary's pattern was to rise early, inspect the sanitation of the cooking and dishwashing facilities in the team house (because parasitic and other GI issues could be easily spread through unsanitary conditions), eat breakfast (usually eggs, coffee, and bacon if they had it), exchange morning greetings with the other members of the team, then participate in morning company formations with the Montagnard fighters, and finally head to the dispensary to get ready for sick call.

After sick call came more training and other duties in the afternoon and sometimes into the evening. Each day ran long. Each night he slept hard. He was glad the team ate well. To augment their diet for lunches and dinners, the men traded Montagnard crossbows to the air force guys for pallets of steak and beer. Sometimes they ate fish pulled from the nearby river. Local housekeepers fixed the food, and meals were always tasty in the camp.

Gary also served as camp dentist, although few Montagnards ever wanted their cavities filled. It was a sign of beauty for Montagnards to have their teeth filed down or pulled and replaced by gold. The Montagnards chewed slivers of betel nuts and leaves that turned their teeth purple and wreaked all sorts of havoc inside their mouths, so Gary ended up pulling a lot of teeth. Novocain was used. A fully trained dentist came out to the camp to grade Gary's work, and the only thing the dentist ever gigged Gary for was that he needed to keep better dental records for the Green Berets themselves. None of the Berets ever wanted their teeth checked.

Another responsibility of Gary's was preventive medicine. In addition to checking the kitchen sanitation, Gary instructed the camp in proper rodent and other pest control. He sprayed for hazardous insects.

His favorite job (years later, he described this with a chuckle) was training the Montagnards in the fine art of human-waste disposal. In Montagnard culture the entire jungle was used as a restroom. But within the confines of a camp, that practice could be a serious problem. Gary worked to introduce the Montagnards to various types of latrines and sanitary disposal systems—and one type eventually caught on, although the plan took a while to gain acceptance.

One of the young Montagnards wanted more than anything to become a medic. He was short, maybe five feet tall, was about eighteen or nineteen years old, and had curly dark hair that always ran over his forehead. Named Tot (pronounced *tote*), he always wore baggy fatigues with his boots unlaced.

Gary worked with Tot for a while to show him how to read a thermometer and take a blood pressure reading, but Tot never learned to do either correctly, and it became clear that he lacked the aptitude to become a medic. Still, Tot pressed Gary to give him a job, and it struck Gary that Tot's eagerness reflected a desire to be needed, to do useful work, to be part of something special. Rather than wasting all that enthusiasm, Gary created a job for him as preventive medical specialist.

Gary, Tot, and the rest of the medics collected spent 105-millimeter shell canisters, each about a foot and a half long and four inches in diameter, bored holes in the bottom, and turned the canisters into "piss tubes" to make the locations for urination more centralized. They dug holes, placed rocks and sand in the bottom of the holes, and placed the tubes atop the holes to funnel the urine. Tot was in charge of the tubes. He took his new job seriously, relished the role, and succeeded in monitoring the tubes and teaching others how to use them.

Then Gary and Tot attacked another major project—where to put human excrement. They decided to build burnout latrines for the camp. Gary ordered all the wood, screening, and other materials needed, and he and Tot and the other medics built eight new latrines. Each was a two-seater, separated for privacy, and complete with toilet seats and screened windows to allow ventilation. Tot was proud of this accomplishment, but he soon came to Gary, frustrated.

"Bac Si ['doctor'], we got a problem," Tot said. "No matter how hard I try or what techniques I use, I can't get the others to use the latrines properly. They just don't know what to do." The young Montagnard was clearly upset.

"What do you mean?" Gary asked.

"Well, nobody wants to sit on the toilet seats. It's not how Montagnards go to the bathroom."

"What do they do?"

"Well, they stand on top and let go. They try to aim through the hole. Drop it right in, you know. I'm sorry, Bac Si, but they just won't sit."

Gary could only laugh. And as disappointing as this setback was for Tot, he promised Gary he wouldn't let up on his education initiatives. Eventually, with all his training and demonstrating, he achieved a measure of success.

Tot became a faithful ally, constantly working in and around the dispensary, and was someone Gary could always depend on to give his best in whatever assigned task.

From Gary's first day in Vietnam, he knew his life was changing. As he worked with the Montagnards, he grew to know people by name. He knew their likes and dislikes, their interests and dreams. He became filled with an overwhelming sense of responsibility—as well as fulfillment and significance. He seldom thought about cars, TVs, big houses, or other things he'd once deemed important back in the States. All that came to matter to him were people. He concluded that he was living his dream in his jungle Shangri-la. He had found a home. He had begun to truly live. One day as Tot and Gary worked side by side in the dispensary, a faraway look came into the young Montagnard's eyes. He cleared his throat as if he might say something, then furrowed his brow as if he was thinking, and finally asked, "You and I are friends, Bac Si, aren't we?"

Gary paused in his work and looked at Tot more fully. In the three months Gary had been at the camp, Tot had hardly left his side. The young man had become part of Gary's life. Gary knew that Tot added strength and an uncommon love to his life.

"We're friends for sure," Gary said with a smile.

———

As much as he enjoyed life at Dak Seang, Gary also looked forward to occasional trips back to Kontum. Doc Nelson or another medic would fly in and spell Gary, and whenever in Kontum, Gary visited two places. One was a hospital run by a female American surgeon who was known simply as Doc Smith. Gary would often spend a few days working with her and three or four other volunteers, some from England and some from Australia.

A graduate of the University of Washington School of Medicine, Dr. Patricia Smith was already a legend among the Montagnards, known far and wide as a miracle worker because of her love for people and skill in medicine. The Montagnards called her *ya pogang tih*—"big grandmother of medicine." Humble, kind, and wise, she had been in Vietnam since the 1950s.

During the Tet Offensive of March 1968, NVA troops had charged into her hospital, guns blazing, shooting patients and staff and ruining wards. Hospital staff hid Doc Smith, fearing she would be shot or kidnapped. When the NVA troops left, she administered aid, helped calm the patients and staff, and spent the next chunk of time rebuilding the hospital. Gary was amazed by her dedication and fearlessness.

Doc Smith and Mac McGinley, the gruff master sergeant who worked at the CIDG hospital, took Gary to a Montagnard leprosarium, the other place Gary often visited in Kontum. The leprosarium had been started by French missionaries shortly after World War II and was now run efficiently by a group of Catholic nuns. The patients made beautiful mosaics of tile, stone, and semi-precious gems and wove fabric and elegant tapestries that they colored with berries and other dyes. The fabric was used to make skirts and long wraps for women.

Every wall of the leprosarium was clean and freshly painted in a yellowish sand color, but strangely none of the buildings had doors that could shut. The reason soon became clear—many of the patients were missing fingers. Although so many of the patients were disfigured by the disease and had lost digits, noses, and other body parts, Gary couldn't help but notice an astounding spirit of joy throughout the leprosarium.

Both Doc Smith and Mac impressed on Gary the need to develop close relationships with the people he cared for. He needed to learn who they were and respect their values and practices. The depth of his relationships would ultimately determine how effective a medic he would become.

———

All these experiences burrowed into Gary's soul. He wasn't able to hear or read much news in Dak Seang, but when he did, the larger discussions surrounding the Vietnam War often sounded controversial and even confusing to him. Gary kept his mind focused on his work. His war had narrowed to the people he was caring for.

It wasn't that he ignored the larger picture. Gary understood the military importance of the Central Highlands. The various Montagnard tribes, more than twenty tribes in all, controlled the highlands, so it made sense for the Green Berets to befriend and train them in weapons, engineering, and communications. For a small jungle region, the highlands were critically important. The prevailing theory about the larger conflict was that if Ho Chi Minh could succeed in bringing all Vietnam under Communism, then the surrounding countries would fall like dominoes—Laos, Thailand, and Cambodia—and with that kind of momentum building, who knew what other countries might fall? So if you saved the Central Highlands, you saved Vietnam. If you saved the Central Highlands, you could win the war.

A medic named Sergeant Blessing worked at the hospital in Kontum. He was an enigma as a Special Forces soldier because he wore a peace sign around his neck and sprinkled antiwar rhetoric into his conversations. In the hospital dispensary he hung up a poster of Nixon riding a pig.

One afternoon while Gary was in Kontum on a supply run, Sergeant Blessing was loudly voicing his political views about Vietnam. Gary shook his head, finished his work, and quietly walked down the hall. He'd come to a new realization: He wasn't fighting for any global ideals or philosophy or economic system. He was fighting for the people he was living with. Them and them alone. The Montagnards were oppressed, and Gary was fighting to help free them.

Gary knew that the Montagnards welcomed American support because the indigenous tribes in Vietnam had been at war for some time. The NVA—professional soldiers trained by the Russians and Chinese—hated the Montagnards and considered them an inferior race worthy of extermination. Vietcong soldiers, the Communists from the south who allied with the NVA, were known to slink into Montagnard villages and commit atrocities. If the Green Berets hadn't come, the Communists would not have simply absorbed the Montagnards into their autocratic political system; they would have wiped them off the map. So the Montagnards' war was not just an exchange of one political system for another but a matter of survival. In many ways, Gary's war, his involvement, wasn't about the bigger political picture. He wasn't fighting for Nixon or Johnson or Kissinger. Yet he was still fighting a war, and his war lay in the Dak Poko River valley, with the people he'd come to care for.

He knew that the people who lived in this environment had survived other wars. They loved, created families, established a culture, village, and community, and they flourished without any of the material comforts that Americans would consider necessities. And they did so with beauty and altruism and freedom and fierce spirits. Dak Seang was no place for arrogance, Gary knew. The Green Berets were indeed well trained to teach the Montagnards about fighting for their survival, but that fight had begun long before the Green Berets arrived.

A larger goal at Dak Seang, Gary knew, was for the Green Berets to humbly transition into the Montagnards' camp, into their lives and histories and futures, and to build real relationships on mutual trust and respect. With this in mind, Gary articulated a new goal to himself. No matter what came, he was going to love and fight for the Montagnards. *Period.* That became his new mind-set, his new mission. He respected them. He supported them. And he would love and fight for them no matter what. As the words from the team house motto continued to sink into him, he realized he would even die for them.

And they would die for Gary too.

———

About a month after Gary arrived in camp, the Montagnard elders planned to hold a traditional rice wine ceremony. Thung brought Gary an invitation from the elders. He explained that it was special to be invited and the elders wouldn't invite just anybody. They recognized trustworthiness in Gary. When the elders shared their rice wine with somebody, it meant that he was a friend of the

Montagnards. He wasn't a stranger anymore. He was accepted into the tribe of the Sedang.

As twilight fell, the elders gathered with Gary in their midst. A large earthen jug, about two and a half feet high, was brought to their circle along with a split bamboo stem laid across the mouth of the jar. An additional stick was inserted through the bamboo stem into the wine, and the depth to which the stick reached indicated the amount of wine the elders wanted you to drink. An elder drank first and continued drinking until the stick no longer touched the wine. As the end of the stick appeared, the Montagnards would break into cheers, then replace the wine and look to the invitee to drink in the same manner.

When the wine first touched Gary's lips, he was shocked by its taste. He was no stranger to bars back in America, yet the liquid in the earthen jar could hardly be classified as a California Riesling. The liquid was bitter, cold, and strong—it had a definite kick going down. *Diesel fuel might be a more accurate comparison,* Gary thought. Using a straw inserted into the liquid, he drew as hard as he could, hoping to lower the liquid's level quickly so he could soon see the end of the stick and be done. He drank and drank, and as the end of the stick slowly came into view, the crowd cheered.

Gary felt overcome. Partially by the wine but also by the realization that he'd crossed a line. Bracelets and beaded necklaces were awarded to him as signs of mutual trust and respect between the Americans and Montagnards. He was a tribe member now.

Years later, Gary would say that there are few possessions he has ever received that he cherishes as closely as the gifts from the Montagnards. Their friendship. Their spirit. Their fierceness and joy. Their simplicity and contentedness. Their rice wine and bracelets. Their respect and invitations.

When it came to the tribe, he had come to *belong.*

6

Man on the Wire

One of the first things each Green Beret did after arriving in camp was to unofficially adopt a Montagnard soldier as a bodyguard.

The locals knew more about the hazards of the terrain and indigenous animals than the Green Berets, and the Montagnards considered it an honor to watch out for the Green Berets. A bodyguard had a Green Beret's back at all times, and real camaraderie and trust developed between them. Bonds were not established based on similar interests such as cars and sports, as they might have been back in the States. Bonds were built on who a person became to you—someone you could depend on, who could say the same about you. Survival, even life and death, depended on these bonds.

Shortly after arriving in camp, Gary had met a Montagnard soldier named Deo (pronounced *day-oh*) and, in a week or two, Deo became Gary's personal bodyguard. Deo dressed in jungle fatigues and a hat and always wore a serious expression. Whenever Gary went outside the camp, Deo went with him. Deo would show Gary what to eat and not eat. Deo looked out for poisonous snakes. He was savvy and smart and always carried his M16 rifle. Already he had experienced three years of combat. Already he had walked the trails outside camp, protecting Green Berets. Already he had protected grown men from tigers and booby traps and ambushes and other dangers of the jungle.

Deo was fifteen.

When Gary first choppered down in Dak Seang, it surprised him how young so many of the Montagnard soldiers looked. He later found out that in Montagnard culture, boys were inducted early into the privileges and responsibilities of tribal manhood. When a boy reached the age of twelve, he was considered an adult and became one of the camp defenders. Some of the best Montagnard warriors Gary came to know were in their mid to late teens and early twenties.

Gary was never fully comfortable with boys being soldiers, particularly the younger ones, although he respected the intricacies and necessities of tribal culture. Often he would try to sort out the differences he saw between Dak Seang and the United States. Back in basic training he'd known American soldiers as young as eighteen. Some even seventeen. Yet his thoughts were of the civilian children and teens he knew in the States. They might play at war with water guns or plastic weapons as Gary had when he was growing up. But in Vietnam he always had trouble grasping the idea that young teens were fighting a real war, with real weapons that fired real bullets.

Deo became extremely protective of Gary, and they talked frequently. One evening the two walked out by the wire near a wall piled with sandbags. They sat down and looked toward the forest to the west and the river to the south. Deo pulled out a can of warm Coke and popped the top. The two split the drink. He said that his dream was to go to the United States someday and become a cowboy like the ones he saw in the western movies. Gary shared that he was already living his dream as a Green Beret in Vietnam with him. Deo liked that, and he smiled knowing that he was a part of Gary's dream. They talked about girls. Gary told Deo about his breakup in college, and Deo expressed sorrow, knowing that the split had hurt Gary so badly. Deo had never had a girlfriend . . . *yet*, he added. He was looking.

Gary wrote home to his mom and asked her to send a pair of Levi's jeans in a size he specified. When the package arrived, the jeans fit Deo perfectly. He loved the gift and gave Gary a Montagnard bracelet as a sign that Gary was now adopted by him. Made of brass, the bracelet had been constructed out of spent M14 rounds. Gary wore the bracelet always. He traded other items with one of the air force guys for a revolver—a .38 Special, just like a cowboy would use— and gave it to Deo. From that point onward, Deo always wore the revolver in a holster around his waist.

On another evening they walked out to the wire. Deo and Gary both had Cokes this time, and the two talked. Gary had noticed that Deo never mentioned his family members—*had they been killed in the war?* But something felt different this night, and Gary chose to make a careful inquiry.

Deo looked away when Gary asked him about his parents. His siblings. His grandparents. His aunts and uncles and cousins. Deo glanced at the stars and his eyes grew moist. Then he said one sentence. It told Gary all he needed to know.

"Bac Si, you are my family."

————

Plenty of good-natured hijinks happened in Dak Seang. Staff Sergeant Gordy "The Rock" Wiley and Gary bonded quickly over one such event. The Rock was the weapons specialist, and one day he got an idea to blow off some steam. He and Gary took the jeep-mounted 106-millimeter recoilless rifle outside the camp and began firing at trees about fifty meters away in an impromptu round of target practice. Just for fun.

They were like two boys with slingshots, except the 106 was basically an antitank weapon. Deo came along and fired a few rounds too. Firing the huge weapon felt satisfying to Gary—the whole process. Loading the round. Zeroing in on a target. Putting his fingers in his ears. Hitting the trigger button with his elbow. Feeling the blast and the jump of the recoil. Seeing the round slam against the tree and watching it disintegrate. The Kid and The Rock were in their early twenties, still crazy in their youth. They whooped and Deo chuckled. In the middle of the mayhem, The Rock turned to Gary and said, "Y'know, if you can't blow something up in the middle of a war, when can you do it?"

Not all bonding involved firing weapons. One day several Montagnards came to Gary because one of their water buffalo had injured its horn at the base near its head. The injury had become severely infected. Water buffalo were prized possessions that aided in farming and other necessary tasks. Because of their great value, they were often the first choice to become sacrifices for the many Montagnard religious feasts. Since Gary served as the camp's veterinarian, it was his job to heal the water buffalo.

Gary's training had never covered work on water buffalo, but he decided to give it his best shot. A small crowd gathered. Deo was there as always, as well as a medic named Pher who was in his early twenties and loved working with kids. Gary called over Tot and Thung and some of the other Montagnard medics and explained that they needed to try to clean the wound, then give the animal a couple of shots of antibiotics. A few of the younger medics tried to corral the water buffalo. The animal resisted. The wound clearly hurt. Someone came up with the bright idea of trying to ride the water buffalo while cleaning the wound. The buffalo switched on his rodeo mode, snorting and huffing, bucking and galloping. Medic after medic flew head over heels. The crowd laughed and clapped and grew. The show was on.

A water buffalo can be huge. Mean. Two thousand pounds. Someone else suggested lassoing the beast to gain control, maybe even wrestling his head down to the ground. This tactic also resulted in flying Montagnards. The crowd had grown quite large and a group jumped in to help. Fifteen Montagnards succeeded in roping the water buffalo, then tried to drag him closer to a nearby tree so they could secure the rope. An amusing tug-of-war resulted. To the crowd this was better than a movie, and they shouted encouragement and support—although Gary was never quite sure whether they were cheering for the water buffalo or the medics.

Finally the water buffalo was securely roped to a tree, although the rope was still long. Gary asked for volunteers to see if they could face the animal, antagonize him, and prompt him to run around the tree, hopefully winding the rope shorter and shorter. The idea was that once his head became secured against the tree, Gary could work on the wound. A young Montagnard ran toward the buffalo, screaming and waving his arms. The tactic worked. The water buffalo began circling the tree. Shorter and shorter the rope became. When at last the buffalo was stuck fast, the entire crowd broke into a raucous cheer.

Gary cleaned the wound and shot the animal full of antibiotics, after which the water buffalo was carefully let go, to his obvious and immense relief. In time the horn healed, and Gary was sure the water buffalo's memorable experience earned it a place in the tribe's oral history.

Each day in Dak Seang brought new adventures. Downtime was spent loading up the deuce-and-a-half with children and driving them to the river for swimming, a welcome relief from the burning daytime sun. Montagnard children didn't engage in many recreational activities, so Gary always enjoyed seeing them swim and play. Deo came along and swam too.

The Green Berets set up a volleyball net on the riverbank, so many of the older kids and even some adults would play. Some afternoons, when it felt as if a regular beach party was underway, it was hard to remember this was a war zone.

One day the camp's new civil affairs officer, First Lieutenant Ed Christensen, threw down a challenge to The Rock and Captain Landers, the team leader. All three were boasting about their experiences and skill as Green Berets. The contest was to see who could call in the most accurate artillery fire on a site picked by one of his opponents. The weapons chosen were 155s and 175s—huge artillery cannons located at another Special Forces camp about twenty miles away. Gary looks back and suspects beer was involved too.

The challenge began. Gary and five of the men climbed up the thirty-foot observation tower in the middle of the camp. They referred to it as their "John Wayne tower" because it looked just like the tower in his movie *The Green Berets*. The tower was reinforced and protected by sandbags and provided an excellent 360-degree view of the camp and surrounding area. In order to prevent enemy troops from sneaking up to the camp walls, the guys had cleared all vegetation from the walls back about two hundred meters. This way they had a clear view and field of fire if attacked.

For the challenge, one guy peered at the terrain through binoculars and picked a site. Another guy jumped on the radio and called the other Special Forces camp, giving the code and coordinates. Then they all sat back and waited for a shell to whistle in and land with a huge explosion.

The artillery guys in the other camp had a bracketing procedure. They overshot the target first. Then undershot the target. Then fired for effect. Even from twenty miles away, they could hit exactly where they wanted to hit. Later, when the higher-ups questioned the expenditure of artillery rounds, the Green Berets told them they were targeting strategic locations to be used in case of an attack.

If they only knew how true this would become.

———

One afternoon the Green Berets received orders to go into the jungle on a weeklong mission. Some CIA operatives had been testing new devices that could detect enemy body heat and movement, then relay the information to headquarters. They'd dropped a bunch of the devices (the Green Berets called them "hens and chickens") out in the jungle, but some weren't functioning properly. So the Green Berets were told to gather a platoon of fighters and go out and bring them in.

The team leader gathered about twenty-five Montagnard soldiers. The Rock and Gary were chosen to go along too—as would Deo since he went wherever Gary went. The platoon geared up, and three helicopters ferried the troops about twenty-five minutes into the jungle, dropping down low—pretending they were landing to let the platoon out—then climbing up again. The helicopters repeated this pattern several times. This was a tactic used to keep the NVA confused as to exactly where the platoon had entered.

The soldiers hiked for a while in the hot sun, then paused to set up camp for the night. Before the sun set completely, Gary observed how pretty the area looked. They were surrounded by smaller trees, and in the midst of the smaller trees were huge-trunked trees rising thirty feet. When the sun rose early the next morning, Gary noticed how the leaves glistened with dew and the foliage provided a beautiful blend of dark and light greens and browns—the same colors as their tiger fatigues.

For several hours that second morning, the men hiked through the forest. They stayed off trails because these paths were too dangerous. Nobody spoke. Everybody used hand signals, and the jungle silence reigned in Gary's ears.

The sun cut through the canopy, and everything quickly grew hot. The men brushed through smaller palmetto plants and foliage that Gary didn't recognize. Every so often a Montagnard would pull up valued roots and stick them in a pack because these roots didn't grow close to home. The Montagnards seemed to know exactly where they were and pointed out the occasional bamboo pit viper, which had a light green color. As far as snakes go, they weren't long but they were deadly. The Green Berets called them "three-step snakes." If you got bit, you'd take three steps, then keel over, dead. Other snakes inhabited that area—boas, pythons, and cobras. But that day Gary saw only pit vipers.

About 10:00 a.m. the brush became so thick that the Montagnards chose to follow a trail for a short while, only to gain some relief from the hard work of hacking their way through the jungle. Gary's heart began to pound. He knew they needed to get off the trail soon. He was positioned in the middle of the pack of soldiers and couldn't see much except the jungle and the man ahead. Deo hiked behind Gary, and The Rock was a short way in front. Each man stayed three to five yards behind the person in front. A thick bead of sweat soaked into Gary's collar and ran down his back. *We're taking far too much time on the trail.* The air was still. Too still. *Why aren't we getting off the trail?*

Kaboom!

Gary heard the explosion, then saw a flash. *Rat-a-tat-tat!* Gunfire broke through the trees. The soldiers each dropped to one knee. Bullets whizzed toward the platoon. More gunfire sounded. Gary couldn't see where the bullets were coming from, only that they were flying in their direction.

The soldiers fired back. Each person alternated shooting to the right, then to the left to try to gain a sense of the enemy's location. Firing his M16, Gary knew they were sitting ducks. If they stayed on their knees more than a moment or two, they'd die. His heart pounded, but his training kicked in too. He found he could think. He knew most enemy ambushes were L shaped, so the allied soldiers needed to determine which direction the fire was coming from, then charge into the point of the L, where the heaviest enemy fire would be.

"Bac Si! Bac Si!" Gary heard the cries for a medic over the gunfire. He stopped firing and charged forward with Deo on his heels.

A young Montagnard lay crumpled in the dirt, blood spurting from his wounds. Both of his legs had been blown off. His name was Hyih (pronounced *he*), and he was about the same age as Deo. Gary scrambled to put tourniquets on the stumps and dowse the ends in epinephrine, which would constrict the blood vessels. Then he hastily bandaged the stumps to control the loss of blood.

Meanwhile, The Rock called in a helicopter and fire support. The NVA had been lying in wait for the platoon of Montagnards, but the resulting ambush didn't last long. Less than ten seconds. Maybe more like seven.

Hyih had stepped on a booby trap or claymore mine. Gary was awed by the strength of the young warrior. He didn't scream or writhe in pain. He simply fastened his eyes on Gary's and focused on every word he said, nodding when Gary told him he was going to be okay.

Gary looked up from his patient and noticed that nobody was firing. Not their side. Not the enemy either. The NVA had simply vanished. All that remained was anger, frustration, the silence of the jungle, and a teenager who didn't have his legs anymore.

Gary knew the booby trap and ambush tactic was meant to create a psychological threat as much as a physical one. It was a terrorist strategy. The NVA wanted the other side to know they were always there, always watching, always able to inflict harm. It felt frustrating to Gary because the enemy was never seen and wouldn't stay around and fight.

A helicopter soon flew overhead, then hovered low. Hyih asked if Gary would visit him in the hospital in Pleiku, and when Gary nodded, Hyih asked if Gary would bring him candy and a carton of cigarettes too. Gary nodded again. He helped load Hyih onto the chopper, where a different medic waited.

When the helicopter left, the men continued with the mission. The team eventually located the sensors, but the lead Green Beret determined that too many NVA troops were in the area to safely retrieve the devices. He relayed the situation to headquarters, and the mission ended. The sensors were never recovered.

It took about two weeks for Gary to be able to visit Hyih in Pleiku. Infection had set in, and more of the boy's legs had needed to be amputated above the knees, but he was going to live. Gary hoped his visit would lift the young man's spirits.

Often, when a Montagnard went to the hospital, his whole family packed up and moved to be with him. Gary was happy that when he entered the ward, Hyih's face lit up and he shouted, "Bac Si, so good to see you!"

But as Gary went closer, Hyih's face fell, disappointed. For a moment Gary was puzzled, but then with dawning awareness, he traced the tribal ethic. He knew that no one in Montagnard culture would ever think of stealing from or lying to a friend. A Montagnard would not even farm an area of the village that was not his. Lies and broken promises were not part of their lives, and words spoken in promise—even a nod—were as good as any contract.

"Bac Si . . . the candy and cigarettes?" Hyih asked. "You gave me your word."

Gary slapped his forehead. He'd forgotten. "I'll be right back," he said. Immediately he went to the PX, where he bought candy and cigarettes for his friend. He became keenly aware of the power of his word.

The Montagnards' survival, their very existence, depended on their ability to trust one another.

Gary never made that mistake again.

———

Encountering—and hopefully *overcoming*—danger was an everyday part of Montagnard life.

One day a young boy fell into a nest of vipers and was bitten by them. Others rushed him to Gary in the dispensary. The main treatment for such a snakebite was to put a tourniquet around the affected limb to limit the blood flow and keep the venom from spreading. Once it started flowing within a body, the venom could quickly enter a person's lungs or heart and stop the neural impulses necessary for life.

The boy was about six years old and covered in bites from head to toe. Gary took a quick look at him and immediately called in a helicopter. He felt helpless. There was no way tourniquets would work. He ran to his medical books and scanned page after page, desperate for any information that might help the boy. The chopper arrived and Gary rushed him on board. The helicopter took off, ascended above the trees, and headed toward the hospital in Pleiku. The boy died before they were halfway there.

His death affected Gary deeply. He returned to his medical books and read everything he could on snakebites, wondering if there was anything more he could have done. Maybe there was something he'd overlooked. There wasn't. Sometimes little boys in Dak Seang fell into viper pits and died.

In Dak Seang, death was a way of life.

———

About a month after the ambush where Hyih lost his legs, Gary and some Montagnard fighters were called out on a reconnaissance mission to check security in the areas outside camp. Recon missions happened regularly, with the Montagnard fighters doing the bulk of the detail. The Montagnards were paid for their work, and there wasn't anything special or unusual about this mission. Gary had been on such missions earlier. Sometimes they walked up toward the mountains, only a few kilometers from the camp. The Montagnards would show him valleys and waterfalls—beautiful areas—and the missions even felt peaceful.

For this mission the men weren't inserted by helicopters; they just walked out into the jungle a few hundred yards. Gary was the only American accompanying about twenty-five Montagnard fighters. Again Gary and Deo walked about midpack. Again the jungle was quiet. Eerily quiet. Again Gary's heart began to pound.

Kaboom!

Booby trap. Another ambush followed. Shots rang out and the din of machine-gun fire. Cries of "Bac Si! Bac Si!" filled the air. Gary ran forward with Deo close behind. The lead soldier was wounded but fortunately had not suffered a significant injury. Gary patched him up, but tension was still heavy. The other fighters fanned out in the forest, and all was quiet for a while before one of the Montagnards called that he'd found a Russian AK-47 rifle, a boot, a hat, and a blood trail. One of the NVA troops had been hit. The Montagnard shouted for backup.

Gary and Deo and another Montagnard were closest and followed the first Montagnard farther into the jungle. He was already running, and they all quickened their pace to keep up. Every three or four feet, they saw broken branches and a good-sized pool of blood.

Historically, Montagnards were infamous for their warlike nature. They'd been known to chop off the heads of their enemies—and worse. The Montagnards with Gary were screaming, yelling, furious. They wanted to get the wounded NVA soldier. Gary found himself screaming, yelling, and furious along with them. A curious new feeling had risen, one he didn't recognize. Although he had no chance to reflect on the feeling as he ran through the jungle, years later he distinctly remembered not liking how he felt. There was something growling inside him, something that felt unleashed and vengeful, something that wanted to hurt somebody.

Only after many years had passed could he look back and name the feeling as his first experience of pure hate. And what that hate might have caused him to do on the trail scared him.

Eventually, the trail ran cold. The wounded enemy was never located. Gary could only imagine what might have happened if they'd found him.

———

A few weeks later, it was late at night and Gary couldn't sleep. The old year had given way, 1970 had begun, and he stole outside to enjoy the cool night breeze that sometimes blew off the mountains. He headed out to the wire to lie down on the sandbag wall of the outer perimeter so he could look up into the clear night sky. He'd spent nights in the jungle with the fighters, nights so black because of the triple canopy that nothing could be seen. But tonight the sky was filled with stars, and their light and the moonglow were enough to reveal much of what was around him.

"You are alone?" came a sudden question.

Gary looked up and abruptly sat up. The breeze blew to his back, and he hadn't smelled smoke, but the figure in the dark was now so close that Gary could smell the strong tobacco from a pipe. He didn't know the name of this man who'd suddenly come near, but he had seen him around the camp. An elder, very old for Montagnard standards, he was slender and had a bit of a beard, dark eyes, and still a good head of hair, although gray. The man wore baggy green fatigue pants rolled up like shorts to his midthighs and a short-sleeved khaki shirt like those worn by Ho Chi Minh. A narrow cape wrapped his shoulders. The elder explained that he was not on guard duty but simply enjoyed walking along the wall late at night. He said that ever since he was a boy, he'd gone for walks in the dark, always checking his surroundings, always making himself aware in case danger threatened.

The walks weren't for exercise. The elder had fought against the Japanese in World War II. After that, he'd fought against the Chinese, who provided weapons and aid to the Viet Minh. After that, he'd fought against the French until France pulled out of the country in 1954. Then he'd fought against other Montagnard tribes. And then he'd fought against the Vietnamese Communists.

Gary sat in silent awe as the man described what it was like to grow up and grow old in a country and culture that was constantly at war. Many of the elder's friends and family members had died in battle. Death was a way of life for him as real and accepted as the gift of each new day. Knowing that death was always near made life so much more precious.

The elder asked Gary some questions about his life back home in the States, but Gary didn't feel much like talking. His past life seemed shallow compared with life in the jungle. The elder asked why Gary was in Vietnam, and again Gary didn't say much. He asked what Gary was learning from his time with the Montagnards, and Gary tried to answer, but the ideas were not yet well formed in his heart. The elder seemed like such a wise man, and Gary hoped he could someday achieve a small amount of the man's wisdom. His mind flashed back to the sign above the team house door. Gary spoke the words out loud in the dark, slowly, quietly . . .

"To really live, you must almost die. To those who fight for it, life has a meaning the protected will never know."

The elder nodded. He placed a reassuring hand on Gary's shoulder. As quickly as he had appeared, he was gone, invisible in the night. Only the smell of his pipe smoke remained.

7

Hours of Darkness

About once a month, Gary went on a supply run. Dizzy often came with him. They choppered from Dak Seang to Kontum, where they needed a jeep. Sometimes they secured the jeep officially. Other times they simply snagged a jeep from whichever US military post had a free one sitting out front.

After picking up the jeep, they drove south along Highway 14 to Pleiku. There Gary visited patients in the CIDG hospital—patients he had treated in Dak Seang and medevaced out—while Dizzy scrounged for supplies. Afterward the two Green Berets often connected with friends in the city.

The trip to Pleiku was business oriented, but the two Green Berets were youthful and wild at heart. The drive often turned into a joyride. With a bright, humid sun shining above, they drove their topless jeep fast on the paved road. Usually they pushed the front windshield down to let more air rush in to keep them cool. Highway 14 was patrolled by the Fourth Infantry Division, and the road was considered "hot," which meant that encountering enemy ambushes and small-arms fire was not uncommon.

One afternoon on the road just outside Kontum, Gary and Dizzy picked up a Vietnamese officer who was hitchhiking. The sun blazed down on them, and the officer grinned at the opportunity to have a lift. Gary and Dizzy were downing beers in an effort to keep cool. Each had his M16 alongside his leg, and they offered a beer to the officer, who gratefully accepted. The three of them flew along the highway with Gary behind the wheel, driving with one hand. They told jokes and swapped stories with the officer, laughing in the heat and sweat of the day. Their jeep had been "liberated" that day, not officially checked out of the motor pool, and the panache of their heist only increased their jocularity.

As they bombed over the crest of a steep hill, Gary suddenly clutched the steering wheel with both hands and hit the brakes hard. Ahead in the road lay a stalled deuce-and-a-half with a convoy of trucks stopped ahead of it. Rockets exploded all around the trucks. Smoke hazed the scene. A jet flew above. The convoy was taking incoming rounds from an ambush of enemy soldiers hidden on the right side of the road, and the soldiers in the convoy were firing back toward the trees.

Gary had been driving at about fifty miles per hour with the accelerator floored, so stopping in time proved impossible. He braked hard yet smashed into the back end of the stalled truck with a huge bang. The firing continued. Gary looked at Dizzy, and Dizzy looked at Gary. They both looked at the hitchhiker in the back, whose eyes were wide, blinking rapidly.

"Let's get out of here!" Dizzy shouted. "Now!"

The jeep's front fenders and grill were crumpled; its radiator hissed. Gary threw the transmission into reverse and backed away from the truck. He slammed the shifter into first gear, spun the jeep off the highway, and accelerated along the dirt shoulder on the left side of the road.

Plunk, plunk, plunk. Bullets hit the side of the jeep. Gary accelerated, shifting into second and third gears. They careened off-road alongside the stalled convoy, drove through the ambush, and roared off down the road.

By the time they reached Pleiku, the jeep was nearly dead. They let the hitchhiker off at the nearest bar. He nodded and climbed out without saying a word. All they needed to do now was to explain the condition of the jeep.

Gary chuckles when he tells this story today and adds, "Boy, did we get in trouble."

What they didn't know (and Gary is quick today to point out that this was no laughing matter) was that in the first few months of 1970 there'd been a buildup of enemy troops in the region. Some of these troops participated in overt hostile acts, such as the ambushes that occurred along Highway 14, while most slunk into the region unnoticed. Those troops were congregating in the hills overlooking the Dak Poko Valley. Waiting. Ready.

———

One of the most gifted medics in Dak Seang was named Chom (pronounced *choam*). He was around twenty years old and was married to a beautiful young woman who'd recently given birth to a healthy baby girl. The joy this infant brought to her family was wonderful for Gary to see. She had huge brown eyes that opened wide with wonder, and she was a happy baby who lived to give smiles and giggles to everyone she met.

Chom's wife wrapped the baby in a blanket, secured her to her back or chest, and carried her everywhere she went, as is the custom of Montagnard mothers. Chom proved a doting father, ever so proud of his child; whenever he held his baby girl, his countenance filled with new purpose, vigor, and manliness.

One afternoon Chom brought his daughter to the dispensary for Gary to examine. The child's skin was damp and hot. Her eyes were closed and she labored to breathe. Her temperature was 101 degrees, but her lungs were clear, and she wasn't vomiting, coughing, or having diarrhea.

Gary was mystified by the combination of symptoms. He drew some blood and ran lab tests to see whether he could detect any signs of bacterial or parasitic infection. The tests all came back negative. He asked Chom if they could keep the child in the dispensary for a few days so staff could monitor her and take blood samples as her temperature fluctuated. The dispensary had the bed space to handle up to fifteen patients, and when the baby moved in, Chom and his entire family moved in too—including grandparents, aunts, uncles, and cousins.

Unfortunately, over the next few days the child grew worse. Her fever spiked to 103 degrees and hovered there, dangerously high. The staff continued to take blood samples, but Gary and his team still could not determine what was causing her fever.

Gary grew increasingly concerned. One morning, Chom drew his daughter's blood and examined it under the microscope. He jerked his head backward and cried out to Gary in broken English: "Bac Si, come look! See what I find!" Gary came running. He looked through the microscope and saw the answer. The baby had contracted falciparum malaria—the deadliest form. Although they now knew the cause of her illness, they worried she might not survive. She was so young. She had been sick so long.

Normally when treating infants infected with malaria, Gary and his team would administer the medication orally. But because of the severity of the child's illness, Gary recommended giving her the medication via injection so it would work faster. When it came to reducing the fever and getting the malaria under control, every moment counted. Chom agreed and administered the medication.

The team waited. Gary explained that the medication would not affect the malaria itself that quickly, but he hoped the girl would soon show some signs of general improvement.

Within minutes the unexpected occurred. The girl's breathing became more shallow and labored. Her arms and legs started to twitch. She gave a little gasp. Chom glanced up at Gary with a fearful face. Was this normal?

Gary sprang into action. He tried not to look panicked, although he knew what was happening. He'd studied this but never seen it firsthand. The baby was having a serious allergic reaction to the medicine and going into anaphylactic shock. Then she stopped breathing. The immediate emergency treatment was to administer epinephrine (adrenaline) to help with breathing and blood pressure. The baby was already hooked to IVs to combat dehydration, so Gary rushed to administer the epinephrine, then began mouth-to-mouth resuscitation.

Chom checked the girl's pulse. Nothing. Gary began cardiac massage and alternated between cardiac massage, mouth-to-mouth, and injections of epinephrine. Desperately he hoped she would take a breath. Her heart needed to beat again. A tense minute passed. Then another. Gary kept working on the girl. Three minutes passed. Four. Five. As hard as he worked, there was still no breath. No pulse.

Gary refused to quit. Six minutes. Seven. Eight. More cardiac massage. More mouth-to-mouth. He felt the entire family slowly gathering around the table. He did not want to look up into all their faces. He knew they were depending on him. More cardiac massage. More mouth-to-mouth. Nine minutes. Ten.

Gary worked and worked. Fifteen. Sixteen. No pulse. No heartbeat. Twenty minutes. Twenty-two. More cardiac massage. More mouth-to-mouth. Twenty-five minutes. Twenty-seven.

"C'mon," Gary said. "Breathe . . . Breathe!" His voice rose to a command, as if he could will life back into her body. Then he felt a hand on his shoulder and heard another voice. This voice was quiet and trailed off, as if the speaker's mind was grasping a reality too difficult to bear. "Bac Si . . . it's okay." It was Chom's voice. "It's okay . . . It's okay . . ."

Chom pulled Gary away from the table. The two men stared into each other's face, then embraced. They held each other, clinging hard in their grief. Each family member hugged Gary. They hugged Chom. They hugged Chom's wife. They spoke words of compassion, comfort, and encouragement.

For years to come, Gary would be haunted by that morning. Something in his own soul had died along with the baby girl. He went over the sequence of events again and again, asking himself with each replay if there was something he could have done differently. *Better.* He felt haunted by the ghosts of self-doubt, plagued by the specters of guilt, trapped by unworthiness and self-hate. He was continually astounded by the words spoken by Chom and his family— how they'd tried to let Gary know that although the child's passing was sad, even tragic, they accepted that death was a constant part of their lives.

Gary sensed that he did not yet know what they knew about life and death. He believed that the death was his fault, yet Chom and his family were still able to see him—not with eyes of hatred or revenge or scorn—but with eyes of compassion. Forgiveness. Love.

———

One of the more powerful people in Dak Seang was the tribal witch doctor. He didn't look anything like a caricature of a witch doctor that might be portrayed on TV. No headdress. No bones around his neck or through his nose. Instead, he wore nondescript army fatigues he'd purloined from an older Montagnard in camp—the pants rolled up above his knees with a wrap across his shoulders. He was an older man, clean shaven and wrinkled, usually barefoot, and hospitable and gracious in his tone and mannerisms.

Thung had introduced Gary to the witch doctor shortly after Gary first choppered into the camp. Gary was hospitable and gracious back, although he noted to himself with a wry grin that they'd never covered "interactions with witch doctor" during army training.

The witch doctor often performed animal sacrifices, and Gary arranged to take him chickens and other animals in the interest of maintaining friendly relations since the villagers looked up to the witch doctor and also referred to him as "Bac Si." Gary's job was to enter and understand the Montagnards' culture, not vice versa, so he and the witch doctor often talked. The witch doctor would recount stories about fighting against the French back in the 1940s, and Gary would tell him about training back in the States.

The Montagnards, when they became ill, would often go to both Gary and the witch doctor, so Gary would sometimes consult with the witch doctor about treating certain villagers, and in turn the witch doctor would invite Gary's input when he experienced something Gary could help with.

Gary did not hold to the witch doctor's beliefs about animism and spiritism, but he noted that the power of belief can have a profound impact on one's outlook, overall state of health, and well-being. Plus, he figured, who was he to say that an unseen world didn't exist? Sometimes, however, the practices of the witch doctor took a darker turn.

One evening toward the end of March 1970, one of the camp's security guards, a young man named Yoih (pronounced *yoy*), came to the dispensary with a look of fear that Gary normally did not see in the young man. Yoih had dark skin and straight hair and always wore a red Coca-Cola T-shirt. He and Dizzy were good friends, and Yoih was known around camp as a capable young warrior, someone who didn't fear anything.

Yoih asked Gary if he could sleep in the dispensary because his family had developed some kind of grudge against him and had him "removed" from their lives. Gary wondered what "removed" actually meant. Yoih explained that it was like shunning, except it was permanent. A removed person was a pariah. An outcast. No longer part of the family or even the tribe. It all seemed very strange.

Yoih refused to explain why the removal had happened. Montagnard family culture was typically very close, yet family members had gone to the witch doctor as part of the removal process and paid him to place a death curse on Yoih. The witch doctor had agreed, performed his secret rituals, and declared that Yoih would soon die. Afterward the family wanted to stay as far away as they could from the curse.

Gary went to the witch doctor to find out why and how this curse was placed on Yoih and to see whether it could be removed, but the witch doctor explained that the matter was something that didn't concern Gary. When Gary pressed him, urging him to lift the curse, the witch doctor said matter of factly, "Once it's done, I can't undo it. Your medicine can't cure him." He asked Gary to leave.

Gary returned to the dispensary, told Yoih that he could stay there for as long as needed, and tried to comfort the young man and assure him that everything would be okay. Yoih thanked Gary for letting him stay but shook his head at the assurance.

"No, Bac Si," Yoih said. "It is true. No hope. He has cursed me. I will die."

Within days Gary saw a dramatic change in Yoih. The young man developed diarrhea and a fever. He stopped eating. Gary started IVs to provide nourishment and rehydration, but nothing seemed to help the young man. Blood work and other lab tests revealed nothing medically wrong.

After a week passed, Gary medevaced Yoih to the CIDG hospital in Pleiku, hoping they might be able to find the cause and begin treatment. Gary suspected psychosomatic reactions and also wondered if simply getting Yoih out of Dak Seang might have a positive effect on him. Nothing helped.

The family's reaction to Gary during this week proved frustrating and puzzling. Whenever Gary tried to talk with them, they simply shook their heads. Gary had seen them act so caring and supportive of Yoih in the past, but now that same care and support were gone. After Yoih was sent to the hospital, his parents told Gary there was nothing anybody could do. The witch doctor was too powerful.

One week later, a chopper returned to Dak Seang. Inside was the body of Yoih. A report came from the CIDG hospital, listing the diagnosis and cause of death as unknown.

A strange transformation happened within the family. Now that Yoih was dead, they believed the curse was lifted. He was no longer considered "removed." They took his body from the chopper and into the bunker where they lived to begin preparations for burial and for the funeral celebration of his life.

A few days later, Dizzy and Gary went to the funeral, which was scheduled to last all night. Americans were seldom invited to Montagnard funerals, although Gary and Dizzy had been to a few. This one seemed different from the start. The atmosphere felt elevated. Tense. Apprehensive. Gary asked Dizzy if he noticed something strange about the mood, and Dizzy remarked that he definitely sensed a similar peculiarity. They wondered aloud whether the mood was due to the situation surrounding the curse or perhaps due to Gary being seemingly helpless to save the young man. The Montagnards, too, were acting peculiar, as if something huge and dark was afoot. An evil lay outside their gates, and the evil was pressing in closer, almost as if it could not be stopped.

It was March 31, 1970. The funeral progressed through the evening and into the early-morning hours. Food was shared. Stories of Yoih's young life were told. People cried. Women in Yoih's family led the ceremonial tribal wailing. Ceremonial drumming echoed throughout the camp. Dizzy and Gary were lost in the emotion and the strange beauty of the ceremony held in this young man's honor.

Dawn broke. April 1, 1970, about four o'clock in the morning. In ten days Gary was scheduled to go on R & R for a much-needed break. Light began to rise over the mountains but without the sense of promise a new day usually brings. Shapes became visible as silhouettes only. The night's deeper darkness still seemed to reign in this shadow time.

Throughout the camp, women and children were first to rise in the dimness, as was customary, to begin the daily chores and prepare the morning meal. The solemnity of the funeral ceremony was just about over. The drumming ceased. The wailing went silent. A moment of stillness was held in the family bunker. Everything went quiet. It was that same eerie silence, Gary noted—the sound of *remoteness*—that he'd heard when he first came to the camp.

Then, without warning, came a different sound, and a bead of sweat broke out on Gary's forehead. He and Dizzy didn't even glance at each other. Their training kicked in . . . and they ran.

8

Siege of Dak Seang

The whistling of incoming rockets pierced the early-morning silence and climaxed with deafening explosions.

One. Two. Three. *Boom! Boom! Boom!*

More rockets whistled in with speed and fury and rocked the camp. A fourth. A fifth. Then everything erupted. The noise of battle became relentless. Rocket after rocket zoomed in. *Boom! Boom! Boom!* Mortars fell all around with defiant blasts. Smoke choked the air. Shell fragments sizzled on the ground. Gary and Dizzy sprinted out of the family bunker and headed to their alert positions. Gary's alert position was the 4.2-inch mortar pit outside the dispensary.

While sprinting to his station, Gary spotted a Montagnard woman lying on the ground, bleeding, trying to shelter two children with her body. As a medic his job was to heal, yet as a Green Beret he was also a weapons specialist.

Gary made an instant decision. He ran to the 4.2-inch mortar pit and began firing illumination and HE (high-explosive) rounds at predetermined locations outside the wire. He hoped that his choice was the right one. With any luck the illumination rounds would help whoever was in the high watchtower in the center of camp to identify the enemy's positions. If that happened, then perhaps the enemy could be stopped right away. Perhaps no more people inside the camp would be hurt.

Enemy shells continued to rain down. Gary ran out of the pit and tried to survey the damage. The barracks were being pounded. The dispensary was taking fire. The communications tower was under attack. The camp's two 105-millimeter artillery cannons were being pulverized. The main generator was already leveled and destroyed. Gary concluded that the North Vietnamese had been informed by someone inside the camp regarding the location of strategic items. The camp was being systematically targeted. These were not random shells. The enemy wasn't even bracketing—overshooting and undershooting a target first to gauge the shell trajectory. They had already zeroed in on everything that appeared important to hit. And the shells only kept coming: *boom, boom, boom, boom, boom.*

Gary raced toward the underground medical bunker. The wounded woman and her children were no longer in sight. He searched for his medics—none were in the bunker. Their plan was that during any attack they would report to the dispensary first and load up with medical kits and supplies, then head out to their respective company areas to treat any wounded. Gary was only one person. But if his medics were with him, together they could help more people sooner. He raced back outside and saw more bodies on the ground now, mostly women and children, more bodies than he could count. He didn't even know where to begin triage. He needed help—immediately!

His mind turned to Thung, his senior Montagnard medic. He needed to reach Thung and bring him back to help. *Why isn't Thung at the dispensary?* Gary turned and sprinted toward the outer wall and the underground bunker system where the Montagnard families lived. He jumped over a wall into a trench near Thung's house and spotted him. It looked as if their house had taken a direct hit. The medic sat outside in the dirt, rocking back and forth, cradling something in his arms. As Gary ran closer, his throat closed. Thung was cradling a torso. The headless body of his wife. She was the one who'd wanted to become a nurse. Every day she'd brought Thung lunch at the dispensary.

Gary ached for Thung and his family, but he shouted at him to get up, get moving. To stay stationary meant certain death. Glazed, Thung didn't move.

"C'mon! You gotta get going!" Gary said and shook him, but still Thung didn't move. Gary spun on his heel and started to run back. A huge rocket zoomed in, exploded, and shook the entire area with a gigantic blast.

Five decades later, Gary still recalls the grit of debris in the air. He can smell the smoke. Hear the screams. But the exact sequence of events from that explosion onward isn't precise in his mind. To him it's like writing down each incident that happened during the siege of Dak Seang on its own playing card. You throw the deck high in the air, scattering the cards. Gary can pick up each card and tell you about it, but he can't place them in order. When he recounts the events, he works to place them in the sequence that seems most logical. Eyewitness accounts and after-action reports help fill in any blanks.

After the debris settled and he realized he was not wounded, Gary leaped to his feet and started running back to the medical bunker. He reached a wall and started to climb over, then saw Pher, the medic who loved kids so much, the man who'd helped with the water buffalo incident. Pher lay facedown on the ground. Gary ran to him and turned him over. A rocket blast had ripped apart the young man's chest, but he was still breathing. A big, sucking chest wound. Gary could see the air escaping and the blood running out. Gary needed to quickly cover Pher's chest with an airtight seal. His mind scrambled to think of something he could use. Maybe the large plastic bags that came wrapped around the camp's artillery shells. He did what he could for Pher in the moment. "I'll be right back!" he yelled.

Gary sprinted across the open yard and made it into the inner security area, where the team house, barracks, and dispensary used to stand. He grabbed several large plastic bags and headed outside again. Gary heard another rocket whistling in. He hit the ground and waited for the blast. *Kaboom!* The ground shook.

As dirt and debris settled from the explosion, Gary scrambled up and ran back to Pher with the bags but, when he reached him, Pher was already dead.

Gary spotted a Montagnard who'd been leveled by the last rocket, although he was still alive. Gary ran to him and saw that the man had multiple wounds to his legs, arms, and chest. His entire body was riddled with shrapnel. Before Gary could do anything to help him, he heard another rocket whistling. By the sound it was making, he knew this one would hit close—really close. Gary threw his body on top of the young man and braced for the explosion. The world turned hazy and high pitched. The rocket exploded. Hot shards of metal entered Gary's body and hit his spine.

Nothing he'd ever experienced had felt like this. Decades later, he tried to explain the feeling of being hit. Before the siege, at the hospital in Pleiku, Gary had visited a Montagnard who had a high fever and a serious infection. The doctor there had done a bone marrow tap, and he'd invited Gary to watch the procedure. Two instruments were involved—the first looked like a hollow screwdriver, and the second was an actual hammer. The doctor anesthetized the patient's skin at the point of the tap and explained that the first instrument would go directly into the bone and that the patient would feel momentary intense pain. "Don't worry," the doctor added. "This will hurt but only for a second. And then you'll pass out."

That's what Gary experienced on the battlefield. One moment of intense, incredible pain that temporarily shut down his body. He may have passed out. Or maybe he wavered between consciousness and unconsciousness, because Gary does remember that during the blast a powerful hurricane-like force picked him up and threw him. While in midair, three thoughts flashed through his mind—wild thoughts that mirrored the craziness of being blown up:

I wonder if this is what it feels like to be kicked by a horse.

Hey, Purple Heart. I hope I live long enough to receive it.

I'm going to die here. Today.

As he flew through the air, Gary's spirit seemed to separate from his body. He remembers being outside his body, watching himself soaring head over heels and landing in the 4.2-inch mortar pit. As his body hit the sandbags that ringed the pit, his spirit reentered his body. He became aware again of who he was and that he was still alive. He didn't feel the intense pain of a moment ago. He thudded against the sandbags and rolled facedown. A moment passed. Another. He tried to move. Head. Neck. Arms. Hands. Upper body. Everything in that sequence moved. Then he tried to move his legs. Nothing. He tried his legs again. He willed them to move. *Legs!*

Legs?

Gary was paralyzed from the waist down. He craned his neck, searching for the wounded Montagnard, the one he had sheltered moments ago. The schoolhouse near where the man had lain was now a pile of concrete and timbers. Gary's gaze raked the area, but he couldn't find the young man to see how he was doing. He searched the area again; then it dawned on him. Parts of a body were spread across the ground. A streak of raw hamburger in the dirt. Gary's mind swirled—*I was on top of him when the blast occurred. To protect him! How did I survive when he didn't?*

He could feel water all around him and saw he was lying in mud. Mud wasn't normal in that area of the camp, and he concluded the enemy had probably hit the water tanks and purification tubs. Each could hold several thousand gallons, and they were always kept full of water.

In the distance he heard machine gun and automatic rifle fire . . . a ground assault was coming. The enemy would pour into the camp soon. He tried to stand so he could move into the pit and fire the mortar again, but he remained on his stomach on the ground. Already he'd forgotten that he couldn't use his legs.

As he lay in the dirt, he felt blood seeping out of his wounds. A moment of utter helplessness. Two moments. Three. His mind churned. *What good is a paralyzed medic on the battlefield?*

Suddenly, he felt hands under his armpits, strong hands lifting him. Gary heard his bodyguard's familiar voice next to his ear. Deo was there, standing, holding Gary upright. Gary threw an arm around Deo's shoulders. Gary was five feet, eleven inches tall and weighed 193 pounds. Deo was a full head and shoulders shorter than Gary. The boy began dragging Gary toward the underground medical bunker.

"Deo . . . what are you doing here? How did you find me?"

"This is where I belong, Bac Si . . . with you." Deo's voice was surprisingly calm.

As the two young men made their way toward the opening of the bunker, another rocket whistled in. Deo dropped Gary and covered him with his body. The explosion shook the earth. Deo stood, hoisted Gary again, and dragged him farther. In another ten feet another rocket flew in. Again Deo dropped Gary and covered his body. The ground erupted. Again Deo stood, picked up Gary, and dragged him nearer to safety. A third time this happened. They were close to the bunker now.

The air was full of bullets from machine gun and automatic rifle fire. The artillery, rocket, and mortar fire had increased. Dust and noise and bullets and smoke were everywhere. Nearby a Montagnard fighter lay wounded. Gary motioned for Deo to drag him closer to the man. He had a chest wound and wasn't breathing. Gary sat near the man, placed pressure on his gunshot wound, and began mouth-to-mouth resuscitation. He paused long enough to utter two words to Deo: "Pull us!"

Somehow Deo pulled both Gary and the man toward the medical bunker. As out of place as it might sound in that moment of chaos and valor, while still giving mouth-to-mouth resuscitation, Gary noticed that his pants were shredded and falling down.

As a rule, most Green Berets didn't wear underwear because of heat and chafing, and in his mind's eye Gary imagined how funny he must look in the middle of a battle, all his private matters blowing in the wind. He quickly yanked his pants back up and secured them with a bandage.

Safely inside the underground bunker, Gary saw Sergeant Dan Noonan— the Green Berets' newest medic. He was triaging the wounded and directing some of the Montagnard medics in how to treat patients. Nearby lay a Montagnard who'd had his leg blown off. Dan was trying to tie off bleeders. He'd been on site for only about two days and was scheduled to relieve Gary fully when his R & R started on April 10.

Dan saw Gary and ran over to begin treatment, but Gary pushed him away. "Work on the others first," Gary yelled above the intense noise. "I'm okay."

"You sure?" Dan asked.

"You got things under control here?"

"Yeah. I got it all set." Dan motioned to the man missing a leg. "This one's okay." Gary nodded, and Dan left to work on another of the wounded. Gary looked around the bunker for Deo. He was close by.

"What do you need, Bac Si?" Deo asked. "Anything?"

Gary didn't answer directly. He looked into the young man's eyes and held them for a moment. The teenager's face showed no fear, only purpose. A sense of mission. They both knew there was much more work to be done.

"Deo . . ." Gary said. "Take me back outside."

9

True Soldier

As Deo carried Gary out of the relative safety of the underground bunker, they saw Montagnard officers directing fighters to defensive positions around the camp. Some of them were running. Others were already dug in, firing back at the enemy. Intense small-arms fire blazed from a multitude of positions.

Quickly, Gary tried to assess what needed to be done. A mother walked by in a daze, holding the body of her lifeless child. As far as he could see, in the midst of all the flying lead, bodies littered the camp—wounded person after wounded person needed help.

Time was meaningless. In the first part of the siege, Gary had felt the constant pounding. The sky had lit up like a city's fairground on the Fourth of July, and the ground shook from one huge explosion after another. But now the tide of the battle was shifting, although Gary didn't know why or to what. Small-arms fire continued, and bullets whizzed through the air.

He could see that every building above ground in Dak Seang was rubble. The team house was gone. The schoolhouse was gone. The dispensary was gone. The generators were gone. House after house was gone. Any wall or beam left standing was riddled with bullet holes. Because of the great volley of artillery and mortar rounds, the ground was cratered like the moon. Only the observation tower remained.

As Gary and Deo determined their course of action, they heard a huge explosion in the middle of the camp. Someone yelled that the Green Berets' civil affairs officer, First Lieutenant Ed Christensen, had been blown out of the observation tower. He was lying wounded and exposed in the midst of heavy fire. The tower had toppled. No one could reach Christensen.

"Let's go!" Gary shouted to Deo.

Deo half carried, half dragged Gary across the open center of the camp. Machine-gun fire burst from all directions. Bullets kicked up the dirt. Deo and Gary reached Christensen and saw he had a number of severe wounds. Gary checked to make sure Christensen was breathing. He did what he could to stop the bleeding, then hung on as Deo dragged both the fallen officer and him back toward the bunker.

On the way Gary heard a crack and felt a bolt of lightning rip through his side. He'd been hit by small-arms fire. Or perhaps a mortar's explosion. Deo continued dragging the two men to the underground bunker.

Dan Noonan rushed to the trio, ordered a medic to attend to the officer, then turned his attention to Gary and wrapped a compression bandage around his waist to stop the newest bleeding. Dan then ordered a Montagnard medic to take Gary's vitals while he turned to care for Christensen.

"Stay in the bunker," Dan added in a shout to Gary. "I'll be back soon to take a better look at your wounds." Dan turned his attention to the officer.

Gary grabbed Deo by the pant leg and hissed, "C'mon. We got more to do."

As Gary and Deo reached the surface again, the smells, sounds, and sights were overwhelming. Explosions. Gunfire. Constant screams of fear and pain. By this time the camp was choked with a gray cloud of gunpowder, but through the smoke Gary saw great need everywhere. Deo dragged him from person to person, and Gary helped each one.

In an eyewitness account, operations sergeant Thomas Drake, a newer member of the team, summarized the action this way:

Sergeant Beikirch, refusing medical aid, rushed back out into the open in search of additional wounded personnel. Making at least seven trips across the open area between the camp's inner and outer perimeters, Sergeant Beikirch repeatedly exposed himself to the enemy fire as he recovered one wounded man after another.

Then Gary heard a frantic shout: "They're in the wire! We need help over here!" The ground assault had begun. The enemy had dug tunnels and ditches to get closer to the camp's outside wall. They'd broken through to the surface during the artillery, rocket, and mortar barrage. This was a tactic similar to one used to defeat the French at Dien Bien Phu, the climactic confrontation of the First Indochina War (1946–54).

Gary instructed Deo to take him to the north wall so they could help block the ground assault. They rushed around a corner and ran into an NVA soldier who'd been running the other direction through the trenches. Deo dropped Gary, unslung his CAR-15 from his shoulder, and brought the enemy soldier down.

On the way to the wall, Gary used M3 medical kits to wrap wounds, put on compression bandages, and administer shots of morphine from syrettes. Sometimes a soldier was too far gone, and Gary could offer only comfort and sympathy.

Gary and Deo kept going and came to the wall, where they climbed over bodies—both Montagnard and NVA—to reach an M60 machine gun.

Gary grabbed the machine gun in defense and pulled the trigger in bursts, firing into the waves of enemy troops that kept pouring over the wire. Deo fired his weapon too. The barrel of the machine gun grew hot and began to smoke, but Gary kept firing.

Other Green Berets and Montagnards were firing too. Gary saw waves of enemy soldiers running toward the camp—like swells and surges of rough water hitting a beachhead.

Enemy faces.

Enemy bodies.

Enemy rifles.

Enemy bullets.

Wave after wave after wave. A human wall of sacrificial flesh. *Carnage.*

Gary spotted his executive officer on the ground trying to call in air strikes and artillery from Ben Het, about fourteen miles away. The camp desperately needed more help.

It was clear to Gary that the enemy was using a suicide tactic to get their troops through the camp's maze of barbed and concertina wire—their first waves of soldiers were almost guaranteed to die. The attackers threw ladderlike objects onto the wire and ran up them, only to be shot and fall flat so the soldiers behind could run over them and into the camp. Other enemy soldiers threw satchel charges against the fences to try to blast their way through. They tried to run through the explosions, often two by two. Some of them made it; many others didn't. Soldier after soldier fell as bullets ripped through them.

In the midst of the mayhem, the camp's defenders detonated barrels of foo gas (sometimes spelled *fougasse*), a mixture of explosives and napalm usually held in fifty-five-gallon drums. As the foo gas exploded, enemy soldiers were doused with the fluid, covered with flames, and burned alive.

Gary had heard that NVA and VC troops sometimes went into battle high on drugs so they wouldn't feel any pain or fear. Apparently, they were told that if they stopped or turned away from the fight, they'd be shot by their fellow troops behind them. A number of soldiers he saw up close appeared glassy eyed and in a kind of trance.

As wave after wave of soldiers advanced, Gary fought the urge to keep the M60 firing on full automatic. He remembered his training—that after 1,500 rounds, the barrel of an M60 turns red, starts to melt, and warps, effectively becoming useless. Gary stuck with the disciplined firing method he'd learned— firing short bursts, one after another. The voices of his DIs came back to him: *"Pick your target. Squeeze the trigger. Don't jerk it. Pick another target. Squeeze; don't jerk."*

Surprisingly, he does not recall feeling fear. Perhaps it was because of all the adrenaline running through his body. Most likely it was also due to the intense training he'd received to become a Green Beret. Back in the States, extreme actions had been drilled into him, minute by minute for a year and a half. Those actions had become part of him, second nature. The military had taught him that training combats fear—and that the first place a battle is fought is in the mind.

Although many of the choices Gary needed to make during the siege were difficult, he knew what his responsibilities were—as a medic, as a Green Beret, and as a member of the Sedang tribe. The predominant emotion he felt on the battlefield was love, a gritty sort of protective love. Love for his people, his team, the women and children in the village that had become his home. He doesn't recall feeling hatred toward the enemy, not then, not even anger because so many of his friends were hurt and dying.

G. K. Chesterton wrote that "the true soldier fights not because he hates what is in front of him, but because he loves what is behind him." Surely on a larger scale Gary hated the evil that had prompted the killing, the atrocities of terror and violence. But hate wasn't the primary emotion he felt during the fight. It was love. Even in the fog of warfare.

———

During the battle it was hard for Gary or any soldier to grasp the full scope of what was happening because the siege had started so abruptly and the shelling and ground campaign played out with such ferocity. The US military later determined that the enemy had been secretly building its force in the region for about two months prior to the attack—with an emphasis on *secretly*. They'd dug a complex network of trenches and tunnels, and some of the tunnels went underneath the wire and led into the camp. So the defenders inside faced enemies who tried to run over the wire, as well as enemies emerging from the tunnels in the middle of the camp.

Ringed by hills as it was, Dak Seang wasn't well suited for defending in the first place. One reason Dak Seang had been built in a valley was that the location was actually part of the allies' larger strategy, although now it is problematic to hear (Gary didn't learn about this strategy until much later). The camp had been built to be a sitting duck, a lure to entice the enemy into a mass attack—and the enemy had taken the bait. The allies' logic was that if the enemy could be lured into gathering to mount a mass attack, then the enemy themselves would be placed in a more vulnerable position. Subsequent fast-reacting allied air attacks could knock out the enemy while defending the camp. A greater number of enemies in one place could yield a higher enemy body count, and a higher body count was a certain yet controversial marker of success in the Vietnam War.

Complicating matters for the defenders of Dak Seang was the fact that the camp was considered critical for border surveillance operations, intelligence gathering, and maintaining the South Vietnamese government's control of the Central Highlands. So orders had been given to the Green Berets and Montagnard fighters to "hold Dak Seang against [any] determined enemy attack." The soldiers inside couldn't flee to safety, even overwhelmed as they were. But staying and fighting was certainly not easy either. In the chaos of battle, it's hard to determine the exact number of attacking troops, although the defenders knew immediately that they were facing a larger army. But how large?

A few days after the start of the attack, the *New York Times* reported that some two thousand North Vietnamese had besieged the camp. But history has shown that this initial number was a huge underestimate. An unnamed reporter for *Stars and Stripes,* Pacific edition, estimated the number of attackers as high as ten thousand—at least two main-force NVA regiments. And after-action reports have shown that this higher number was much more probable. These ten thousand enemy soldiers were fighting to overrun some four hundred Montagnard fighters and twelve Green Berets, who stood in defense of some 2,300 women and children.

The perfect storm had gathered at Dak Seang. The enemy surrounded the camp, surged forward, and sought to flatten it. Could those inside the camp, along with air support, repel the throng? Or would all those inside Dak Seang be doomed?

The defenders were outnumbered twenty-four to one.

———

Manning the machine gun, Gary felt another bolt of lightning blast into the right side of his abdomen. The bullet spun him around, and he collapsed and rolled to the bottom of the trench. He'd been hit for the third time.

Deo dropped beside him, grabbed another bandage, and wrapped it around Gary's middle, then hollered for another Montagnard to help. In spite of the pain, Gary twitched a slight smile when he saw that the new corpsman was Tot, his old friend, the camp's preventive medical specialist. Tot and Deo carried Gary toward the underground medical bunker. Halfway there, they spotted an abandoned stretcher. They threw Gary onto it, picked up the ends, and rushed for the bunker.

On the way they passed the schoolhouse, which had been leveled by a rocket. Bodies were scattered on the ground. Five children, bleeding but still alive, huddled by the blasted-out timbers. "Let me down!" Gary hollered at Tot and Deo. Tot did what he could for the group while Deo brought the most severely wounded child—a boy—toward Gary. Deo cradled the boy in his arms so Gary could examine the wounds. Reflexively, Gary started to work on him, but then he stopped and examined the boy's wounds more thoroughly. He sighed inwardly and looked into the boy's eyes.

"Is he going to be okay?" Deo asked.

Gary held the boy's gaze. The child looked to Gary for reassurance. Gary tried to smile and said, "Don't worry. You're going to be okay." He stroked the boy's hand. His forehead. The side of his face. A relaxed expression came over the boy's face. He saw genuine love in Gary's eyes. The boy breathed deeply a few times, then closed his eyes. He was dead.

By now Tot had rushed the other children into the medical bunker, and he came back to help with Gary. Tot and Deo picked up Gary's stretcher and carried him into the bunker. Deo shouted "Bac Si!" Dan Noonan rushed over to Gary and looked him over yet again.

"Well, you've got internal injuries," Dan muttered. "Your stomach's blown out. You've got internal bleeding. External bleeding. Everything." He turned to Tot and Deo and added, "Keep him here this time!" They nodded, and Dan ran to get some instruments to start IVs and care for Gary's wounds.

Lying on the stretcher about two inches off the ground, Gary sensed that all kinds of water had run into the bunker, because the ground was soaking wet. He let his hand dip into the liquid, then looked at it. His hand was covered in blood. Gary shook his head. He looked at Deo and Tot and said, "If I'm gonna die, I'm not going to die down here. Take me back to the battle!" He could tell by the looks on the two Montagnards' faces that they understood.

Fifty years later, Gary described the feeling of that moment this way: "How amazing it is when a man knows he's going to die. He knows he's not going to have power over whether he dies or not. Yet he still wants a say in where and how he dies."

Gary was a Green Beret. A warrior. A medic. He wanted to die in the battle.

Deo and Tot picked up the stretcher and carried him back outside.

———

The battle was now much worse. Low-flying allied gunships rumbled overhead and strafed the ground with wide, systematic rivers of bullets. These Douglas AC-47 Spooky fixed-wing aircraft were painted light and dark green, nicknamed Puff, and full of firepower. Gary could hear the whir of the bullets coming down fast. He could see the streams of tracer bullets against the smoky sky. They looked like steady streaks of lightning.

Deo and Tot picked up some discarded weapons lying next to soldiers who were dead. They rushed to a crater, lowered Gary inside, and handed him a weapon. All three began firing at the NVA, who now seemed to be everywhere.

The medic Dan apparently had called in a medevac by then for some of the most seriously wounded, and the three watched as a Huey lowered itself, rotors whirring, into the black cloud that surrounded the camp. Suddenly, the blackness was broken. A tremendous light erupted as the chopper exploded.

"We're too exposed!" Gary yelled to Deo and Tot. "We've got to move!"

Deo and Tot picked up Gary and headed toward a deeper, semisafe mortar pit that was surrounded by sandbags. The rockets, artillery, mortars, and automatic rifle fire were deafening. They were on the run, maybe ten feet from the mortar pit, when they heard another incoming rocket. Deo and Tot dropped the stretcher, and Deo flung himself on Gary. The rocket exploded. Gary felt his body rise off the ground.

Even before the dust and debris settled, Gary called out, "C'mon—let's go!" He shook Deo by the shoulders, but Deo didn't move. Gary felt torn clothing on the boy's body and warm fluid. Deo's back was riddled with shrapnel. Gary shook Deo harder—"Deo!"

Tot was by Gary's side now. He rolled Deo's body off Gary and said, "He's dead, Bac Si. Deo is dead."

Gary went numb.

Tot was still moving. Still working. He yelled something in Sedang. A Montagnard fighter ran over. The two of them grabbed Gary's stretcher and carried it the rest of the way to the mortar pit. Gary passed out on the way—he'd lost so much blood. Once in the pit, Gary came to and snapped into action. He and the two young men continued to fire their weapons as they'd been trained— choosing their targets, firing in short bursts.

Gary's mind began to swirl again. He drifted in and out of consciousness. He remembers the incessant sound of gunfire. Shouts and screams. He saw faceless shadows falling around the pit. He remembers the strafing of the gunships overhead. The rockets and the artillery and the blood and the pain form a jumbled mess of memories. Gary recalls clearly the feeling of being numb after Deo died. Part of his numbness came as the result of a decision: he chose to stop feeling—*anything*. He also chose to stop caring. Today, he explains those decisions this way: "If I did not care about anyone ever again, I would never have to feel the pain, the hurt, the guilt."

His next solid memory is of lying in the mortar pit with Tot, but the sequence of events is jumbled. Dizzy was there now too. Gary is sure of that—Dizzy still chewing the stump of an unlit cigar.

They were all nearly out of ammunition. They told Gary he was going to be okay—a chopper was coming to get him. Two silhouettes ran toward them. The evening fog swirled with smoke and gunpowder, making visibility tricky. Two soldiers emerged, sprinting toward the crater. *Which side are they on?* They charged closer. Gary guessed what Dizzy and Tot were thinking: *Make sure of your target. Be accurate. Don't go crazy.* They spotted black and green pajamas. Pith helmets. Tot took down the first. Dizzy fired a short burst from his M16 and leveled the second.

"Chopper's coming," Dizzy said. "Get him ready."

Tot glanced at Gary. "Bac Si, you must go now."

Gary raised his hand in protest. He said—or maybe he only thought, *Don't do it. It's too risky. Stay away.* The chopper broke through the thick black clouds.

"There it is." Tot motioned with his chin. "You will make it, Bac Si."

This chopper was smoking, leaking fuel, its side riddled with bullet holes. The pilot reversed course and lifted the chopper up and out of harm's way, limping toward safety.

"Don't worry," Dizzy said. "Another will get here."

Gary heard another chopper make its approach, but once again the sky erupted in a deafening explosion. The chopper crashed in flames. Gary remembers thinking about the crews on those choppers—the men who flew into battle, their great sacrifice for him. In firefights the helicopters were huge targets for enemy fire.

Gary wondered why he was still alive when so many others had already died.

———

A half hour passed. Maybe an hour. Gary heard shouts. Screams. Explosions. Dizzy's radio crackled. *Support the north wall. Now! Move!* Another breach of defense. More enemy soldiers were overrunning the village. Gary sensed unconsciousness overtaking him again. He heard Dizzy firing his rifle. Then Tot's voice again:

"This one's yours, Bac Si. Get ready."

Gary braced himself. As the chopper dropped from the sky, Dizzy and Tot grabbed Gary's stretcher and started running to the open area where the chopper would land. Gary doesn't remember the skids even touching the ground. He saw an American soldier jump out and help carry him to the chopper. They all threw Gary aboard—and the word *threw* is accurate. The chopper quickly climbed almost straight up. "You're going to be okay!" the medic in the chopper yelled.

Gary felt cold. Freezing. He lost consciousness on the chopper, everything swirling in a mix of blood and screams and cries of the wounded. The medic's words were the last words Gary remembers hearing for a long time.

"You're going to be okay."

———

Sergeant Bob Hill was a Green Beret weapons specialist, and although like every Green Beret he'd had a smattering of training in all the disciplines, being a medic wasn't his primary job. He was with the C Team in Pleiku at the beginning of April 1970, when the siege of Dak Seang began. There he'd been healing from a gunshot wound to his shoulder.

Life around a C Team can turn boring quickly, especially for someone used to being on an A Team. While sitting around wishing he were someplace else, Bob heard a colonel shout for a volunteer.

There's an unwritten rule among soldiers never to be a volunteer if an officer calls for one, but Bob yelled, "Here I am, sir."

The colonel grabbed him by the arm, dragged him down to the helipad, and managed to explain a bit about the mission. An American medic was badly wounded at Dak Seang. They needed to get him out ASAP, but it wasn't going to be easy. They had already lost two choppers but were going to try to land another. Walking briskly, the colonel said, "Sergeant, this is your mission. You get that American. And no matter what—you stay with him to the end!"

"Yes sir," was all Bob said. He grabbed a .45, an M16, and some ammo, jumped on the chopper, and settled in for the thirty-to-forty-minute ride to Dak Seang.

The helicopter flew at treetop level and fast—at a speed he'd seldom flown before. When the colonel had explained it to him, the mission had seemed basic enough, but now Bob wondered about the exact nature of what he'd volunteered for. He glanced around at the pilots, crew chief, and door gunners. The gunner closest to him caught his eye. He was a younger kid, red hair with freckles. He reminded Bob of the *Howdy Doody* show. Bob wondered how a kid like that ever became a door gunner in Vietnam. Bob spotted threatening dark clouds ahead, and he asked the door gunner, "Are we going to fly through that storm?"

Howdy Doody laughed. "That's no storm. That's Dak Seang. Where we're going."

Bob swallowed. The pilot said to him in the headset, "Sergeant, if we get in, I'm only staying on the ground for ten seconds. You got that? Once ten seconds are up, I'm gone. With or without you."

"Roger that," Bob said.

As they entered the black cloud, Bob wondered if they would even make it to the landing zone. Antiaircraft, machine gun, and small-arms fire lit up the dusk. Bob and the door gunners began firing at the flashes coming from below.

Bob zipped through all his ammo quickly, then sneaked a glance at Howdy Doody. He had a crazy look on his face and was laughing hysterically. Five decades later, Bob says he can still hear that crazy laughter accompanied by the distinctive sound of an M60 machine gun.

The chopper hit the dirt. Today, with a chuckle, Bob clarifies that regardless of what Gary thought he saw, the skids of the chopper did indeed touch the ground—albeit only for a second. The chopper actually bounced because it came in so fast and hard. On the first bounce Bob jumped out and met Dizzy and Tot coming from the other direction, carrying Gary on the stretcher. He joined in, and as they were running toward the chopper, enemy rockets and machine guns focused on destroying the Huey.

The ten seconds were almost up. Bob was counting under his breath. Right before they reached the Huey, Bob spotted an RPG (rocket-propelled grenade) coming right at them. It careened through the farther open-door of the chopper, flew out the door nearer them, and went screaming right by their heads.

The chopper started to lift up. All three threw Gary on board. Bob leaped for the skids as the chopper went airborne. The soldiers had always heard that a Huey cannot perform a vertical takeoff. It needs to take off at about a thirty-degree angle—or surely not much more than a forty-five-degree angle—and gradually gain in speed and elevation. But this pilot performed a miracle. The chopper rose straight up and disappeared into the black cloud.

Once inside, Bob threw flak jackets under Gary, then over him, and covered him with his own body because he knew they were not out of danger yet. He remembers the ground fire and explosions being the worst he'd ever seen.

Since he'd had some cross-training as a medic, Bob started an IV to keep Gary alive until they made it to the Seventy-First Evacuation Hospital in Pleiku. When the chopper landed, the hospital staff rushed out and carried Gary into the building. The remains of Gary's clothes were torn off. The Montagnard bracelets were cut off his wrists. His bandages were removed so the doctors could determine the extent of his wounds. More IVs were started in both arms and in his neck. Tubes were inserted through his nose into his stomach, and a catheter into his bladder. An oxygen mask was placed over his face. Gary remembers a voice over him saying, "You're a mess."

While all this was going on, two hospital corpsmen in the emergency ward grabbed Bob and started to strip him to look at the extent of his wounds. He pushed them backward and yelled that he was okay. None of the blood covering his body was his. It was all Gary's.

As Bob watched the doctors wheel Gary away, he felt that he could now leave. His mission was complete. He had gotten Gary and stayed with him no matter what. But he shook his head. He thought, *There's no way that guy's going to make it.*

Gary was transferred to a cold flat surface so X-rays could be taken. He had been shot at least three times. He'd been blown up and thrown through the air. He'd been hit by shrapnel near his spine. His insides were full of jagged metal. Much of his stomach and intestines had been ripped out and hung in clusters outside his body. He'd lost most of his blood. He wavered in and out of consciousness.

In spite of all that damage, the greatest battle Gary needed to fight still lay ahead.

10

Wounded

Black. Dark.

Dim. Light.

When Gary awoke, he felt intense pain piercing his abdomen. Cautiously, he moved his hand so he could try to massage away the pain, but his hand felt tethered by a cord, or a tube perhaps. His mind felt cobwebby, and he struggled to comprehend what held him back. His eyes saw the tube, and he followed it upward to a bag of red fluid. He tried to focus on the printing on the bag. *O positive.* His blood type. But it wasn't his blood flowing into his system. Someone else's blood now gave him life.

He tried to move his other hand toward his abdomen, but his hand was stopped by something resting on his stomach. He lifted his head slightly and glimpsed a clear plastic bag with some sort of murk inside. Part of his large intestine was exposed, raw, outside his body. He laid his head back against the pillow.

He couldn't tell if his legs were still attached. He tried to move his free hand to check if they were there. His hand touched one leg. Then reached over to the other. His legs were there, but he couldn't feel anything in the limbs. He felt other parts of his body. He couldn't move from the waist down. Everything he touched was numb.

Gary tried to swallow, but his throat ached and his breathing felt restricted. He reached up and discovered a thick tube jutting into his nostril. He struggled to remember what the device was. A nasogastric tube. It ran through his nose and into his stomach. He'd inserted an NG tube into himself once during medical training.

He felt dizzy, his thoughts scrambled. His eyes refused to focus, and everything blurred. He felt himself passing out.

Black. Dark.

Dim. Light.

He heard sounds. Coughs. Moans. The whoosh and hiss of machines pumping oxygen into damaged lungs. *How much time has passed?* Now the room was dim, and only the green and red lights of the machines showed. Maybe it was nighttime.

"How're you today?" a voice said from above. The voice was gentle, quiet, female.

Gary tried to speak, but his mind felt far away. His tongue and throat couldn't get behind the necessary sounds to make words.

"You're in Pleiku," the voice said. "At the Seventy-First Evac Hospital. You were shot up pretty bad. Just rest now. Rest." The hospital in Pleiku was less than an hour's helicopter ride from Dak Seang. Maybe the nurse said more, but Gary's head started to spin again, and unconsciousness overtook his mind.

Black. Dark.

Dim. Light.

His mind worked again. *How long have I been out this time?* He felt a strange wetness. Smelled an odor. *Am I in a bathtub?* His eyes opened and he saw daylight. He heard swearing. A gruff voice. Male. A brawny figure stood over him and rapidly wiped sections of his stomach and side. The wiping hurt.

"Listen up," the male voice said. "You have an ileostomy, okay? Know what that means? Your guts are in a bag. You can't go moving around from side to side. You gotta lie still. If you don't, you'll make a mess again, and I'll have to clean it up again, and I might not be so nice. Got it?"

Gary wished the gentle female voice would return. If Gary had been more awake, he might have reached up and grabbed the male nurse by the throat, but Gary's strength was leaking away again. He needed to clutch whatever strength he had left to stay awake, to stay alive, to fight death.

Gary's thoughts swirled again and his vision blurred. The darkness was overtaking him, ushering him to a place he did not want to go. He had passed out before. Lots of times in college when inebriated. But this didn't feel like passing out drunk. It didn't even feel like going to sleep. This was something new and frightening.

Accompanying the darkness was a feeling of sliding down a chute, of traveling through space and time, of journeying to another location. His mind swirled, and he fought against the darkness, but his eyes closed, and he remembered no more.

Black. Dark.

Dim. Light.

The face of Dan "Mac" McGinley emerged. Mac was standing beside Gary's bed, looking down but with his eyes averted. This was the crusty old master sergeant who'd first assigned Gary to Dak Seang, and the old soldier wouldn't look Gary in the eye. Gary sensed Mac's feelings of guilt and tried to tell him that it was okay, but no words came out.

"You don't have a beret," Mac said. "Where's your beret? It's the symbol of what's inside you. You need a beret." An ache layered his voice.

Gary hinted at a shrug. His beret had long since disappeared in the fighting.

Mac wore jungle fatigues that had side pockets on the outside of each leg. He'd stuffed his own beret in one of the pockets, and he took it out, smoothed it in reverence, then set it on top of Gary's hand lying on the hospital bed. "I don't want you ever to be out of uniform," Mac said. "Hang tough. You're going to make it through this."

Gary tried to convey his gratitude, but his mind was already heading down the chute. He closed his eyes and his head swirled.

Black. Dark.

Dim. Light.

This was not daylight but light that punctured the dimness here and there, here and there. He saw small flashlights moving around the ward. Nighttime again. To his left Gary heard a deep, guttural gasp. The soldier in the bed next to him was choking. He gave another gasp. Choked again. Then Gary heard silence. Silence. Silence. Silence.

Gary tried to call out, but his voice was weak and hollow. He wanted to press the button that rang the nurse, but every movement was slow. Besides, he'd already spotted the flicker of a nurse's flashlight dashing toward the next bed.

More figures ran toward the other soldier. Shadows. They congregated around the bed and worked feverishly. For some time all Gary could see or hear to his left was a commotion. Then came a sudden letdown of activity, almost like a balloon deflating. The activity was over, and the congregation of shadows drifted away. Only one figure remained . . . and pulled a sheet over the soldier's head.

Gary stared at the ceiling. He blinked and vowed not to surrender to the same fate. Death might be advancing on each soldier in the ward like a swordsman on a galloping horse, but Gary swore he wouldn't lie down and die. He was a Green Beret, one of the best-trained warriors in the world. He'd endured the most challenging situations devisable by military minds. He'd been taught to be resourceful, resilient, strong, able to survive any situation—even a fight against death.

I will not lose this battle, Gary told himself. But the darkness again approached. Gary braced himself and tried to fight, but his mind swirled. His strength was gone.

Just before he lost consciousness, he thought he heard a voice asking, "Is this all you got?" Death laughed. Gary slipped into the dusk.

Black. Dark.

Dim. Light.

Is this what it's like to die? Gary wasn't aware of time passing, but it must have been hours until he became conscious enough to open his eyes. He didn't know what he would see. Would it be heaven, hell, or only total darkness? He felt stripped of all his resources, leveled, rid of all self-sufficiency.

He was glad to see the bright light of the hospital ward again. *At least I'm not dead yet.* He heard the familiar labored breathing, moans, and coughs of wounded soldiers in the ward. Nurses comforted patients and did their rounds. He did not want to die. He desperately wanted to stay alive.

"Glad to see you're awake, son," came a sudden voice from his right. The figure advanced, pulled a chair to the bedside. "I've been coming by your bed for a few days now and praying for you."

Gary's eyes focused. He saw the gleam of captain's bars on the man's fatigues and an embroidered cross on his collar, the marks of a chaplain. The man smiled. He was young and holding a baseball cap with a cross on it. He tucked the hat into his belt and sat down. For the first time in days, Gary found his voice. It sounded raspy, and his words emerged stilted and slow. "I'm . . . glad . . . to be awake . . . sir."

"Would you like to pray?" the chaplain asked.

Gary managed a thin chuckle. "Pray? I don't know . . . how to pray, sir. I don't even know . . . who . . . to pray to."

The chaplain smiled again. "That's okay, son. God knows how to listen." His voice exuded reassurance and confidence. He reached toward Gary and handed him a small Celtic cross. It was no more than an inch and a half tall, dangling from a chain.

Gary took hold of the cross. He had determined to take anything anybody gave him that might help him live, and he liked the thought that God knows how to listen. The chaplain's words helped Gary picture an attentive God, always ready, always listening for the cries of those in need. Back at Dak Seang, soldiers had established listening posts outside the camp at night. The function of those who manned the posts was to remain vigilant, always listening for any sounds. Even in the dark, if one was listening, communication could happen.

The chaplain took hold of Gary's hand. Gary kept his eyes open and looked up. He didn't want to close his eyes for fear of losing consciousness again. He gripped the chaplain's hand as hard as he could and whispered, "God . . . I don't know . . . if you are real . . . or if you are there . . . but I'm scared . . . And if you are real . . . I need you."

Gary was nearly twenty-three years old. It was the first time he had ever prayed. Then he closed his eyes.

Something felt different. Definitely different. Gary knew no miraculous healing had occurred. He didn't suddenly pull all the tubes out of his body. His intestines were not all suddenly back inside his abdomen, and the feeling below his waist didn't suddenly return. But he sensed a distinct presence he'd not felt before.

Gary opened his eyes and glanced around, searching for answers. The new presence filled the room, but Gary couldn't see any person except the chaplain. The captain was still holding Gary's hand, still with an expression on his face that matched the peace Gary now felt in his heart.

Five decades later, Gary described the experience this way:

When I first prayed in the hospital, I could actually sense God in the room. I had never experienced this before. There was someone outside of me who was greater than any fear or pain I felt. That same someone was able to reach across whatever separated us. He began to change the chaos in my heart and mind, and I felt a peace that passed my ability to understand it. This new presence in the room gave me this peace, and with this peace I wasn't afraid to die anymore. I wasn't afraid I'd never be able to walk again. I no longer felt afraid. The peace I now felt was real, and although I had a long way to go in my journey of faith, the peace stayed with me.

Gary doesn't remember if the chaplain prayed too or how long he stayed or if they said goodbye. Soon enough the chaplain was no longer there, and when Gary's eyes closed again, he fell into a deep sleep. It was real sleep this time—not unconsciousness—and while in his sleep, he felt his body resting, his mind at ease.

When he awoke, he was still clutching the cross. He reached over to the table beside him and placed it on top of his green beret.

————

One doctor had jet-black hair. He was a major and always wore a white smock with a stethoscope around his neck. He sat down beside Gary, flashed a crooked smile that felt somehow nasty, and ran through a chart, explaining the extent of his wounds.

A lot of muscle and tissue had been removed from Gary's right side. Shrapnel was still embedded in his spinal column, but fortunately the jagged chunks of metal hadn't severed the spinal cord. Surgeons had decided not to operate to remove all the pieces because some of the shrapnel lay too close to the cord. Gary probably would be able to walk again, but the doctor didn't know how long it would take for him to regain feeling in his legs.

Some sort of bullet or projectile had gone through Gary's large intestine, much of which had been removed, and some of it still lay exposed. The ileostomy had been done to allow the damaged organ to heal. Hopefully the large intestine would be reattached soon.

Multiple pieces of shrapnel were still in Gary's abdominal cavity and buttocks and might work their way out over the next few years. The doctor announced that he wanted to take him into the OR right away to remove some of the pieces closest to the surface.

Gary nodded. He felt uneasy around this doctor, although he didn't yet know why. Orderlies wheeled Gary into a small room off the main ward, where he was rolled onto his side. The orderlies scrubbed him down with Betadine, an antiseptic wash, which felt cold and came as a shock. But it was nothing compared with the pain Gary felt as the surgeon with the jet-black hair dug pieces of shrapnel out with probes and tweezers. No local anesthetic was given. Nothing.

Gary won't swear to it, but he thinks he heard a weird, sadistic laugh as the doctor dug into his back.

A few days later, the same doctor came by Gary's bed and ordered him to cough. Gary had been immobile for too long, and the doctor was concerned that pneumonia might set in. Because of Gary's weakened condition and his susceptibility to infection, pneumonia was a real possibility. They'd started him on a new antibiotic called Keflin, but it wasn't having the quick results hoped for. Fluid was gathering in Gary's lungs, so the doctor ordered him to cough it out.

"No way," Gary said. The pain was too intense. His abdomen had been split open and was only partially closed. He could hardly move, much less cough.

A few hours later, the same doctor returned and went to the soldier lying next to Gary, who'd already been diagnosed with pneumonia. He, too, was unable or unwilling to cough, so the doctor had a nurse pull up his traveling surgical tray. He picked up a scalpel, made a quick incision in the guy's throat, took an NG tube, and shoved it into his trachea. The doctor jerked the tube up and down until the guy coughed violently.

When Gary saw this, he yelled, "I'm coughing! I'm coughing!" and he started to hack up fluid. His esophagus burned. His stomach felt on fire.

The doctor's mouth twisted into that crooked, sadistic smile.

One morning, two weeks after being wounded, Gary awoke and saw Captain Paul Landers sitting by his bed. The captain had been the Green Berets' team leader back at Dak Seang. He had been shot in the throat and medevaced to the Seventy-First Evac.

In a raspy voice the captain explained that Lieutenant Ed Christensen had survived, thanks in great part to Gary's battlefield actions. Christensen was already on his way to Japan and then would head back home. Landers was going to stay in Pleiku because his wound was not serious enough to be sent home. Gary asked about Dak Seang.

"The fighting's still going on," Landers said. Gary was surprised. Landers explained that during the first week, the enemy had controlled the runway at Dak Seang and had also encircled the camp. Air drops were the only way to get ammo, food, and medical supplies to the troops and women and children inside. Only three helicopters had been able to land that first week.

Ten days after the siege began, an Australian-led cadre of Montagnard ground troops had reached the camp from the south. Simultaneously an American-led battalion had fought its way through from the east. Supply and medevac choppers were able to land a little more easily that day, and about half the defenders and women and children who'd been wounded were evacuated.

But according to Landers, the fight was still hot. More than two thousand enemy rounds had already fallen on the camp, mostly 82-millimeter mortars and 122-millimeter rockets, and the camp was nothing now but a fortified pile of rubble. Corpses littered the ground. The enemy was determined to win the battle, and there appeared to be more fighting to come.

Gary could only shake his head. He ached for the people he knew and loved. He thought of Chom and his wife. Dead.

Thung and his wife. Dead.

Pher. Dead.

Deo. Dead.

So many other friends. Dead.

The next morning a three-star general came by with an entourage of officers and pinned a Silver Star and a Purple Heart on Gary's pillow. Gary said thanks but felt unworthy. He thought of Dak Seang, his family still fighting. A soldier doesn't want to be in a hospital. He wants to be back in the battle.

Later, Colonel Lawrence, the Fifth Group surgeon, came from Special Forces headquarters in Nha Trang to see Gary, along with the group's Sergeant Major Bowser. Gary felt honored that they'd come all the way to Pleiku to see him, although his heart was still heavy. He knew it was unusual for them to travel so far to visit the wounded. They both asked if there was anything they could do. Gary told them that he did not want to be sent back to the States and would love it if they could pull some strings so he could stay and heal in Vietnam. He wanted to head back to Dak Seang as soon as possible.

They both smiled. Sergeant Major Bowser said, "I know how much you want to stay, Sergeant. But it will be much better for you to go home now. Heal, get strong again, and then come back."

Gary knew the sergeant major was right. Still, he did not want to leave the place and people he'd grown to love.

———

A day or so later, Gary found himself on a plane headed to Camp Zama, Japan. There, doctors continued to monitor his treatment for pneumonia, and he underwent minor operations on his abdomen to remove dead tissue and improve the function of the ileostomy.

Gary was able to speak to his mother by phone. The first conversation was short, matter of fact. She was glad to hear he was still alive and coming home. After the call she wrote him letters, but he wrote back only once, a short note. Difficulty of expression had to do with more than just his injuries. He was still feeling too contained within his heart.

At last Gary was able to sit up and get around in a wheelchair, although walking was still not possible and he still couldn't feel his legs. The hospital had a series of long hallways, and Gary rolled through the corridors for hours. He liked being out of his room. In Japan he was able to read newspapers for the first time. Dak Seang was the top story in *Stars and Stripes,* the military newspaper available to all service personnel. As he read, he felt renewed feelings of hurt, guilt, and anger. Why was he alive when so many others were dead? He saw pictures of people he knew, people he'd fought with, people he loved. He wanted to be back in Dak Seang so badly, not in a hospital and not in a wheelchair.

The feelings nearly overwhelmed him. He didn't know where to turn, whom to talk with. The embryo of faith conceived within his initial prayer seemed real but undeveloped, smaller than a mustard seed.

Some days later, Gary was wheeled out to a C-141 airplane and placed on the top of the three levels of bunks that lined the aircraft. At first he was told he was going to be sent to St. Albans Medical Center in New York. This was the naval/marine facility where his stepfather had been sent when he was injured in the naval reserves. But at the last minute, plans changed, and Gary was flown to Walson Army Hospital at Fort Dix, New Jersey, where he'd gone through basic training, where his service had begun.

On his first morning at Fort Dix, Gary found himself in a sterile-looking ward. A wheelchair was near his bed, and he was able to lower himself into it and roll out into the hallway and past a few rooms. Other army guys lay in beds, and Gary said hello to a few, but he didn't get many responses. Mostly guys just looked at him with faraway stares.

He rolled up to a closed door, opened it, and rolled through. The door swung shut behind him with a loud *click*. Inside the room a medic in a white outfit sat behind a desk. Gary mentioned to him that the other guys on the ward didn't seem too friendly. The medic explained it was probably because of the medication they were on and asked, "Has no one told you where you are yet?"

Gary shook his head.

"You're on a locked ward for psych patients."

Confused, Gary asked if the medic could open the outer door so he could leave.

"Nope. Not till a doc talks to you," the medic said.

Gary never found out whether his placement in a psych ward was standard procedure to screen all wounded soldiers coming back from combat or whether it was because of the serious nature of his wounds and the circumstances he'd endured to receive them. Either way, he was troubled.

A little while later, a doctor came in and asked Gary a series of questions. Apparently Gary answered them satisfactorily, because before long he was transferred to a different ward. This one was filled with soldiers with a variety of serious wounds from the war, mostly spinal cord injuries and amputations. These were guys without arms and legs, guys paralyzed from the neck or waist down.

One soldier had burns over 80 percent of his body. His hands were twisted and his face was scarred. He would soon be sent to Brooke Army Hospital at Fort Sam Houston in San Antonio.

A day passed and then another. Gary noticed that a number of the patients just sat around and got high. He stayed in that ward for a couple more days until he was transferred to a facility that would become his home for the next ten months—Ward 9B, Valley Forge General Hospital, Phoenixville, Pennsylvania.

In Valley Forge, though Gary's physical wounds began to heal, he soon faced another raging battle. He was out of intensive care, and his hand-to-hand fight with death was all but over. But next he would fight the pain of a wounded heart, soul, and spirit—the stress of having been through trauma, the kind of stress that can't be readily seen. In time, although he didn't know it just yet, the battle with his emotional pain would prove more destructive than any of his physical wounds.

PART II

The Cave

11

Seeking

Though it felt good to be home in the United States, a significant part of Gary still felt left in Vietnam, and it would remain there forever. His heart longed to be there, viscerally, in time and space.

At Valley Forge General Hospital, he began his struggle to make sense of it all—a struggle that would last for years. Ward 9B was strictly for spinal cord injuries and orthopedics, and among the paraplegics, quadriplegics, and amputees, Gary felt troubled in spirit, not because he might never walk again but because he *would* be able to walk again. He still had all his limbs while so many others did not.

Why am I not paralyzed?

Why am I even still alive?

Many guys on the ward spent their days outside in wheelchairs, huddled in groups underneath the trees, drinking and smoking dope. Gary sensed a bonding experience taking place, a camaraderie, but it felt different from what he'd experienced in Vietnam. Here, as a Green Beret, he felt distanced from the other troops. He chose not to connect with them or use drugs and alcohol.

It wasn't a status thing or a moral thing. He just didn't want substances to change the way he was feeling. He wanted to try to capture his feelings, understand them—and deal with them. He wanted to remember the love and good times he'd shared with the Montagnards.

One day a young amputee missing one leg asked Gary what he'd done in Vietnam. Gary said he was Special Forces.

"I thought so," the young man said and laughed. "I knew you were either an officer or a Beret."

Gary didn't know how it showed and didn't know how to respond.

He began to feel tingling in his legs, and doctors said it was a good sign. Gradually more and more feeling returned. Eventually, the paralysis ended, although parts of his lower legs and back stayed numb.

The day came when therapists urged Gary to stand. It took everything he had, but he made it up onto his feet. His head felt woozy; he took a look around the ward, then sat down. That was enough for the first day.

Each day afterward, he practiced standing. Everything hurt. Then came the process of learning to walk again. Therapists got him standing again and pushed a walker in front of him. Gary was hesitant. He found he needed to consciously speak to each limb. "Okay, right leg. Move." The leg moved, and he planted his foot on the ground. "Okay, left leg. Move." His left leg moved, and he planted it. He moved the walker forward. He repeated the commands, step by step by step. Gary felt exhausted and wanted to sit down, but he didn't want to stay in the chair forever, so he willed himself to continue.

Days passed, and each day he practiced walking. Sometimes when he moved a certain way, sharp pain shot down his back and legs because so much shrapnel was still inside his body. Sometimes a leg gave out entirely and he fell. Every movement affected his ileostomy, and he felt pain in his stomach. Stomach acid seemed to slosh around, burning him with each step.

When he wasn't in physical therapy, he rested in bed or moved about the hospital hallways in a wheelchair. He liked being outside his room.

Gary had a long way to go. At five feet, eleven inches tall, he'd weighed a trim 160 pounds in college. After he finished Special Forces training, he'd tipped the scales at a muscular 193, a weight he'd maintained in Vietnam. But now after being wounded and in the hospital, the scale showed 132 pounds.

———

One day Gary was lying in bed, lost in thought. He'd just returned from a walking session and felt exhausted. His bed was against the back wall of the ward, situated in such a way that he could look down the length of the ward to the door that opened to other areas of the hospital.

A large figure appeared in the doorway and walked toward his bed. Their eyes locked. As the man came closer, Gary's heart raced. The man was tall and powerfully built, trim, and strong across the shoulders. He wore a dapper suit with a white Stetson.

Gary knew immediately who he was, although he had not seen or heard from this man in almost twenty years. The man smiled as he came to the side of the bed, but Gary saw neither warmth nor sadness in his expression—there was something more like apprehension, as if the man knew what he wanted to do but wasn't sure how to go about it.

"Hello, Gary. I'm not sure if you know who I am," the man said. "I'm your dad. And I want you to know that I love you."

"I know," Gary said. He couldn't say anything more.

George Beikirch didn't try to explain anything about the past. He talked about how he'd heard reports about Gary from his brother, Gary's uncle, in Rochester. The first reports were that Gary was killed in action. Later reports said Gary was alive and at Valley Forge. George added simply, "I'm sorry you were hurt, but I'm glad you're still alive."

His father worked as a sheriff in St. Johns County, Florida, and Gary was glad that he'd traveled all that way to see him.

George paused, then added, "If you can find it within yourself to forgive me, I would love that. And if you'd like to meet me and talk with me later, I'd love that too."

Gary waited. His father hadn't exactly apologized for leaving him in the past, but his coming felt almost like an act of contrition.

Gary stayed silent this whole time, stunned although not angry. He felt more confused than anything. He was trying to sort through so many thoughts about the war, and this meeting felt like one more thing to add to the confusion pile.

His father set his business card on the bedside table and left.

———

Stateside, Gary was able to catch up on some news about the siege of Dak Seang. Other than extensive coverage in *Stars and Stripes* and several mentions in the *New York Times,* the siege was largely ignored in the American press and quickly became another forgotten overseas battle.

The coordinated surprise attack that began on April 1, 1970, ended up raging for thirty-eight days and officially ended May 8, 1970, although the area was considered unsafe and gunfire was heard until mid-June.

Air support ultimately played a key role in turning the tide toward the allies, although the insertion of allied ground troops proved indispensable too. In thirty-eight days of fighting, American and allied forces flew a whopping 2,829 fighter sorties, 154 gunship sorties, 114 Arc Light (code name for the B-52F Stratofortress) bombing sorties, and 164 aerial resupply sorties. The entire siege proved brutal, and casualties were heavy.

In the end, Dak Seang stood and stayed under allied control, but success came at a high cost. More than eight hundred houses, other buildings, bunkers, storage areas, and caches were destroyed or damaged in Dak Seang, and the village was turned into a mass of pits and rubble. An eyewitness described how after the siege Dak Seang was filled with "a tickling sour smell of raw vegetables and rot mingled with the acid smell of smoke."

Remaining were only the 2,922 enemy dead, along with the corpses of 338 allied fighters and Montagnard women and children. The wounded were not counted. There were too many.

———

About two months after being wounded, doctors told Gary that, if he wanted to, he could go home for a few days, although he'd need to return to the hospital. He was using a cane to walk, and his wounds still weren't fully healed. Since coming from the hospital in Japan, Gary hadn't seen any friends or family other than his father. He was eager to go home. He made a few phone calls, and a couple of days later was headed for Rochester.

As Gary slowly climbed off the airplane, his legs, back, and stomach ached. He was worried about what questions people would ask. He didn't know what he would say when asked about the war.

He walked through the doors to the waiting area and scanned the crowd for any familiar face. He saw two: his mother and Steve Hess, a friend since fifth grade.

Steve had already spent two tours in Vietnam—the first as a door gunner and the second, after he'd smartened up, as a supply clerk. When Steve mentioned his switch to the last job, he always drew a laugh. Steve was huge, six feet four and 220 pounds. Out of the army for a year now, he had a shaggy mustache and goatee, and his hair hung to his shoulders. A crocheted belt looped around the waist of his bell-bottoms, and his tie-dyed T-shirt was already fraying at the seams.

Gary hugged his mother and Steve, and they all talked a bit. Gary sensed that Steve would not ask him any tough questions, so when Steve offered to take Gary home in his car, Gary accepted. His mother nodded. She knew it would do Gary some good.

Steve loaded Gary's duffel bag into his big black two-door Pontiac Bonneville convertible and slipped an 8-track cartridge into the player. Jimi Hendrix's "Purple Haze" filled the air with electric guitar distortion. No conversation was needed. Gary climbed into the passenger seat, and the two friends sped down the road. Steve drove to Rochester's college district and stopped in front of The

Bungalow, a small bar where they used to go before being sent overseas. There they met another friend from high school, George, who'd also recently returned from Vietnam.

Instant mutual respect settled among the three veterans because they knew they shared something so deep. Yet each man's experiences felt unique, even sacred. A boundary separated their Vietnam experiences from the rest of their lives and somehow also separated each man's experiences from the others'. None of the three would violate that boundary without being invited in. It was too early to share that sacred space.

They ambled into the bar, got beers and seats, and talked about friends still in town and what boring lives they must be living in the Rochester rut. Steve and Gary planned to buy Harleys and ride across the country like Peter Fonda and Dennis Hopper in *Easy Rider*. George was getting serious with a girl and talked about settling down. The others good-naturedly gave George a hard time for it but half envied his relationship. The three weren't intending to get drunk; they merely wanted to celebrate Gary's homecoming. But Steve and George were big jokesters and loud, and the more the three drank, the louder they became. Gary didn't know George as well as Steve did. George was a year older and had a bellowing voice, particularly when he laughed. Steve and George were reminiscing about some wild R & R trips to Japan and Bangkok, and some of the stories were coarse and ribald.

Three college-age guys were sitting a table away. From time to time they shot dirty looks at Gary and his friends. After about an hour the college guys stood, sauntered over, and asked Gary and his friends outright if they were Vietnam vets. Gary nodded, and the guys peppered the table with probing questions.

"Did you see any gory stuff?"

"Did you kill anybody?"

The veterans ignored the questions and went back to their beers.

"Ya kill any babies?" one of the college men asked. The question hung in the air like an unexploded grenade.

"What did he just say?" George asked Steve.

Steve looked at George, and George looked at Gary. Gary shook his head. His mind flashed to the death of Chom's daughter—how he'd worked so intensely over the little girl. He remembered the devastation he'd felt afterward. He wasn't a baby killer. He was the exact opposite. "I got this," George said. His voice was casual, and he stood up and said to the college kids, "Let's take this outside."

Steve was big. George was even bigger, about six feet seven and 260 pounds. Evidently the college guys hadn't noticed George's size while he was sitting down, but now that he was standing, they collectively gulped. One cowered and slunk away, but two said they'd take George up on his offer. Steve and Gary started to stand, but George shook his head and told them not to bother. George and the two guys walked toward the door and exited the bar.

A couple of minutes passed. Steve sipped the last of his beer. Gary stared at a wall absentmindedly.

"You think we should go see what's going on?" Steve asked. Gary nodded.

He and Steve walked outside. One of the college guys was already sprawled out cold on the pavement about two steps from the front door. Steve and Gary stepped over him. The other guy was holed up in a telephone booth about ten yards away. George was bear-hugging the telephone booth and shaking it violently. The guy inside looked about ready to wet his pants.

Steve and Gary laughed. They managed to get George calmed down enough to get him into the Pontiac. A police siren sounded in the distance. Steve cranked Jimi Hendrix again, and the three roared off down the road.

Welcome home from Vietnam.

———

The three vets cruised over to the Park Avenue area of Rochester to the house of Steve's friend, Linda, so they could all calm down. She was sweet and slender, a few years younger than Gary, with long brown hair and an alternative vibe.

"So what's new?" Linda said when the guys walked in. She wasn't asking Gary to share anything he didn't want to, so he decided to risk it.

"I think I met God," Gary said.

Steve's mouth dropped, and George just laughed, but Linda smiled and said, "Groovy. So now what?" Her boyfriend, Bill, was lounging in a chair and jumped into the conversation. His black hair hung past his shoulders, and a long beard covered half his face. Bill was into the pursuit of God, too, and began talking about all these cool "spiritual realms" he'd been exploring, some through meditation, others through drugs. He'd been studying the writings of a former Harvard psychologist named Timothy Leary who'd been experimenting with LSD and other psychedelics. Leary believed drug use expanded the mind, and Bill was also interested in the many revelations now being brought to the Western world through Eastern cultures. Gary was baffled by the mix of options Bill was talking about, but it all sounded right up his alley.

Their conversation was cut short when Gary felt something wet around his waist. He excused himself and went to the bathroom. The hospital did not have appliance bags with large enough openings to accommodate the size of his colon still outside his body, so a larger opening had to be cut in the bag and then sealed with tape. Unfortunately, as the bag filled, the tape shook loose and the waste leaked out. Gary was in the bathroom for quite a while.

Steve came in to check on him. When he saw Gary's intestine hanging outside his body, Steve said with his characteristic humor, "Wow, how cool is that!" The intestine was moist with a lot of fluid around it, about three inches wide and extending out a good inch and a half. It looked like a big red piece of rippled meat.

Gary often visited Bill and Linda over the next few months, and their apartment became a safe place for him. Although their beliefs and practices would prove an eclectic mix of yearnings and experimentation, Gary appreciated their friendship. They talked about music and traveling, religions and drugs. The couple accepted his presence without asking too many questions about the war. Gary tried to talk with them more about his initial encounter with God, but he was still sorting out the whole experience himself. He found he could not convey very well what had happened in his soul in that hospital bed. Mostly because he himself didn't yet know.

———

Life at home was strained for Gary. His mother, younger brother, and stepfather had moved into Gary's grandfather's house during his last few years to care for him. His grandfather had died, so for Gary, staying at his house felt weird. The grandfather had lived through the Great Depression, a hardworking man but not warm emotionally. He and Gary had never been close.

Gary stayed in the third-floor attic, the bedroom where his grandfather had slept. Gary felt as if he was trespassing on a restricted floor.

After his three-day pass, Gary headed back to Valley Forge General Hospital. On the return trip he drove his Karmann Ghia that his stepfather had kept for him while he was away. Steve had encouraged him to invest in a new sound system for the car, so Gary had a stereo and speakers installed. He bought a collection of 8-track tapes—Led Zeppelin; Iron Butterfly; Crosby, Stills, Nash & Young; and James Taylor. Steve had also introduced Gary to the soulful sounds of Leonard Cohen, who quickly became a favorite, although Gary mostly felt out of touch with the music scene. In Vietnam the bulk of the music he'd heard was country and western. When Woodstock had happened, he'd been administering antibiotics to a rogue water buffalo.

After being away from the hospital for a few days, Gary found it difficult to be back. The doctors checked his ileostomy and the status of his other wounds, performed a minor surgery, and ordered him to bed for a few days' rest. Then they gave him another pass—this time for thirty days.

Gary drove back to Rochester and went straight to Steve's house. They went to a nearby biker bar with a long line of people trying to get in. Steve said it was the coolest place in town, so they waited in line and finally made it inside. Normally Gary loved being in a bar, but that night nothing felt familiar. Gary felt hemmed in by the crowd; the noise was unsettling—even overwhelming. He felt chaotic and unsafe, and visions of Vietnam flitted through his mind. He knew he needed to be someplace else—somewhere he could be more in control of his surroundings. But where?

He walked outside, sat on the hood of Steve's car, and looked up at the black sky. It was a clear night, and Gary searched the multitude of stars for the few stars and constellations he'd recognized as a kid. It was easy to find the Big Dipper, the Little Dipper, the North Star, and Orion, the hunter.

Gary closed his eyes. Just as early navigators used the stars to guide their journeys, he was trying to find something to guide him through the chaos he felt. His mind went back to the many nights he'd sat on the bunker walls in Dak Seang, looking at the sky and talking to the Montagnards. How he missed his Vietnam life, the depth and wisdom of their conversations.

"Gary, you okay?" Steve's voice brought him back to Rochester.

"Yeah, I'm okay," Gary said. "I just had to get out of there."

"You want to go somewhere else?"

Gary looked at the sky again. How do you convey to anyone—even a great friend, even a fellow veteran—what's going on inside you? How do you talk about anger, guilt, fear, confusion? Things you've seen. Things that happened to you while away. Nothing felt the same anymore. *He* was no longer the same.

Gary shook his head and said, "I just don't know how to explain any of this."

Steve thought for a moment. "Let's go to Linda's," he said.

Wordlessly they climbed back inside Steve's car and headed over to Steve's friend's. Gary was still thinking about how to explain things, how to sort out the craziness in his head, when Linda greeted them at the door with hugs. Gary was still lost in his thoughts when Bill encouraged him to take something to help him relax and find the spiritual life he was seeking. "It might help open up some doors" was all Bill said.

Gary put the tab of mescaline under his tongue. The Beatles were cranked up loud on the turntable, and soon Gary's head was filled with pigs running from a gun and sitting on cornflakes and a crabalocker fishwife jumble of words and guitars. The mescaline took hold, and the Beatles came alive on the album cover as Gary stared at it while they played a private concert just for him.

No spiritual insights came from Gary's first drug trip. After a while he was aware enough to notice wetness spreading on his chest. A snort of incredulity came out of his nose, and he fumbled his way to the bathroom to empty his ileostomy bag.

So much for enlightenment.

12

Broken Hallelujah

On those nights at home when Gary couldn't sleep, he stayed up late in the tiny attic peak of his grandfather's home, journaling, reading, thinking, listening to Leonard Cohen, trying to sort things out and heal, wondering whom he could ever talk to about what he had witnessed.

Gary's ileostomy was giving him a lot of trouble. The bag continually leaked digestive acids onto his stomach, resulting in severe burns and blisters on his abdomen. Technically, Gary was still in the army, although home on convalescent leave. After the thirty days' leave, he would need to report back to Valley Forge again so he could finish getting well.

But on a particular night, a Tuesday, with seven days of leave left, Gary listened to Leonard Cohen's "So Long, Marianne" and "Hey, That's No Way to Say Goodbye," searching for whispers of empathy within the lyrics.

Tonight, he wasn't thinking much about his physical wounds, although surgeons had already gouged seventeen pieces of shrapnel from his back—even a rusty nail from a jerry-rigged NVA claymore mine had been lodged near his kidneys. Some thirty-four additional pieces of shrapnel had shown up in X-rays and would need to be precisely located and dug out. But he could focus on all that later—the debridement for the infections, the resections on the ileostomy, the treatments for the spinal concussion.

Tonight, he was on a more personal quest. Hopefully, within the lyrics he could find that somebody else knew something about the sadness and loneliness he felt. The loss of love and innocence. The quest for hope.

Gary cracked open his grandfather's upstairs window, rolled a joint and lit it, puffed and inhaled. The bedside clock read 3:00 a.m. The music helped, but he still felt unsatisfied. His spirit roamed, searching for something more. Gary sighed, switched off his turntable, and padded downstairs. He slid on his tennis shoes, ambled to the garage, climbed onto his ten-speed bike, and headed out for a ride.

The first street was deserted, and Gary rode down it in silence. He turned left and kept going. One hour passed. More. He lost track of time as he rode and rode. The cool air felt good against his forehead and cheeks.

In Cobb's Hill Park he stopped, leaned his bike against a tree, and sat down on the dewy grass. Nearby lay a reservoir, with the surface of pooled water as smooth as glass. In the distance were the lights of the city skyline. Twinges of calm finally came. There he stayed until the sun rose. Watching. Waiting. The dawn felt more hopeful than the night.

After sunrise he climbed back on his bike and rode home to shower, change, and grab a bowl of cereal.

At 7:00 a.m. Steve rumbled up in his Bonneville, parked at the curb, honked, and peeled back the Pontiac's convertible top. Gary climbed into the car next to Steve and banged the door shut. Gary wore straight-legged jeans and a button-down shirt. His hair was buzzed short—"whitewall," they called it in the army. He still strongly identified as a Green Beret and carried a sense of military stature and decorum. Steve was the perfect counterpoint in appearance with his long hair, ripped flares, and beads. But the strangely paired young men felt an unspoken bond.

Today, they had no particular place to go. Steve often came by to take Gary for a drive. Sometimes Steve simply said, "Let's go for a ride," and at other times no words passed between them. This morning Steve kept his mouth shut and plugged in an 8-track. The metallic sounds of Iron Butterfly blasted through the speakers as the car pulled away and gained speed. Steve kept one hand on the wheel and lit a marijuana pipe with his other. They passed the pipe between them, and Steve switched out the Iron Butterfly for some Led Zeppelin.

"Let's go to Montreal," Steve said, almost absentmindedly.

"Okay, that sounds cool," Gary answered.

The destination didn't matter. They didn't know exactly where Montreal was, only that it wasn't far away. Neither had been to Canada, but it sounded like something fun to do for the day.

They drove up through New York, through Watertown, to the edge of their country, pausing before they reached the border only long enough to stow the pipe under the seat. Both guys kept on their sunglasses while talking to the border patrol, who waved them through after a few simple questions.

Soon they found themselves driving down one of the main streets of Montreal. Gary spotted a sign for Sherbrooke Street and remarked, "Hey, that's where Leonard Cohen used to live. Go there. Maybe we'll see his house." Steve nodded and turned onto the street. Cohen's poetry and songs had felt critical to Gary's healing. The artist's passion, love, and honest pursuit of meaning in what happens to people were offering Gary comfort and encouragement.

The day suddenly developed intrigue. They drove by the historic mansions in the Golden Square Mile district, along the edge of Plateau Mont-Royal, and past the lush arboretums of the Jardin botanique de Montréal.

Two hitchhikers stood by the side of the road. Women and young. One was tall and slender with hair to her waist, wearing huge John Lennon glasses. The other was shorter with long curly hair. She reminded Gary of Janis Joplin. It was still morning when Steve stopped the car.

"Hi," said the first girl, showing a cute dimple. The other smiled. Steve grinned and motioned with his chin, and the girls climbed into the back seat. Gary liked their quick friendliness. The shorter one introduced herself as Audrey; the taller one, Margie.

"You guys both from the States?" Margie asked.

"Yeah," Gary said. "We're vets. We don't sightsee much. We just wanted to know what it's like to live in Montreal."

"Well, come over to our apartment." Audrey flashed another smile. Her tone didn't seem salacious. The girls were both students at Loyola College, they explained, an English-speaking Jesuit school in the city, and their apartment was almost a hostel, with people always dropping in and hanging out. A place for anyone on a journey. Anyone passing through. Anyone trying to "tune in" and find himself. Gary and Steve both nodded.

By the time the Pontiac pulled up to the apartment, five students were already there, smoking, eating, drinking wine, engaging in earnest conversation. Gary and Steve sat cross-legged on the floor, engaged the group, and somewhat warily introduced themselves as Vietnam veterans. Right away the tone of the rap session changed, but not as Gary expected. The Canadian students, mostly from Loyola and nearby McGill University, said they were familiar with American deserters and draft dodgers, but they'd never met anyone who'd actually fought in the war. They wanted to know more.

Gary and Steve simply stared at each other for a moment. Neither had encountered many listening ears in the United States, except from Bill and Linda. Back home not many had welcomed them and truly wanted to know what the war was like.

"Yeah. Just start anywhere," Audrey added. "Gary—you go first."

He gave a slow, disbelieving shake of his head. Where would he even begin? Sure, there was horror. Tragedy. Despair. *But so much of the war wasn't about that,* he thought. Here in Canada he'd found people who really wanted to know what Vietnam was like, and he knew he couldn't shuffle his way through this. He needed to get past the media-portrayed war zeitgeist. He had to dig deeper to discover and convey meaning in what he'd experienced—for their sakes, perhaps, yet most assuredly for his own sense of well-being.

In this atmosphere of acceptance, he dared to allow images to surface. No one rushed him, and the constant music provided an easy backdrop.

The first image that came to his mind was the jungle. The ever-present jungle. Sights and sounds flooded his heart and brain. Children riding in the back of a deuce-and-a-half as the Berets took them to swim in the river. Laughter and cheering as the Montagnards watched a western movie projected on a bedsheet in the middle of the jungle. Evenings spent looking up at a star-filled night sky and listening to the wisdom that the Montagnards had learned and passed along generation to generation.

The memories were strong, overwhelming, and Gary found that words started pouring out from somewhere within him. He talked and talked, and the students truly wanted to hear more.

Steve talked, too, about his experiences as a door gunner, all pretty crazy. On Steve's first tour he'd often fought in the heat of battle, especially serving with an airmobile unit like the 101st Airborne. Whenever they had choppered into a landing zone, especially when the LZ was hot, it was Steve's job to begin firing right away, providing cover for the troops who were inserted.

As Steve talked, Gary realized that his war had been vastly different. He and Steve might have both fought in Vietnam, but its impact on each of their lives was unique, and the process of healing would be just as unique.

Steve and Gary stayed in the apartment for a few days and in that short time felt that many hearts became one. Acceptance created a kind of unity. When they said they needed to get back to the States, the students all seemed sad that they'd have to separate. Audrey and Margie said to come back anytime. Gary felt as if he'd found a home again, a home almost like what he'd experienced in Vietnam. And it all came from a compassionate presence.

As Steve steered the Pontiac south from Montreal, he mused on how dissimilar their war narratives were. "Gary, how come your time in Nam was so different than mine?" Steve asked. "It sounds like you truly loved those people in Dak Seang and they truly loved you. Are you sure we fought in the same war?"

Time slowed down in the next months for Gary. At the hospital, doctors would monitor Gary's progress for a few days; then he'd receive another thirty-day pass. He'd head north to Rochester to pick up Steve and return to Montreal. The apartment of Audrey and Margie felt like the only place where life came close to making sense.

In the days in the hospital, most of Gary's time on Ward 9B was spent staring at the ceiling or wishing he was somewhere else, but a few times Gary tried to bond with the other wounded soldiers. Once, he ordered twenty pizzas for the guys on his ward—deluxe, with all the toppings. The guys all chowed down and said thanks; then Gary spent the next few days at the mercy of his ileostomy bag, sick and unable to leave the hospital.

Another time, Gary became fed up with a nurse, a major, who acted perpetually angry toward all the wounded soldiers. Whenever she entered the ward, the atmosphere soured. Guys would roll over and try to melt into the wall, afraid she'd come hassle them. The nurse was sarcastic, unprofessional, and belittling. Whenever she changed their sheets, she slammed the guys around, making sure they felt pain. She also had a nasty habit of helping herself to the soldiers' care packages without being invited. The men in the ward nicknamed her Nurse Ratched, after the fictional antagonist in *One Flew over the Cuckoo's Nest*. There were no good days with her.

After a few months of Nurse Ratched's harassment, Gary decided enough was enough. He bought a can of peanuts, ate most of them without chewing, let them go through his system, then fished the peanuts out of his ileostomy bag and placed them back inside the peanut can. The other guys on the ward watched with raised eyebrows. He then set the can on his bedside table and hit the call button. Nurse Ratched tromped into the room.

"You've just interrupted my favorite TV show," she said. "Whaddya want?"

"Oh," Gary said in a small voice. "I just wanted to know when I'm going to get my next thirty-day leave." It was a nonmedical question, stupid in her eyes.

"How should I know?" she growled. "I'm not your doctor." She spied the open container of peanuts, swiped it with her paw, grabbed a huge handful, and poured them into her mouth before adding, "If you're leaving soon, you won't be needing these." She tromped back to her show, still clutching the can.

The guys roared.

———

Every chance he got, Gary drove to Montreal. The conversation with the students soothed him, but his time there wasn't always healing. Sometimes American draft dodgers and deserters came by the apartment to talk and hang out. Gary chose to listen without judgment, to learn what he could about what had transpired in their lives to cause them to flee the war. One evening a tall guy with long greasy hair became vehement. He announced that he was a deserter and spewed condemnation at Steve and Gary. Steve looked as if he might pummel the guy, but Gary asked simply, "What did you do during the war? You must have seen some really bad stuff."

The deserter squirmed, flushed, and said, "Well, I never actually went to Vietnam . . . I was in the army band."

Steve and Gary burst out laughing.

Other students frequented the apartment. Some sought enlightened experiences and a higher sense of consciousness from chemicals and organic hallucinogens, such as LSD, psilocybin, mescaline, and peyote. They heard that Gary was searching for God and encouraged him to go on trips with them. Gary experimented with drugs for a season but never found what he was looking for while tripping. Others introduced him to a 1970s technique of enlightenment called soul tripping, which felt similar to Transcendental Meditation. Soul tripping involved a candle, incense, music, and hours of trying to locate your "center" somewhere between your eyes. Gary never found anything of substance, but he kept trying.

One day while lying on a balcony, Gary was tripping on psilocybin. The balcony morphed into a coffin, and the coffin filled with rats and closed up around him. A Vietcong soldier appeared. He dug a hole, buried Gary up to his neck, and put a cage with rats around Gary's head. The enemy let the rats gnaw on Gary's face. The trip finished, leaving Gary sweating, shaking, and sick to his stomach. Had he actually seen the Vietcong? Or was it all from the trip?

On another trip, a Buddhist monk appeared and asked if he could join Gary's journey. In a soothing voice, the monk asked Gary about his story. Gary told of the Dak Poko River, about loading Montagnard children into a deuce-and-a-half and taking them swimming. Gary saw the mountains that surrounded the valley. So beautiful. So real. The children were laughing in the sunlight. Then a couple of black helicopters came over and began shooting at the children. The children were bleeding, screaming, dying.

Gary felt helpless. Furious. The psilocybin wore off, and Gary saw that the monk was real after all—he had stopped by the apartment. Was the massacre on the river real too? The monk continued to talk to Gary about the experience.

Gary felt empty, shaken, powerless.

For almost a year Gary journeyed back and forth between the hospital and Montreal. From time to time, he spent a few days at home with his mother, but mostly he stayed in Canada. One day back in the hospital, the doctor told him, "I think we can get rid of your ileostomy." This was great news to Gary. He'd grown accustomed to the leaky bag, but it was always a nuisance. He had another surgery and a week's rest, and then the bag was gone. It meant he was deemed fit for duty again, and he still had almost two years left on his enlistment.

Before Gary left for his final thirty-day leave, he was asked where he wanted to go next. "You mean I get a choice?" Gary asked. He was assured he did and was told to provide his top three choices. Gary's first choice was to go back to Vietnam with the Fifth Special Forces. His second choice was Okinawa with the First Special Forces. His third choice was Panama with the Eighth Special Forces.

Gary's orders came through: Tenth Special Forces. Fort Devens, Massachusetts. Nowhere on his list. *So much for being able to make a choice,* he thought.

He drove to Montreal one last time and stopped at the apartment. Eight students were hanging out, and Gary piled them all in his Karmann Ghia and drove up to Mount Royal Park. On top of the hill was a huge cross that lit up at night and could be seen from most of Montreal. The sun was setting, and the students relaxed on the lawn, passing around joints. Gary reflected on how he longed to return to the Montagnards. He had almost died in Dak Seang, but he had also experienced a quality of life there that he'd been unable to recapture since returning home. He realized that here in Montreal was the closest thing to a deeper life he'd found so far, and the students from the apartment were mostly kind, welcoming, and receptive. But his contact with them wasn't enough. He still hadn't found what he was looking for.

The sun went down, and the darkness surrounded them, pierced only by the light from the cross.

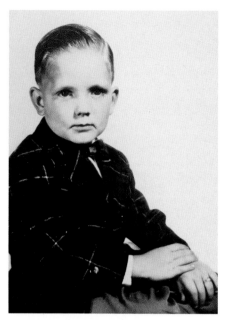

As a boy, Gary survived a fall out of a second-story window.

Gary was told, "The military will either kill you or make you a better man. You have to decide." He enlisted. This is him just out of basic training, ready to serve.

Special Forces training involved ten weeks of unbelievable torment designed to take a man past his breaking point. This is Gary, cold, wet, hungry, and exhausted in the woods during Special Forces training, winter 1968.

For His Honor
Gary Bukirub, Jer 9:23-24

An official Green Beret, a few days before he left for Vietnam. Here, Gary is a specialist fourth class, US Army, Company B, Fifth Special Forces Group. (He would eventually become a sergeant.)

Aerial View of Camp A-245, Dak Seang. The airstrip is along the top. Rows of barbed and concertina wire surround the camp. *Dak Seang* means "river of blood."

Dak Seang was home to 400 Montagnard fighters and some 2,300 women and children. Here are some of the below-ground living quarters.

A Vietnam version of the Band of Brothers, 1969. Back, L–R: Hyih, Deo (in hat), Chom, Brer. Front: Gordy Wiley, Pat Dizzine, Bre (the team's fourteen-year-old interpreter), and Gary (in hat). Bre is the only Montagnard in this picture who survived the siege.

The Montagnard fighters were tasked with defending the strategically located Camp A-245, along with twelve Green Berets. Here the fighters are getting briefed during morning formation.

When Gary discovered that the Montagnard children loved trucks, he sent $400 home to his mother, and she mailed back a hefty supply of Matchbox trucks.

Poignancy lay everywhere. The photo of these Vietnamese children was taken by Gary during a supply run to Pleiku. He loved the expressiveness of their eyes.

The Montagnards were considered an inferior race by the NVA and VC, so the Montagnards' war wasn't a matter of trading one political system for another; it was a matter of survival. Gary took this picture of Montagnard children and the elderly in front of above-ground living quarters near Dak Seang.

Green Berets Captain Paul Landers (L) and Lieutenant
Ed Christiansen (R) are shown with Montagnard friends.
Deo is wearing the hat. During the siege Landers was shot
in the throat and Christiansen was blown out of a tower.
Both survived.

Escort Captain Thornberry (L) came to Lancaster, NH, to take Gary from his cave
to Washington, DC, for the Medal of Honor ceremony. The madras sports coat
was from high school, and Gary's mother sent it to him for the ceremony. A haircut
would soon follow.

Medal of Honor ceremony. The original handwritten caption (not pictured) beneath the photo read, "To Sergeant Gary B. Beikirch, with admiration and gratitude on behalf of a grateful nation, Richard Nixon."

The picture of herself that Lolly placed in Gary's mailbox in Lancaster, NH, to let him know what she looked like before they met.

Gary and Lolly tie the knot.

Gary reunites with Green Beret weapons specialist Sergeant
Bob Hill, who fearlessly helped medevac him from Dak Seang
to the Seventy-First Evac Hospital in Pleiku.

Gary and Lolly at a joint fund-raising event for the Special Operations Warrior Foundation
(supports the families of fallen Special Ops troops), the Gold Shield Foundation (supports
the families of fallen law enforcement and emergency responders), and Guiding Eyes
(trains service dogs for people with vision loss, including wounded veterans).

Gary and Lolly, present day, with their three children, fourteen grandchildren, and in-laws. Each Christmas it's a tradition that they all take a photo wearing hats.

Sergeant Gary Beikirch, Medal of Honor recipient, at a pregame ceremony, Atlanta: "My story is God's story. This medal is not about me. This medal is about him. Without God's grace, I wouldn't have been able to survive Vietnam. Without his forgiveness in my life, I wouldn't have been able to live with myself. Without his love, I wouldn't have healed from my wounds. This medal is about him, and I wear it for his honor."

The Breaking Point

As the leaves were changing in fall 1970, Gary was on his way to Fort Devens, Massachusetts, and his mind swirled with emotions. He was happy with his degree of physical healing, happy to be reinstated on a Special Forces team, but he wasn't content with his stateside duty assignment. Fort Devens would mean formations, inspections. As a professional soldier Gary wanted action; he wanted to make a difference.

He parked his car in front of the headquarters of the Tenth Special Forces Group, climbed out, and surveyed his surroundings. Row after row of brick barracks fenced him in. Courtyards of grass shouted that they couldn't be walked on. Drab gray pavement where soldiers stood at attention for reveille taunted him. As is customary when reporting to a new duty station, Gary wore a class A dress uniform with all his awards and decorations. He straightened his uniform and sighed.

Behind the desk in the personnel office, a young specialist fourth class clattered away on a typewriter. Peach fuzz shaded his upper lip. His skin looked bronzed by the sun, his blond hair was longer than regulations allowed, and his insignia indicated that he was neither Airborne nor Special Forces. A baseball cap worn by conventional unit troops lay on the desk. Gary tried to make a connection anyway and said in his best nonmilitary voice, "Hey, man, how you doing?"

The spec 4 didn't even look up. The clatter continued.

Gary stared at the young man. He was fairly sure the spec 4 had never been to Vietnam. It looked as if he spent most of his time at the mall. Gary refused to repeat his salutation. He looked at his watch. A minute passed. Then another. After a full three minutes, the spec 4 stopped typing and glanced up. Gary's fuse was already short—and lit.

"201 file," the spec 4 said. His voice was flat.

Gary handed him his file. It contained his entire military history and followed him from location to location. The spec 4 thumbed through the file, scrutinizing the information. Gary tapped his foot. The spec 4 reached the end of the file and said, "You're going to have to take that Purple Heart ribbon off. There are no orders in here for that award."

The lit fuse hit the dynamite stick. Gary leaned forward, placed his fists on the spec 4's desk, and growled slowly, "A three-star general pinned this on me in Vietnam . . . You're gonna need a three-star general to get me to remove it."

The spec 4 started flipping through Gary's file again. Gary didn't move. Crazy thoughts ran through his head. Uncontrollable thoughts. He was so mad he was afraid of what he might do to the punk. The spec 4 stopped again, scribbled a few notes, pushed his chair back from the desk, stood, and tucked Gary's file in a cabinet behind him, then handed Gary the scrawled piece of paper. "Here you are, Sergeant," he said. "Your orders."

Gary read the orders, and his eyes narrowed. He had expected to be assigned to a regular company, where he'd be placed on an A Team, but the spec 4's scrawls were all too clear. He'd assigned Gary to headquarters company with a recommendation that he be given a physical and a mental exam to determine his fitness. The spec 4 had based his recommendation on Gary's experiences, the severity of his wounds, and the length of his hospitalization.

Gary wanted to hit something. Throw something. He glanced around for the spec 4 so he could show him exactly how fit he was, but the guy had already stepped out a side door. Gary felt the same kind of rage boiling up within him that he'd felt in the jungle when he ran after the enemy soldier who'd fired on their team during the ambush. They'd followed the bloody trail to the end, but it had disappeared. Gary had wanted to destroy something then, and he wanted to destroy something now. This level of rage scared him, and he didn't know what to do with it. Instead of reporting to headquarters company, he got back in his car, slammed it in gear, and headed out the front gate.

Gary roared up the road, not knowing where he was going. He spotted a sign for Boston, only twenty miles ahead. *Why not?* he thought. Soon he found himself driving down beautiful old cobblestone streets in the heart of the city. He stopped in front of Boston Common, the large public park. Still churning, he climbed out to take a walk. In downtown Boston in 1970, the sight of a soldier in uniform was seldom greeted with gratitude. The park was a popular location for antiwar protests and demonstrations.

Just a few months earlier, on May 4, 1970, National Guardsmen had shot and killed four unarmed students during an antiwar rally at Kent State University. Some four million students across the country responded by holding sit-ins, blocking intersections and freeways, vandalizing buildings, and burning down ROTC buildings. Boston had been a hotbed of activity for student protests. Tensions still ran high.

A group of college-age students in the park started following Gary. Some sped up and kept pace with him. Some closed in on his heels. Gary glanced around and counted at least fifteen of them surrounding him like wolves.

"Hey, look at that—a soldier!" one of the pack sneered. Gary continued walking, his face set hard.

"Why don't you go back to Vietnam and stay there!" another chided. The whole group began shouting at him.

Gary kept silent. He'd been yelled at so many times during Special Forces training, he'd learned how to put up walls. He silently walked onward, and finally the students harassing him broke apart and left him alone.

About two hours later, Gary returned to his Karmann Ghia. It had been broken into, and his new cassette deck and speakers and all his music had been stolen. He made a mental note: *Next time in Boston, don't wear a uniform.*

———

Gary returned to Fort Devens later that day. Going AWOL for an afternoon wasn't exactly an act of quitting the military, he reasoned to himself. His decision had been made spontaneously. Gary knew he'd needed to get away, calm down, and sort things out. He still wanted a full career in the Green Berets and didn't consider his action desertion. Not yet anyway. He likened it to taking a break, like jumping in a jeep with Dizzy and heading up Highway 14 to Pleiku.

At Devens, the CO reviewed his orders and scheduled the physical and mental exams for a few days away. In the meantime he listed Gary as "excess" in the company, meaning not attached to any one unit. Gary was assigned a room on base and told to go to supply and draw his gear.

As he waited for the tests, Gary's hopes rose for an appealing assignment. Gary hoped to be sent to Bad Tölz, Germany, where the Tenth Special Forces detachment responsible for western Europe often worked with NATO forces. But he soon learned that because of snafus he was scheduled to leave for Alaska for winter training instead—even before his tests were performed. With this news his attitude toward soldiering sank. He missed his friends in Montreal. He didn't want to be stuck at Devens playing soldier. He particularly didn't want to be sent to Alaska in winter.

He met a guy in headquarters named Chief, who seemed to have connections. Chief winked and said he could "get things." He kept an apartment in Boston and said that if Gary lay low for a while—at least until the team left for Alaska—then most likely Gary could take his physical and mental exams afterward and get a limited-duty profile. Hopefully, then, things would all work out, and the military wouldn't gig him for skipping town. The plan sounded good. The day before he was supposed to leave for Alaska, Gary headed to Chief's apartment to hide out.

The team departed. Gary returned to Devens and, sure enough, Chief's plan worked. The medical professionals decided that given how his wounds still affected him, Gary should be placed on limited duty. This meant no prolonged standing, no heavy lifting, and no running.

Because Gary was still listed as excess, it was harder for the military to keep track of him. The CO assigned Gary to work as an assistant to the base's dentist. Gary had done some dental work in Dak Seang, but he hated his new assignment. Over the next few weeks, he skipped base more often, took more trips to Boston, and hung out with Chief more. Gary's attitude worsened.

Gary discovered that, similar to Margie and Audrey's place in Montreal, Chief's apartment was a place to hang out and connect, but the people who congregated there were definitely rougher. Chief's pals were into hard drugs—cocaine, meth, and heroin. Gary never dipped into hard drugs himself, but he was around the drugs and the subculture that often accompanies them.

Over time Chief led him to nightclubs and seamier areas of town known for violence and organized crime. Today, Gary simply describes this time of life as his lost season. Through a mutual friend, Gary partied with the Hells Angels for a time. Gary and Chief were at a bar once where a fight broke out. The bouncers took baseball bats and began clearing the club, swinging the bats with no regard for anyone they hit. Another time a young woman Gary knew overdosed on a mixture of meth and PCP and died. The experiences shook Gary up and the death haunted him.

Gary's life felt out of control, and he wanted out—out of everything. Out of the military. Out of the darker side of life. He realized he needed to put some serious distance between himself and Chief. He loaded some things into his car and took off for Montreal.

His old friends welcomed him and helped him regain focus. He stayed for three weeks in Canada and wanted to stay forever, but his friends convinced him that deserting the army and running away from life wasn't the best path forward. One friend said, "Gary, change is good, but make sure if you leave the army that you leave in victory . . . not in defeat."

Gary took those words to heart. He packed up and headed back to Devens, not knowing what consequences awaited him for going AWOL. He could be reduced in rank, fined, or even kicked out of Special Forces. He pulled into the parking lot of HQ company and gulped when he saw his team sergeant (the NCO who took roll call in formation each morning) walking toward him. The team sergeant merely said, "You better go over to the mail room and pick up your mail. There's quite a stack waiting for you." Gary was shocked. He was sure the NCO knew he'd been missing.

Gary headed over to the dispensary to face the head NCO there. He was a friend from Pleiku days who simply smiled and said, "Glad to see you, Gary. I told them you'd be back."

Perplexed, Gary could only grin. The friend pulled him aside and quietly told Gary that after he'd been missing for two days, the team sergeant and the military dentist had set up a meeting with the NCO in charge of the Tenth Group dispensary, who'd explained everything Gary had been through in Dak Seang. The three of them had agreed to cover for Gary. Their warm support flooded him with surprise and thankfulness.

Today, Gary wishes he could say that after he returned to Devens he became an exemplary soldier and role model, but his old behavior pattern cut deep. From time to time he still left base without permission—although he went to Montreal, not to Boston. His buddies still covered for him while he was gone, and his attitude still ran a troubled course.

After almost a year at Devens, Gary knew his military career was drawing to a close, although he still had time left on his enlistment. He wanted something more from life, although he didn't know exactly what, and desperation dogged his heels. Memories of Vietnam were always in his mind, and he concluded he didn't want to be a soldier for the rest of his life. Someday in the future he wanted to get married, and he knew that Special Forces guys often have a hard time with family life because of multiple sudden deployments. He knew a lot of Special Forces personnel who'd been married and divorced more than once. Gary decided he wanted to become a doctor. Maybe someday, with those skills, he could return to Vietnam and help the Montagnards.

Gary spoke to the chaplain on base and a psychiatrist, explaining he didn't think he was going to last through his final year at Devens. Gary described to them his despondency, rage, and confusion. He hoped they would recommend him for a 212 discharge—inability to adjust to the military. The chaplain said no. The psychiatrist just shrugged and said, "Well, you sound normal to me."

Normal? Gary thought. *I've just come out of combat—what's normal anymore?*

After being turned down for the 212, Gary searched for another avenue out of the military—on his terms and legally. He heard about a new army program that allowed a Vietnam vet to be discharged if he was accepted into an approved college program. This seemed like a light at the end of the tunnel. Gary reapplied to SUNY Brockport and switched his major to premed. Two months later, he received a letter from his congressman saying that because of Gary's exemplary service to the nation, he was being granted an early out to pursue his new goal of becoming a doctor.

Altogether, Gary had spent almost four years in the army—a year and a half in military training, almost a year in Vietnam, ten months in and out of the hospital recovering, and almost a year at Devens. He would stay in the reserves and finish his enlistment, but when it came to active duty, Gary was done.

He had a swirl of emotions: sadness about not being able to pursue a lifetime career as a Green Beret, apprehension about returning to college after being gone so long, gratitude for all that Special Forces had taught him, and honor that he'd been allowed to serve and defend the cause of freedom.

Mostly he felt relieved. No one was ever going to tell him what he could or couldn't do with his life. He was in control again.

Or so he thought.

———

Gary gave his Karmann Ghia to a friend in Special Forces and bought a 1965 Volkswagen van, the kind with roof porthole windows and a canvas sunroof. He took out two rows of seats and built a platform bed in the back, then loaded up a group of friends and took off to Newport, Rhode Island, for the annual jazz festival—four days of music and fun. It was 1971, and many top artists were scheduled to perform, including Ray Charles, Roberta Flack, Miles Davis, Duke Ellington, Dizzy Gillespie, Buddy Rich, Aretha Franklin, the Allman Brothers, and B. B. King.

The festival had grown over the years, which caused a strain on the small Rhode Island community. Halfway through the event, the crowd became so large and unruly that officials stopped selling tickets.

Gary and his Special Forces buddies were sitting on blankets down in front, passing around pot and bottles of wine while talking with acquaintances from Rochester. Dionne Warwick was on stage singing "What the World Needs Now Is Love" when she stopped midsong. An announcer took the stage and said that the show was halted because too many people were pushing in and that the whole crowd needed to exit the space in an orderly way and return to their campgrounds or homes. The concert would start again the next morning.

The group from Rochester was already pretty loaded. One of them yelled to his buddy, "What did they say?" And someone yelled back, "They're going to shut down the show!" One of the bigger Rochester guys yelled, "We paid good money for this!" and chucked his bottle onstage.

Suddenly, there was all kinds of shoving, yelling, and throwing. Gary and his friends made a quick retreat toward the gate, leaving the pals from Rochester to duke it out with the crowd. The riot had already spread. People were climbing the chain-link fence, tearing down barricades, jumping up and down on the hoods of police cars.

Gary and his buddies maneuvered back to Gary's bus, climbed inside, and shut the doors. They pulled back the canvas top and stuck their heads out so they could watch the bedlam. When police started to use tear gas, they hunkered down under the top.

On the drive home to Rochester, Gary named his van Newport in honor of their crazy experience.

Back in Brockport, classes were to start in three days, and Gary busied himself with registering, applying for financial aid and veterans' benefits, buying books, and finding a place to stay. He accomplished everything except finding housing, so he opted to live in his van for a while, usually parking in a lot on campus near the gym. He didn't have much money, so a friend at Devens contributed a few cases of C-rations and LRRPs (dehydrated field rations), along with winter boots and a coat, a sleeping bag, and fatigues—so that took care of food, bedding, and clothes.

Gary was excited about his premed program. Classes began. Gary showered in the PE building and studied in the library or by candlelight in his van. Life felt set on a purposeful track at last. But two days into the semester, as Gary walked to classes wearing his army fatigues, he encountered glares, taunts, and whispers. A student looked his way, locked eyes hard, and wasn't embarrassed by the stare. It happened again. And again. The message was *We don't like you and what you represent.*

Then things took a turn for the worse. Gary didn't have money for civilian clothes, so he kept wearing the free army fatigues. Ironically a lot of army gear was being worn on college campuses, although most of the shirts had peace sign patches sewn onto the shoulders and most of the pants had an American flag stitched upside down across the buttocks.

One afternoon Gary was walking down a hallway, and a thick-necked student bumped hard into his shoulder. The student didn't apologize. It happened the next afternoon. And the next. One evening while he was studying in the library, two students walked by and knocked Gary's books onto the floor. He wondered if it was an accident until the next night when the same students walked by and did it again.

With each incident Gary told himself what he'd learned during Special Forces training. *Just hold it in and wait for it to pass. This won't be forever.* And he chose to study in his van.

One morning he was awakened by loud yelling outside Newport the van, which still had the Fort Devens military decal on the bumper. At first all Gary heard was a loud commotion. He stole a look out the window. More than a dozen students had encircled his van.

"Hey! Come out and talk," yelled one. "We want to know what it's like to kill babies."

He stole another look. "Yeah!" shouted another. "Ya burn down any villages lately?"

The students started pushing Newport one way and then the other. Banging on the sides. Scratching her paint. "Hey, baby killer, come on out!" another yelled. "We want to talk to you about killing people!"

Anger burned in Gary's heart. He envisioned himself jumping out of the van. With all his training, he knew he could get in more than a few solid blows before the rest of the group took him down. Along with the anger, he felt disbelief at the things he was hearing—and sadness, incredible sadness.

Before too long, campus security came and chased the crowd away. The officer checked in with Gary, determined there were no injuries, and ordered him not to sleep in the parking lot anymore. After the officer left, Gary slunk behind Newport's steering wheel. He wondered, *Would it have been better if I'd stayed in the army? Here I am with no job, little money, no place to stay, no friends on campus. Is this the life I'm supposed to live?*

He started up the engine and headed forty minutes up the road to his buddy Steve's house in Rochester. Steve had gotten married recently. When Gary walked in, Steve lit a joint and handed it to him, then put some Led Zeppelin on the turntable. Gary crashed there for a couple of days.

After sorting out his thoughts, Gary decided to return to school. On the way back he saw a hitchhiker wearing an army field jacket and picked him up. The hitchhiker's name was Tony. He'd never gone to Vietnam, but he'd worked on the wards as a medical tech and was now majoring in psychology at SUNY Brockport. He offered to let Gary stay with him and his wife, Nancy. Gary shrugged. *Why not?* Their apartment turned out to be another gathering place where students came and went, rapped, argued, smoked, drank, and hung out. Half a dozen of the regulars lived on a farm outside Brockport. It was a working farm with chickens, goats, and vegetable gardens.

After the students came by a few times, Tony and Nancy said they were packing up their apartment to live on a farm too and encouraged Gary to join them. The plan sounded good, so Gary moved out to the farm with his new acquaintances. There he spent his free time doing chores, playing guitar, drinking wine, and smoking marijuana. He found a bit of peace and started to get into the groove of school again, although life on campus did not become any easier. Students still glared, taunted, and called him names.

Gary decided to get a job to supplement his meager monthly VA benefits. He applied to work at a hospital, figuring that as a premed student and with his training as a Special Forces medic, he'd be a shoo-in for a good position. But he was hired to work in housekeeping. He swallowed his pride and took the job, emptying trash, mopping floors, wiping up barf, and scrubbing toilets. His attitude slowly deteriorated.

Something else gnawed at him—something more than the lousy job and problems at the university. He thought about Vietnam all the time. Many nights he woke in a cold sweat from nightmares, and the images stayed with him during the day. Gary felt socially removed from everybody, and he stopped talking to his friends at the farm.

Often he would take off for days without telling anybody. Sometimes he bought a couple of bottles of Pagan Pink Ripple wine and headed for Steve's house to camp out. Steve was concerned. "Hang in there, bud. It'll get better," Steve said more than once, but it didn't get better.

Gary felt as if he couldn't talk to anyone about what he was feeling because he didn't know what to say. All he knew for certain was that life was confusing. He hurt. Any free time he had he spent holed up in his room, scribbling in journals. One entry read,

It's now been two weeks, and not one word has passed over these lips to anyone. The only words formed come from my own heart, only to return back to me and bring hurt and guilt.

One night, Gary went drinking with some guys. They drank all night, took amphetamines to stay awake, and kept drinking the next day. A second day and night passed, then a third. They drank the entire time.

Gary remembers driving Newport. He heard a loud crash and was thrown forward. For a moment he wondered if he was back in Vietnam. Maybe a rocket had exploded. The night was dark—morning was still some time away. He saw sparks and smelled smoke.

"Wow, what a rush," Gary mumbled and, along with the guys, crawled out of the van. A hard rain fell, and Gary saw that they'd slid off the road and crashed into a utility pole. The pole lay on top of the van, and the electrical wires buzzed and arced. A VW van's engine is in the rear, and only the shattered windshield and a thin piece of crunched metal separated the driver's seat from the utility pole. Gary wondered why they hadn't been killed by the crash or electrocuted. The police came and sorted out the accident. Gary was taken to the hospital with three broken ribs. Newport the van was totaled. He never saw those drinking buddies again.

Gary knew he was going downhill. A cousin loaned him money, and he bought a red Chevy van with a stripped inside. Because of the drinking binge and accident, he'd been gone from college for more than a week and away from his place at the farm for even longer.

He drove back to the farm first, where the others started a fire in the wood-stove in the living area, sat Gary down, and held an impromptu intervention. They told Gary they worried about him, worried about his drinking, worried about his seclusion—even when he was with them. They cared for Gary but believed they couldn't trust him anymore. They asked him to leave.

Gary felt as if he'd let his family down. He wanted to cry, but he stuffed everything deep down inside and said he'd go. He drove back to the parking lot on campus and slept in his Chevy, anxious that security might catch him and tell him to leave. The next morning he tried to go back to classes, but he couldn't concentrate. He sat wrapped in undeniable hurt.

One afternoon a few days later, Gary left his van and headed toward the student union building. It was a place of gathering, of tables and clubs and people talking—the lifestyle of the early 1970s. Anybody was welcome to hang out and rap. Gary wanted to get lost in the crowd and hoped simply to be around people—even strangers—if only for an afternoon.

It was spring, near the end of the second semester. Feeling lonely, even desperate, Gary headed up the walkway and saw a group of students hanging around underneath a tree. Somebody recognized him from a class they'd had together. "Hey, you're that soldier," the guy said. "What're you doing around here?" He strode over and stepped into Gary's path, blocking his way.

Gary stopped and stared at the young man. The rest of the students formed a ring behind Gary. Gary sensed they were committed. They wanted something to happen. He turned around, broke through them, and started walking away. The first guy followed Gary, yelling and swearing. The rest of the pack came with him.

Gary kept walking. Then he heard a guttural sound, like someone clearing his throat. Out of the corner of his eye, Gary saw one of the students run up to him and spit. Saliva hit Gary's face and dripped down his cheek. The other students laughed.

Gary felt like a volcano about to erupt. The lava had been building for months, and any second, fire and lava would explode. His anger frightened him. He didn't know what he would do if he went after the students. Pulling together every ounce of remaining self-control, Gary kept walking. He reached his van and climbed in, started the engine, and slumped in his seat.

"This is crazy," he whispered. "I'm just . . . so . . . done."

He didn't know what to do or where to go—only that he couldn't stay where he was. As he drove away, he heard gunfire and rockets, the deafening sounds of grenades and mortars. He shook his head and tried to stop the memories, but the air seemed full of bullets, and blood pooled in potholes on the road.

He kept driving, and the van's tires swerved onto the shoulder; the ground rumbled with a huge explosion. Images blasted into his head and played with his mind. He saw his medic sitting on a fence post, cradling the headless body of his wife. He felt hot shards of metal explode into his own body and slam against his spine. He felt helpless, powerless. The images kept coming. They occupied his mind and wouldn't leave.

Gary grabbed the steering wheel, lurched back onto the road, and found he was pulling the trigger of his machine gun in bursts, firing into waves of enemy troops that poured over the wire. Bodies lay everywhere. Children. Whole families. They were lying on the road, sitting in the Chevy van alongside him. Gary hollered for Tot and Deo to stop the van. He needed to get out.

Sitting by the side of the road in his van, the engine running, Gary knew he was in trouble. He was breathless. Spent. Exhausted. Hated. How was he supposed to control any of this? How could he make it all stop—the taunting, the rejection, the images thrusting themselves on him again and again? So many hard memories and feelings filled him with pain. So many dark experiences insisted on being a part of his life. Always. He could never leave them behind.

He switched on the radio, found some familiar rock and roll, and turned up the music to a deafening level. He tried to drive on. But even the loud music could not keep the memories from bombarding his mind.

Gary stared at the road ahead, trembling. He had tried numbing the pain with drugs and alcohol, but these had proved a temporary diversion at best, destructive in the long run. He'd tried forgetting, putting the past behind him, but the experiences wouldn't leave him; they'd taken on a visual reality of their own. He had tried to move forward in life, attempting to think positive thoughts and make new connections. But positivity didn't have the power to wipe the past away. He couldn't make it stop.

Gary drove and drove, and a resolution formed in his heart and mind. It felt like his last hope of survival: an agreement with isolation. The logic seemed straightforward: if he didn't care, then he wouldn't feel; if he didn't feel, then he wouldn't hurt.

So that's what it would be, then. From here on out, he would not care about anything or anybody. He would push everything and everybody away. He would lock himself behind impenetrable walls. He would place large signs around him, warning anybody who tried to come near: "Stay away!" "Danger!" "No one allowed!"

He focused harder on the loud music. He'd reached his breaking point. All he needed to do now was shut down.

Blaze of Light

After a man hits a breaking point, profound and dark as it may be, he still needs to go on to the next thing. But as Gary drove away from school, he had no idea where to go. He was concentrating on building walls, on shutting down. Even so, common sense told him he needed respite, a place where he could catch his breath and figure out life beyond SUNY Brockport. He vowed he'd never go back there.

Gary thought about going to Steve's place again; he'd always been a good friend. But Gary sensed he shouldn't lay this on Steve. In fact, Steve's life was becoming so different that maybe he wouldn't even be able to help. Steve had tried to forget Vietnam by immersing himself in a normal life. He was working a nine-to-five job and was married, and Gary didn't want to burden Steve with his problems.

He considered driving up to Montreal. But Audrey and Margie and many of his Canadian friends had graduated and gotten jobs by now. They were settling into new lives, and the magic of the compassionate presence in their apartment was gone.

Gary considered driving to California to see Steve's friend Linda, who had moved there recently and always seemed like a mother full of wisdom and kindness. Maybe he could try California. It seemed like the best way forward, although he doubted his old Chevy van could make it across the country.

He'd heard that students could scan the personal ads in Boston and find people traveling to different locations who wanted to share a ride—maybe he could get to California that way. He drove to the city, changed into civilian clothes in the back of his van, and headed into Boston Common. As usual the park was filled with young people, some sitting in groups and smoking, some studying, some walking hand in hand.

A web of haziness hung over the park. Gary's mind felt muddled. He was constantly trailed by loneliness, anger, hurt—and now he was hungry. A group of young adults sat in a circle, singing, holding hands while one played guitar. Their hair was long, and they wore beads and simple clothing, and as Gary stopped and listened, they seemed so happy. One of the guys walked over and invited Gary to join them. The guy explained that they were part of a larger group called the Children of God and that a prophet named Moses David had sent them from Huntington Beach to Boston. He invited Gary to stay with them for a couple of days, and Gary shrugged and said, "Sure. Why not?"

Gary spent a day with the group. They fed him and cared for him. The girls gave him hugs, and the guys seemed sincere in their acceptance. Group members talked a lot about a coming apocalypse, which they predicted would occur in 1993. Meanwhile, life consisted of revolution and fulfilling sexual desires and being into "free love," although they didn't trust the rest of the world, which they called "the system."

A strange imperative overtook Gary, and he thought, *Forget the free food. Forget the group.* He left and returned to the common to pick up a newspaper so he could get back on track for California.

Haziness still hung over the park. There he met another group of young adults who were talking to anyone who'd listen. They belonged to a church started by a sci-fi novelist named L. Ron Hubbard. They told him about a technique called Dianetics, which they promised could help erase memories from Gary's subconscious and give him a more satisfying life. They invited him to their spiritual guidance center to go through an initial process called auditing. Curious about anything that promised help, Gary went and proceeded with the audit. After twenty minutes he walked out, figuring that whatever pap they were selling wasn't what he was looking for.

Gary stayed at the park for several days, sleeping in his van, doing a lot of hard thinking. Nightmares plagued him. Flashbacks happened regularly throughout the day. Almost anything could trigger the memories—the smell of gasoline or diesel, a particular song, the sound of a helicopter hovering over the city.

His interaction with the two religious groups caused him to think more about God. He didn't know all the specifics of the groups, but he sensed they were wandering from truth. His mind kept returning to his experience in the hospital bed when he had prayed with the chaplain. Gary's encounter with God then had felt honest and rational and left him feeling peaceful and supported. That same sort of experience was what he wanted to pursue now, if more of it could be found.

He decided not to go to California after all. He wanted to know more about this God he'd encountered within the prayer, even after barricading himself within walls as he'd vowed to do, and although Gary didn't know exactly how to continue his search, he slowly concluded the answer didn't lie in running away.

———

One afternoon while sitting under a tree in the common, wrestling with his confusion, he remembered that his cousin Jan and her family had recently moved to Marshfield, Massachusetts, about thirty miles from Boston. Jan was the one who'd knelt beside her bed as a young girl and begged God to spare Gary's life when he fell out of the window as a toddler. She and her husband, Buck, were the ones who'd driven cross-country to see Gary before he left for Vietnam. Their visit had always meant a lot to him.

His first inclination was to forget about them, to push them away, just as he pushed away everybody else. But he decided to take his chances and was soon heading for Marshfield. He found their address in a phone book and decided just to drive by and take a look.

Jan and Buck lived in a small renovated Cape Cod farmhouse on five acres. *Well, since I'm here, why not drop in?* he thought. As Gary drove up the gravel drive, he felt a strange mix of emotions. He knew he was showing up unannounced, carrying with him a world of hurt. Maybe his plan was foolish. He hadn't seen them in almost three years. Maybe he should just turn around. But two ponies beckoned from a corral by the barn, and a number of dogs surged around his van, yipping and smiling and sniffing as he pulled to a stop. Maybe he'd step in for a few moments to say hi.

Their property was not the sort of manicured farm that might be pictured on a New England postcard but rather a working collection of outbuildings and kids' bicycles and animals and vegetable plots. Around the property's perimeter lay a circular track with mounds of dirt built up like ramps—Gary later found out it was a track where Jan and Buck's older son could ride his dirt bike. Jan would later describe the farm as a "flea market," and Buck would say to her quietly, "Jan, we are raising children . . . not a pretty yard." And they were raising children indeed—three girls and two boys.

When Jan opened the front door and saw Gary standing on the stoop, she laid a hand over her heart and burst into tears. She pulled Gary close in a warm embrace. Gary's instinct was to pull back, but her actions were so genuine that he let himself be held. Buck wasn't far behind, and he clapped Gary on the shoulders and said "Welcome!" Jan laughed and hugged Gary again, and when she released her embrace and looked at him more closely, she said, "Gary, your presence at our farm is no coincidence."

They talked for a while, and their conversation was full of laughter and warmth. They had heard bits and pieces from relatives about Gary's story since his return from Vietnam, but they were looking forward to learning about what was happening with him now.

Buck asked Gary how long he could stay. Gary shrugged. Since Gary had no real plans beyond the moment, Buck invited him to stay for a few weeks. Gary could sleep in a trailer on the property, work with Buck during the day, and help take care of things around the farm. Gary didn't have to think—he accepted the offer.

Quickly, Gary settled into living with Jan and Buck. What amazed him most was the respect and consideration evident within the family. Meals began with a simple prayer, then food was passed, then Buck and Jan listened as each child shared things that had happened throughout the day. The kids knew their parents were sincerely interested, and the children freely shared jokes, thoughts, and dreams.

Each meal was straight from the farm or surrounding areas—salads of tomatoes and fresh spinach, cucumbers and squash. Potatoes dug from the garden. Plenty of roast chicken, local milk, and free-range beef. Delicious and comforting.

After each meal, with the dishes washed and put away, the kids would dash away to play games or do chores or finish their homework, and Buck and Jan would linger and talk with Gary over jasmine tea.

Jan told Gary that his showing up was an answer to years of prayer. Ever since he was a toddler and had fallen out of the window, she had prayed for him. She had prayed for him while he was growing up. She'd prayed for him as his mother and stepfather moved from house to house. She'd prayed for him when he joined the army, when he was in Vietnam, and when he was wounded and recuperating in the hospital. Lately she had been praying for Gary more than ever, although she couldn't explain exactly why. She simply felt compelled.

Gary was intrigued to learn more about this unique family.

He came to appreciate Buck as a genuine Renaissance man. He had his master's degree in education and had worked as an administrator and teacher but become restless in his career. He'd traveled to Brazil and helped set up a school; then he'd run his own business for a season and succeeded, but now he liked being free to organize his day without a clock. In addition to the work around the farm, he collected items to sell at flea markets. He liked to talk with the people he met there about philosophy and literature and God—and when he wasn't out collecting items or restoring them, he remodeled bathrooms, cleaned up basements or attics, or dismantled old buildings marked for demolition and salvaged whatever he could find. Each day was different for Buck—and he liked life that way.

Working with Buck meant Gary started each morning by driving with him to the nearby pancake house. Jan worked as a nurse and would often join Buck and Gary for breakfast before heading to the hospital. They talked about what Gary's life had been like in the army and with the Montagnards in Dak Seang. They asked about his studies, why he'd wanted to attend med school, and what had prompted him to leave the university. Their questions were deep, and often Gary could not give full answers. He was still searching for the answers himself.

After breakfast, Gary and Buck headed to whatever job Buck had lined up for the day. They'd drive over to the site, work for a few hours, then stop work and take what Buck called a "word break." It was like a coffee break, although Buck would pull out a book and read for fifteen minutes. He encouraged Gary to do the same.

Gary hadn't brought any books with him to the farm other than the medical textbooks he'd tossed into the back of his van, but while cleaning out an attic, he'd found two books that caught his attention. One, the complete works of Emerson, and the other, a work of Thoreau. He brought Thoreau to work the next day to read during their break.

After a few days, Buck asked Gary what he was learning from Thoreau. Gary had come to know Buck as a subtle intellectual, very deep, who wasn't intimidated by anything. He reminded Gary of Socrates, a wise guru who taught through dialogue. The more students talked, the more students learned.

Gary described to Buck how Thoreau had written, "The mass of men lead lives of quiet desperation," and what that warning meant to him personally. He admitted he was leading a life of desperation, although his mind and heart weren't exactly quiet.

Buck asked him what he thought the solution to the desperation might be, and Gary said he had no idea.

They talked about philosophy, about what the purpose of life was, and about how so many people are searching for insights into life. Buck's demeanor fostered openness. Gary was impressed that Buck was patient during these conversations, a genuine listener and thinker. He was years down the road from Gary in terms of insight into life, but he never spoon-fed Gary any answers. Buck seemed interested only in readiness, and Gary wasn't sure he knew how to offer that. But he sensed that Buck knew that if there was no readiness, if Gary's trace of receptivity disappeared, then anything Buck might say would not help Gary find his way to solutions.

———

One afternoon Gary and Buck were working at an old armory, taking apart containers to resell the wood. They stopped for a word break and sat side by side on a wooden coffin that had stored artillery shells.

When they finished reading, Buck spoke first. "Gary, do you consider me a friend?"

"You're the closest thing I've had to a friend in a long time."

Buck handed Gary a paperback. "Do me a favor, then." He paused and pointed to the book. "Read this. Let me know what you think."

Gary shrugged without looking at the book's title and said, "Sure. Be glad to."

That night, Gary started reading the paperback. It described a man who lived a disruptive, extravagant, and even playful life. He reminded Gary of the Green Berets he knew. The man wasn't afraid to toss over tables and clear a room. He gave funny nicknames to his friends.

Once, he showed up for a dinner party at the home of a fastidious lawkeeper and immediately insulted the host. Gary found himself amused, then shocked, then intrigued.

After reading for a few days, Gary was also puzzled. They were back at the armory, and he asked Buck, "What kind of book is this anyway?"

Buck shrugged and said, "Just keep reading, Gary. Keep reading."

That night after work and supper, Gary was in the camping trailer where he stayed and found he couldn't rest. Usually he read until he felt sleepy, but that night he felt wide awake. He started reading again and found he couldn't put the book down. In his mind he heard Buck's voice. *"Just keep reading, Gary. Keep reading."*

As Gary read, a powerful experience filled his heart and mind. He dialogued with the words of the book—reading a section, stopping, then discussing the section out loud—the way a musician and an audience feed off one another in a performance. The method seemed Socratic to Gary, the best way of getting to the heart of the material.

Gary read, "Do not let your hearts be troubled."

"Am I troubled?" Gary asked into the air. "Yeah. I've had way too much trouble in this life already."

"You believe in God," continued the protagonist of the story.

"Yeah. I'm pretty sure I met him at the Seventy-First Evac Hospital in Pleiku."

"Believe also in me."

"Well, I want to. But how? And where exactly are you?"

Then he read how a friend of this man asked him, "We don't know where you are going, so how can we know the way?"

"Your followers sometimes felt confused too?" Gary said. "Man, tell me about it. Did they ever figure out who you were or where you were going?"

"Jesus answered, 'I am the way and the truth and the life. No one comes to the Father except through me.'"

"Wow, that's a bold statement. What kind of man would ever make such a claim? If the man wasn't a liar, he had to be crazy. Or maybe there was another option. Maybe he was telling the truth." Gary finished the chapter and continued reading the next.

"Greater love has no one than this: to lay down one's life for one's friends."

"Have you ever experienced this greater kind of love?" Gary asked himself. "Sure, that's what happened in Dak Seang when Deo laid down his life for me. One man gave his life so another could live."

"You are my friend."

"Me? Gary Beikirch? A friend of God's?"

"You did not choose me, but I chose you."

Gary stood up, stared at the paperback, and answered in a rant: "Why would God choose me as a friend? Don't you know—you, God—what I've seen? I'm not the easiest person to be around. I hold people at arm's length. I push people away. I've done drugs, fought with the law, and walked on the edge of destruction. War is a terrible thing, and those who go to war sometimes have to do terrible things. Sure, I killed people . . . I killed too many to forget. And now I'm tormented by memories I can't get out of my mind. Who would ever want to be friends with me?"

As an answer, the last few words he'd read lodged in Gary's mind and repeated themselves:

I. Chose. You.

Those words from God struck Gary with power. They became his turning point. The receptive insight grew strong in Gary's heart, and the same presence that had filled the hospital room in Pleiku filled the trailer in Marshfield.

At 3:00 a.m. on July 2, 1972, Gary set the book on his bed. He knelt on the cold tile floor of the trailer and bowed his head for the second time in his life. He prayed that he would find comfort for the pain and memories that tormented his thoughts. He prayed to be given peace for the rage he knew he couldn't control. He prayed to be forgiven for all the wrongs he had done. And he prayed that God would restore him and make him new.

Fifty years later, Gary describes the experience this way:

As I was reading through the book of John in the trailer, it felt like the ethereal took shape and took on a form I could identify with.

God became a person. I couldn't describe the person fully yet, but I knew that God was not an abstract idea to me anymore. God became a person in the form of Jesus Christ, and that person was now my friend who had laid down his life, dying on a cross for me. He had extended the greater love so that I might truly live.

The date was marked. From that moment forward, Gary sensed that something had changed within him. The old ways of living were gone. The new had come. In those early-morning hours, when he finally closed his eyes, he slept in peace.

But Gary's problems weren't behind him completely. Life's poisonous residues often seep away slowly. Gary might have had a genuine conversion experience in the trailer, yet ahead of him still lay a vast wilderness—one of the coldest, most isolated experiences he'd ever encounter.

15

Trailhead

The next morning at breakfast, Gary told Jan, Buck, and the children that a few hours earlier he had dedicated his life to God. Their smiles and words were joyful, and there were hugs all around.

Later, as Buck and Gary worked on remodeling a bathroom, Buck asked Gary if he had any new plans for the future. Gary indicated he still didn't know what to do, and Buck suggested that he stay on with them for a while. That sounded good to Gary.

Over the next months, Gary realized he had a lot to learn about trust and forgiveness. He sensed the presence of God in new and good ways, yet impenetrable walls still surrounded his life.

One day Buck was scheduled to speak to a group of about a hundred students at a conference, and he invited Gary along. When Buck finished his talk, he asked Gary to tell a bit about what he'd been through. Gary panicked, froze, then mumbled a few words. He'd taken speech classes and generally could do an okay job of public speaking, but to talk about himself—well, there were still large pieces of his heart he wanted to keep hidden. Gary knew God loved him, but he didn't trust that strangers would.

Afterward, when they were alone, the ever-Socratic Buck asked Gary,

"What needs to happen in your life before you can learn all that God wants you to know? Do you think maybe you should leave us for a while? Maybe God wants you to go somewhere alone so you can grab hold of him and him alone. Will you pray and ask God what he wants you to do?"

The words echoed in Gary's heart. He didn't want to leave Buck and Jan and the kids. Staying with them had brought healing, affirmation. But as for "what needs to happen," he knew that, for starters, one big relationship needed to be faced. He was clutching anger and resentment toward one person. And although Gary wondered if it was too late to restore that relationship, he felt he must at least try.

"Buck," he said. "You're right. I need to go to Florida."

———

Gary packed a few clothes into his rucksack; grabbed Thoreau's book, his Bible, and his guitar; and started hitchhiking. He still owned his old Chevy van, but Buck had been using it a lot at work, so Gary decided to leave it with him.

It took Gary a while to reach Florida, and he had time to think on the journey. He wondered how he'd act when he saw his father. Would he confront him for leaving when Gary was just a child? Would he lash out with words? He didn't know.

When Gary was still about fifteen miles from his dad's house, he decided to call and give his dad some warning. A woman answered. She said that her name was Millie—and that she was married to Gary's dad. This was the first Gary had heard of the marriage. Millie said she was glad Gary was in the area and invited him over.

George Beikirch was still at work when Gary arrived. Millie invited Gary in, hugged him, and started telling their story. She'd met George twenty years ago. He was newly divorced from Gary's mom and working as a groundskeeper at a country club where Millie worked as a waitress. Their romance was a whirlwind from the start, and they were married shortly thereafter. Things turned tough financially, and sometimes they collected bottles on the beach to make ends meet. Eventually, Gary's dad worked his way up at the country club to security officer. He liked the work, went back to college, earned a degree in criminal justice, and was hired at the St. Johns County sheriff's department as a patrolman.

Inspired by his example, Millie went back to college herself, earned her own degree, and joined George as his partner on patrol. They were the only husband-and-wife road patrol team in the state.

A car pulled into the driveway. The screen door swooshed open. When Gary had last seen his father in the hospital at Valley Forge, he didn't get a sense of how big he was. George was six feet, two inches tall and a trim two hundred pounds. He wore his tan sheriff's uniform, a sidearm in a leather holster, and cowboy boots. His figure filled the doorway.

As the father walked toward the son, Gary didn't know whether to shake his hand, give him a hug, or just say hi. He played it safe and extended his hand. His father clasped it with both his huge hands and said, "I want to show you something. C'mon." He led Gary out to the sunroom, sat him down on the couch, and motioned toward the center of the room, where a large chest sat, seemingly in an honored position. George pushed the chest toward Gary, opened it, and said, "I'd like you to look through this. Read some of the things here. We'll talk later." Abruptly he left the room.

Gary picked up an envelope. It was addressed to him but never mailed. Inside was a card with a handwritten message: "Happy birthday to a swell 7-year-old. Love, Dad." Gary pulled out another card. And another. Each card was addressed to him. Each was from his father. One for every birthday his dad had missed. Gary took out Christmas cards. Letters. "Thinking of You" cards, and Post-it notes with scraps of handwritten wisdom. "Things I want you to know" was scrawled at the top of notes. There were newspaper articles about Gary cut from the Rochester paper, mostly about Gary's success as a high school soccer player. In each article Gary's name was highlighted. At the top were scrawled a few words about each article with "sent by Bob" underneath. Bob was Gary's uncle. He'd been keeping track of Gary and forwarding articles to Gary's dad.

Gary read and read. An hour ticked by and then another. He stopped every so often to think and pray. Then he kept reading. Before Gary knew, it was late in the evening. George came in. "You look too tired to talk tonight," he said.

Gary nodded. He had no idea what to say.

"Well, get some rest," George said. "We can talk in the morning before I go to work."

Gary nodded again. Questions packed his mind. Why weren't the greeting cards sent? Why had his father never telephoned? So many years had gone by, and all Gary had ever received from his dad was silence. Gary didn't know if things would be different in the morning, but he was glad for some extra time to try to figure things out. He lay on the couch and fell into an uneasy sleep.

In the morning he awoke to the sounds of Millie fixing breakfast in the kitchen. She poured Gary a cup of coffee and he sat down. His father joined him.

"How'd you sleep?" he asked.

"Okay," Gary said. "I guess."

His father wrinkled his forehead, looking perplexed as to how to proceed. In front of him sat coffee, oatmeal, and half a grapefruit. He cleared his throat. "Gary, I've prayed about this moment for so many years. If you could, I'd like you just to listen for a minute to what I have to say."

Gary nodded.

"I've always loved you," George blurted. "When I was married to your mother, I was a jerk and a terrible husband, and all your aunts and uncles knew it. I drank too much. I wasn't faithful to her. But I always loved you. When I left her and you, it was the hardest thing I've ever done, but I felt at the time that it was the best thing I could do. I was ruining her life—and I didn't want to ruin yours."

George paused, gathering himself to continue. "In my decision to leave, the only thing that gave me hope was knowing the rest of the family was very close. I knew that your aunts, uncles, and cousins would always be there for you.

They'd give you the support I couldn't. Knowing that, I made the tough choice to stay out of your life, because if I had tried to come back, it would have only caused problems. Each birthday and holiday, I made a card for you and put it in that chest. Whenever I thought of something I wanted you to know, some bit of wisdom I could pass on to you, I wrote it down and put it in the chest. With each card and note I placed in the chest, I also said a prayer that one day we would have a chance to talk so I could explain why I did what I did."

He stopped, sipped his coffee, and waited, again with his forehead wrinkled. Gary could see the honesty in his father's eyes but still felt conflicted. Gary thought he should say something, but all that came out was "I don't know what to say."

"I understand," George said. "I need to go to work. But I'll come home early—I have a place I want to take you."

After he left, Millie poured herself a cup of coffee and sat. She asked if she could say a few things, and Gary nodded. Millie told how she'd seen a profound change in George over the past twenty years. When they'd met, he was an unyielding man, full of hurt. Her faith was important to her, and she began praying for George when they started dating. He went to church with her. After a while he stopped drinking too much. He became active in several church programs. A few years later, George decided to follow Jesus. He'd been growing in his faith ever since.

This news just about knocked Gary over. He told Millie about his own faith journey. She telephoned George to tell him the news. And George relayed where he wanted to take Gary that afternoon—to the office to show all his colleagues how proud he was of his boy.

Sure enough, George took Gary to the sheriff's office and beamed as he introduced him all around. The frost began to thaw, and Gary spent the next several weeks in Florida with his father and Millie.

Gary rode with his father and Millie on patrols throughout Palm Valley, a rural and depressed area known for drug use, violence, and criminal activity. Gary was amazed that in every place they stopped, people greeted his father and

Millie with warmth and respect—showing Gary how much this couple cared for people. George took Gary to his weekly prayer group, and folks he met there indicated they'd been praying for him ever since he went to Vietnam.

Sometimes when they were patrolling together, George simply pulled over the cruiser, and he and Millie and Gary walked over the dunes and around the swamps and saw grass, talking and catching up. Gary loved those times best. He didn't understand every action his father had taken over the years, but Gary sensed his call was not to understand everything about what his father had done but to forgive him—and to love him. He knew that his father had never stopped loving him. It wasn't too late to restore the relationship.

———

After several weeks, George offered to get Gary a job at the sheriff's department, but Gary still felt restless, and the need to roam still tugged. He thanked George and Millie, bought a bus ticket, and headed back to Massachusetts.

When he got back to Buck and Jan's place, he began researching educational options. He knew he wanted to return to Vietnam someday to work with the Montagnards, and the urge to pursue a degree in medicine felt strongest. He discovered a physician's assistant program at nearby Dartmouth College and decided to apply.

A few days later, on the drive up to Hanover, New Hampshire, where Dartmouth was located, Gary reviewed the past several weeks. So much good had happened during his visit with Millie and George. But Gary's thoughts felt clouded too. The war kept plaguing his mind. He looked out at the mountains and other scenery, but his mind snapped back to the highlands of Vietnam, and other memories rushed in. Screams. Explosions. Dead bodies. He shook the thoughts away and pulled into the parking lot of Dartmouth's admissions office.

Inside, Gary was handed an application to fill out and mail back. He explained he'd just driven up from Massachusetts and asked if he could begin the admission process immediately. The clerk said yes and, if Gary could get all his paperwork organized and filled out that day, he'd get him an appointment with an admissions officer first thing the next morning. Excited, Gary headed to the library, copied all his military records, filled out his forms, and made it back to the office just before closing. He handed the clerk his packet along with a Coke and a bag of chips to say thanks for expediting the process. The clerk smiled, and Gary left, feeling as if he'd found direction.

At 9:00 a.m., Gary was back in the office. A different young man introduced himself as Gary's admissions representative. He wore khaki pants and a collared polo shirt with a Dartmouth logo. He took Gary back to his office, the two sat down, and the clerk thumbed through Gary's file. All was going fine until the clerk paused and said, "You mind if I ask you a personal question?"

Gary nodded.

Gary remembers the next line precisely. Exactly. He would never forget a single word. In later years, he wondered if the clerk had been an avid antiwar protester or if somehow the clerk had merely come to an erroneous conclusion about veterans. Perhaps it was an honest question but poorly worded. Perhaps not.

"I'm wondering," the clerk asked, "after killing all those people in Vietnam, why do you now want to help people?"

There it was.

For a moment Gary stared at the clerk, his mouth ajar. Then his vision grew blurry. The next memory Gary has is almost out of body, watching himself from a distance. He's standing up, glaring into the clerk's face. The clerk is six inches off the floor. The clerk's face is blood red and he's shaking. Gary is holding him up by his shirt collar, ready to blast him with his fist. Gary's vision blurred again. He remembers setting the clerk down. He remembers turning around and walking out the door. He wasn't escorted by security, and he wasn't handcuffed by the police, but Gary was badly shaken—by the clerk's question and by his own reaction.

He climbed back into his van, slammed the door, and headed back to Marshfield. He knew he could have badly hurt the clerk. What he didn't know was how to control himself. A deep fear gripped him. Maybe the volcano had taken control of him; the rage would always be there, always ready to erupt. *Forget Dartmouth,* he told himself. There was no way he could go there now.

———

Gradually, Gary calmed as he drove back to Buck and Jan's house. A program came on the radio hosted by a New England minister and educator named Clinton White. Buck and Gary sometimes listened to him when they worked, and since Buck admired the man and his ideas, Gary had grown to respect him too.

Reverend White mentioned he was beginning a Bible seminary to prepare people for pastoral ministry. The school would start that fall near the small town of Lancaster in the White Mountains of New Hampshire and would offer a two-year program leading toward a degree. The school would be affiliated with the Bible Institute of New England and draw adjunct professors from Dallas Theological Seminary.

Gary was intrigued. He wanted to get more education. He wanted to learn more about God. He particularly wanted to do something with his rage. Maybe this school would be a safe place to accomplish all three things.

He applied and was accepted. Early in September 1973 he loaded up his van and headed toward Lancaster. As he drove north, he was awed by the rugged beauty of the White Mountains, part of the northern Appalachians. Snow topped the higher peaks, and already in the foothills, the leaves bore hints of red.

Lancaster consisted of one main street, a couple of shops and diners, two gas stations, and a grocery store. Near the end of the street, he stopped by a large colonial-style building with a wraparound porch. A sign over the door read "White Mountain Seminary."

Gary closed his eyes and said a quick prayer. When he opened his eyes, three college-age young people stood outside the van, waving and smiling—two guys and one girl. Gary opened his door. The students welcomed him heartily and chattered with excitement about the start of classes. They were all huggers. Gary could be a hugger with friends and family members but not with strangers. There were too many walls up in his life at this point, and having these people he didn't know hug him made him feel uncomfortable. When the hugs were finished, the guys walked around to the back of his van, grabbed Gary's stuff, and carried it into the building. Gary wondered what he was getting himself into.

Inside, he met another twenty new students. Everybody was talking, asking questions. It was a diverse group—different ethnicities, men and women, some younger students, some older. Some had already graduated from college, and some had come with their spouses and children. Everybody hugged him again. Gary was peppered with good-natured questions. He knew the atmosphere was positive, but already he felt claustrophobic. He was trying to create a safe space around himself, but those invisible boundaries felt violated.

The two guys who'd grabbed his stuff showed him to his dorm room, then left him to get settled. Gary shut the door. He looked at the bookshelves, the desk, the twin bed. He glanced at his guitar, books, and belongings. He didn't want to unpack. Someone knocked on the door and announced that everybody was gathering downstairs to get better acquainted.

"I'll be down in a minute," Gary said through the door. He could hear them downstairs. They sounded like an enthusiastic bunch, but he couldn't make himself join the group. The thought of entering a room full of strangers, of answering deep questions about his life . . . He shivered.

Gary left his belongings packed, walked out the front door, got into his van, and drove away. He didn't return to the school but slept that night in his van, parked beside a gas station two doors down from the seminary.

Gary tried to talk himself into staying. He wanted to be there. He wanted to study. He wanted to learn new things and meet new people. The next morning he walked back to campus, showered in his room, grabbed a pen and notebook, and headed to classes. He enjoyed the teaching. The professors were strong academics, and the course content was robust and practical. But when the day was over, Gary itched to take off.

He resisted leaving and tried to fit in. Another informal gathering was held that evening, where students talked about the day, and Gary grabbed a chair near the edge of the circle. Students talked about struggles. Things they were learning. Ways they were growing. Hopes for the future. Others responded with words of encouragement, empathy, and wisdom. Gary wanted to enter the discussion, but he just couldn't. Years later, he articulated his struggle this way:

Some of the things that had happened in Vietnam had destroyed me. They'd destroyed my sense of who I believed I was. My ability to feel and care had been affected, and I still wrongly believed that if I could just forget what had happened in Vietnam, all would be fine.

At the school I didn't know who I was yet. I knew I needed people in my life and that, to have them in my life, I needed to let people see the real me. That's what a true relationship is about. But I was afraid to open up. I didn't want anybody to see the parts of me that I'd closed off behind walls. I just couldn't do it.

On the morning of the third day, before breakfast, another gathering took place. Once again Gary tried to participate but couldn't. When the gathering finished, the other students headed to breakfast. Gary got into his van and started driving. He didn't know where he was going. He just knew he needed to get away. Again. He sighed. *Maybe I'm destined to wander forever.*

———

Gary left town and headed east on Route 2. Off to his right were the majestic mountains of the Presidential Range—the tallest peaks in the northeast. Gary looked from side to side out the windows. The scenery calmed him. He didn't want to miss any of it.

About forty-five minutes from school, he spotted a sign: "Appalachia Parking Area." It had the figure of a hiker on it with an arrow pointing to the right and the words *Appalachian Trail*. He'd first heard of the trail back at Devens. Some of the Special Forces teams went to the White Mountains and hiked parts of the Appalachian Trail on training exercises. He pulled into the parking lot, turned off the van, walked to the trailhead, and paused. Warning signs loomed tall.

STOP. The area ahead has the worst weather in America. Many have died there from exposure even in the summer. Turn back now if the weather is bad.

ATTENTION: Hike this trail ONLY if you are in top physical condition, well clothed, and carrying extra clothing and food. Many have died above timberline from exposure. Turn back at the first sign of bad weather.

There were no cars passing by and none in the parking lot except his. The woods felt hushed and inviting. The trailhead looked like the dividing line between two worlds. On the side of that divider where Gary stood, he sensed restlessness and claustrophobia. On the other side lay potential danger yet also an unknown adventure. The other side beckoned.

Gary passed the trailhead and walked into the woods, letting his senses bathe in the wilderness. The smell of pine trees quieted his soul. He stopped walking and closed his eyes. He heard red squirrels running through the trees, leaping from branch to branch, playing in the foliage overhead. He heard a bird flapping its wings. Far away he heard water sliding over rocks and splashing as it collected in a pool. He took a deep breath, opened his eyes, and kept walking. He felt more alive than he had in days.

Gary headed toward the sound of the water by following the Snyder Brook Trail. Soon enough a creek ran alongside the trail, and Gary envisioned how frost and ice had melted on the peaks of the Presidentials and the water had descended to rush here by his feet. He passed a small waterfall, then a slightly larger waterfall, and then an even higher falls.

On the mossy bank he stopped to listen to the roar of rushing waters. When Gary inclined his ear, he heard something within the water, something that sounded new yet familiar. The sound was indescribable, yet he felt a need to put words to it. It was the sound that brilliant light would make if it emitted speech. The sound a rainbow might make when it pierces the clouds after a rainy day. The sound glowing metal might make when full of fire. A sensation moved his spirit. Words came from something he'd read somewhere, and when Gary recognized who was speaking, he wanted to fall facedown, but instead he listened—then answered.

I know the plans I have for you, the voice said.

"What kind of plans?" Gary said out loud into the wilderness.

Plans to give you hope and a future.

"Sounds good. What do I do?"

You will seek me and find me when you seek me with all your heart.

"But where will I seek you?"

Come and see . . .

Come and see? Gary thought. *What does that mean?* He kept walking.

He followed the trail across a log bridge that traversed the creek. On the other side a wooden sign pointed the way to Dome Rock. Gary had no idea what he would find at the rock, but he had a distinct sense that it was a special place. He wanted to go farther but hesitated. He glanced at his watch, then at the sky. Dome Rock would need to wait for another day. It was getting late, and Gary worried that the other students would be concerned about him since he'd missed classes all day.

He turned around, hiked back to the trailhead, and climbed into his van.

Already he missed the solitude of the woods. He'd felt calm in the wilderness, free from trying to prove himself to others—or even to himself.

———

By the time he got back to the school, dinner was over and a group of students had gathered again to talk about the day. Gary glanced at the group, shook his head, and headed back to his van. He spent the night there and in the morning went to a diner for breakfast to avoid any discussion about where he'd been.

He headed to class, and when students asked about his whereabouts, he answered vaguely, requesting politely that they give him some space.

He spent another night in his van. The next morning he arrived at some conclusions. He wanted what the other students had in the way of relationships, but he sensed he wasn't ready. And the only way he could prepare for something deeper was to immerse himself in solitude.

At first he didn't have much of a plan. Gary shoved his belongings into his van and headed out again on Route 2. He stopped at the post office in Lancaster, rented a PO box, and filled out a change-of-address notification so he could receive his monthly VA check. Then he drove to the same Appalachian parking area. He climbed out, looked at the trailhead and the sky, then decided not to chance it that night. For now the trailhead was enough. He spent the night in the van. The proximity of the forest lulled him to sleep.

In the morning he headed back to Lancaster for classes. He was cordial to the other students, and they were cordial back. That evening he drove to the trailhead again and slept in the van.

For a few days this became his routine. But he knew the trailhead was beckoning him to something more. Something wilder.

The next weekend he passed the trailhead again and followed the Snyder Brook Trail up to the log bridge that crossed the brook. The autumn morning was clear and bright, the air hinting at crispness. He continued hiking toward

Dome Rock. The farther he went, the more difficult the trail grew. In places he needed to climb hand over hand over large granite boulders. Above the tree line, the climb grew easier and he could see blue sky again. The closer he got to Dome Rock, the greater his sense of anticipation became.

About an hour from the trailhead, Gary stood at last in front of a massive granite boulder, perhaps twenty-five feet in diameter, smooth and rounded, steel gray. Dome Rock seemed to have erupted from the forest floor itself, and when he climbed to the dome's top, he could see the length of Route 2 from Vermont to Maine. He calculated that the dome would be hard for casual hikers to find but that he could find it again. Smaller boulders encircled it, and as Gary moved down from the dome and back into the tree line, he came across a different arrangement of boulders—highly unique.

A cave.

These boulders were perhaps eight feet tall, forming three walls. Roots and moss grew between the rocks and made a roof atop them. Trees had grown up from the roof. The entire structure looked sturdy and timeless.

Gary entered the cave and surveyed the interior. Spacewise, he had about four feet from side to side and seven feet from the entrance of the cave to where it ended in impenetrable rock. From the floor of the forest, the little room was about five and a half feet tall, so Gary needed to stoop. It wasn't a big cave. Just a cleft in the rock. This was it. He felt it. This was where he needed to "come and see."

Gary hiked down the trail and drove to the nearby town of North Conway to a hiking store. He told the salesperson he needed every bit of winter camping gear he could recommend. Gary left the store loaded with down jackets and pants, hats, gloves, a face mask, a waterproof outer jacket to wear over the down jackets, a winter backpacking tent that would be stable in high winds, camping stoves, good boots, insulated socks, crampons and an ice pick, a suspension cord and ropes, snowshoes, a couple of boxes of dehydrated food, and a sleeping bag good to fifty degrees below zero.

Immediately he drove back to the trailhead, hiked to the cave, and set up the equipment he needed for that night. The weather was still relatively mild, and that first night he didn't need much. Gary stretched out his sleeping bag, lay back, and made himself comfortable. Next summer after classes let out, he'd reevaluate his plan, but for now this felt right. It was the only plan that gave him peace. The only plan that made sense.

He would live in the cave.

16

The Cave

As a Green Beret, Gary was used to sleeping outside.

It was late September 1973, and he felt comfortable in the mountains—as comfortable as he'd felt in the jungle, anyway, and more comfortable than in four walls. Gary wasn't looking for a challenge—he'd already had plenty of those. His quest wasn't to survive—he already knew how to do that.

Back in Dak Seang, Deo had often stressed that the jungle was never a place to be feared. Challenges existed in the jungle, sure. But when a person accepted and undertook the challenges, the jungle became a teacher and would supply what a person needed to learn about life. Similarly, Gary believed the Appalachian Mountains would become his professor. He decided to live in the mountains for what the mountains could teach him.

During his first night in the cave, he didn't sleep much. For an hour he lay down, closed his eyes, and dozed, but for the next hour he sat awake, listening, peering into the dark. The tree cover was heavy around the cave, and even with a bright half-moon, it was hard to see the sky. He got up, slid out of the cave, and walked around the perimeter, learning the area inch by inch by the feel of his boots.

Like a Green Beret would with any new experience, Gary wanted to establish a baseline of normalcy because then he could gauge other experiences. If something occurred that was out of the norm, he would be aware of it. He carried a long multibattery flashlight with him, but he frowned on using it too much. He wanted to remain inconspicuous, blending in with the environment.

As he walked in the dark, he established routes and patterns in his mind. This was his Special Forces training in action: *know your norm.* He could hear water running in the creek. He walked to the creek, timing himself. Fifteen minutes one way. His closest freshwater source. He figured he could make it in ten minutes in daylight, if needed. The creek was spring fed and flowed year round, so he didn't worry about its cleanliness, although he made a mental note always to throw an iodine tablet into whatever he drank. Special Forces had a rule: if the water is moving, use one tablet; if stagnate, use two.

He hiked back to the cave and listened. Tama Fall was not far away, a huge waterfall, and he could hear the faint majesty of rushing water. He heard branches cracking and swaying in the wind—were any animals nearby? Already, he could judge whether a certain sound was the scamper of a chipmunk or the patter of a squirrel running across the leaves. He listened for crunching—any larger animal would make that noise. Bears roamed the area, also moose and fisher-cats—a vicious cross between a wolverine and a weasel. Wolves were known to range down from Canada.

He heard a crunch and held his breath, listening, his heart pounding. By the light of the moon, he saw two eyes ringed by black. A raccoon sauntered past. Gary chuckled and headed back inside the cave.

———

Morning dawned early. He didn't need an alarm. The sun rose, and Gary rubbed the sleep out of his eyes. The cave faced west, and from his sleeping bag, all he could see outside the entrance were trees.

He slid outside, cracked open a C-ration, and broke out the toilet paper and the pound cake, which he would save for later. He ambled some distance from camp, dug a hole, did his business and buried it, washed his hands using his water bottle, and went back to the cave. He heated water on his backpacking stove and mixed up one of his dehydrated LRRP military meals. He had plenty to choose from. Beef hash. Beef and rice. Beef stew. Chicken and rice. Chicken stew. Spaghetti with meat sauce. A turkey noodle mix was his favorite. It came with something like alfredo sauce. He finished his meal with coffee and a handful of gorp—a high-energy mixture of nuts, raisins, dried fruit, and seeds.

Gary read for a while, then hiked down the mountain the hour it took to reach the trailhead and drove back to the school. It was only 7:30 a.m. He took a shower in a school bathroom and headed to his first class at 8:00 a.m. He made a mental note to skip the shower from here on out. He wanted to be self-reliant and could always wash up in the stream.

For lunch he mixed with the students in the dining hall, but he knew he could always eat in the van if the hugs became too much to handle. By 3:00 p.m. his classes were finished. Evening activities were posted on bulletin boards, but Gary declined those, walked back to his van, drove to the trailhead, and parked, then hiked back for his second night in the cave.

He ate dinner first and then, while he still had daylight, explored the surrounding areas, the paths and woods that led away from the cave. It was soon dark, and he switched on his flashlight and hiked back, suspended the flashlight from an overhead root in the cave, and read until he grew sleepy. He bundled up in his sleeping bag and crashed hard.

In the morning he could see fresh snow in the higher elevations. Although it was only early October, the air was cold. He wasn't overly concerned that winter was coming, although he knew the weather would soon truly test him. A light mist fell, and Gary knew he could use his tent's rain fly as a door to the cave to help keep out the cold and wet. Cardinals and hawks flew past in the morning air. He hiked to the stream, washed up, went back to the cave and made breakfast, read for a while, then headed down to his van and another day of school. He didn't feel lonely at all. He was absorbing the peace.

Another day went by like this and then another. Students didn't ask where he went. Already it seemed to Gary that they sensed he was a bit different. Plus, he was learning whom to avoid. The introverts were easier to take, but the outgoing types were the worst. One bubbly girl who led with her hugs was constantly smiling, asking hard questions, trying to peer under his surface. Whenever Gary saw her coming his way, he headed the other direction.

The first weekend living in his new outdoor home, he hiked far out into the wilderness and spent Friday night in his tent, then headed in a new direction on Saturday and spent the night in his tent again. His tent weighed about five pounds, and he carried it and anything else he needed in his rucksack.

On Sunday he hiked back to the creek near the cave, spent some time listening to the rhythm of the flowing water, then headed back to the cave to spend the rest of the day reading. His back hurt on the longer hikes as the remaining shrapnel mixed around in his torso, and his legs didn't quite work as they used to, but overall he felt good.

He kept his guitar in the cave, and he strummed for a while, mixing the music with the melody of the forest, then went back to reading. He had his textbooks from class, his Bible, Thoreau, a few biographies, and guidebooks on plant and animal life.

Near suppertime, he hiked to Dome Rock and gazed at the landscape. It was growing dark, and in the distance he saw a twinkle of civilization. He thought about how his new life living in a cave seemed to be going so well. Days in class felt meaningful, and his time in the mountains felt calming and rewarding. He hadn't had a nightmare in some time now, although the nightmares never completely stopped. The daytime memories of the horrors of the siege weren't creeping into his mind as frequently either.

A huge hawk glided by. Gary grinned. He thought about how he was learning to see God everywhere—not only through the words of Scripture but also within nature. He could sense God by the still small voice within himself but also within the wind of the evening, the water that rippled over the moss-covered rocks in the creek, and the roar of Tama Fall.

On top of the rock, Gary prayed with his eyes open: "God, you told me that if I seek you with all my heart, I'll find you." He paused, listening.

I'm here, Gary, came the response.

"I was in a hospital bed in Pleiku and sought you there that day when the chaplain asked me if I wanted to pray. I traveled to Massachusetts to seek you, and I found you at Jan and Buck's home late that night in the trailer. I hitchhiked to Florida to my father's house to seek you, and I found you in our reconciliation, as well as this new truth that I didn't need to understand people so much as I needed to forgive and love them. And now I'm here in the north country of New Hampshire to seek you. What will I learn about you now?"

Come and see.

"Come and see?" Gary thought about that a moment. "I believe you've led me here, God, to hike these trails and live in a cave, and I don't know exactly what 'Come and see' means, but I want to say I'm all in."

All in? Tell me more.

"I'm giving my life back to you, God. I want nothing else in life except what you want for me. From today onward, God, I am all yours."

The wind continued to blow, and another bird flew by. The prayer felt highly significant to Gary, an act of complete dedication, although his prayer ended without any apparent response.

Today, Gary explains his prayer on Dome Rock this way:

It might sound strange to hear it, but I sensed that God wanted me to live in the cave. He wanted me to be at the school, too, but I couldn't handle the closeness of the students yet because their love and attention overwhelmed me. By living in the cave, I could stay at the school and still make sense of life.

I knew difficulties lay ahead, so my prayer that evening on Dome Rock was me saying, "Okay, God, if we're going to do this, then we need to do it together. The only way I want to do this is by giving everything to you. Whatever you want, God—that's what I want too."

Over the next two years, I needed to go back to that prayer again and again. I needed to remind myself of my act of surrender. I had given God all I was. My call from then onward was to receive all he had for me—whatever lay ahead.

Gary doesn't remember feeling different after that prayer. But he does know it was sincere. He meant every word. He did not realize, however, how swiftly God would act.

———

One week later, Gary hiked out from his cave, drove to Lancaster, and stopped to check his post office box. In this small town anyone could scribble a note and pop it into the letter slot. The postmaster would deliver it without a stamp to the appropriate box. There wasn't any mail this day, but there was an anonymous handwritten note: "Please be down at the seminary building tonight by 6:00 p.m. There's an important phone call that will be coming for you."

Strange. He decided the call must be coming from Buck or Jan. He had no idea what the important news was. Aside from one or two administrative folks at the school, Buck and Jan were the only ones who knew where he was staying. He hadn't been in contact with his mother since coming back from Florida, and he hadn't contacted his father or Millie since then either. He shrugged.

That night, Gary ate supper with the students, then hung around the dining room with a cup of coffee, waiting for the phone call. His hair hung past his shoulders by then. His clothes were dirty. He'd washed up that morning in the creek, but even he had to admit he stank a little.

Promptly at 6:00 p.m. the pay phone rang. One of the students answered, then motioned to Gary.

"Hello?" Gary said.

"Is this Gary Beikirch?" a man asked.

"Yeah, that's me."

"Did you serve with the Fifth Special Forces in Vietnam?"

"Yes."

"This is the Pentagon calling."

"Okay."

The caller identified himself as a colonel, gave his name, then added, "It's my pleasure to tell you that you've been awarded the Medal of Honor."

"Oh" was all Gary said. He thought it was a joke. A few moments of silence passed.

"Are you still there?" the colonel asked.

"Yeah."

The colonel told Gary that at a specific time two weeks later an escort officer and army photographer would come to Lancaster to pick him up and take him to Washington, DC. The colonel made sure Gary understood all the information he'd just relayed, then asked if he had any questions. Gary did not. Slowly it dawned on him that this was no hoax. The colonel added that he was looking forward to meeting Gary soon, then hung up.

For a moment Gary stood motionless, stunned. He glanced from side to side. None of the other students were looking his way. He hunched his shoulders, walked out to his van, and drove back to the mountains.

In the parking lot near the trailhead, the shock wore off and the reality of what had just happened hit Gary with full force. He was basically a hermit, a caveman, a recluse of the wilderness, but now he was to receive the Medal of Honor, the United States' highest and most prestigious military decoration given for acts of valor. He knew that recipients must be people who have distinguished themselves at the risk of their lives above and beyond the call of duty in action against an enemy of the United States. Given the nature of the medal, it was often awarded posthumously.

On that date in early October 1973, Gary didn't know the exact number of recipients, but he knew there weren't many—maybe three thousand since the medal was created in 1861 during the American Civil War. He hadn't been watching the news lately, but he didn't think many service personnel from Vietnam had received it.

With the reality came a flood of questions: *What just happened? Why me? What did I ever do to deserve the Medal of Honor?* Then Gary directed his questions to God: "Did you know about this? I was seeking you, God, not anything else—what am I going to do now? I'm trying to heal, trying to forget about Vietnam—and now I'm going to get a medal for what happened there? Why did you let this happen, God?"

Gary had no immediate answers. He did all he knew to do. He shut his van door, hiked up the trail, and went back to living in his cave.

The Medal

That night, after receiving the phone call from the Pentagon, the nightmares returned without mercy.

For hours, Gary's mind swirled with explosions, screams, and visions of horror. Sleep evaded him, and morning brought no relief; even in daylight the memories would not flee. The morning sky was gray and a few flakes flitted down, the snow like powdered sugar, as Gary huddled by his backpacking stove and waited for water to boil. Strangely he also felt supported, held up with two strong hands, almost like after he'd been paralyzed and Deo had carried him around Dak Seang.

Gary made coffee with the boiled water, flipped open his Bible, and read, "When anxiety was great within me, your consolation brought me joy." Those words had been written thousands of years ago, perhaps by David, the famous king of Israel. Gary admired David, a warrior who'd once taken shelter in a cave before he was a king, in a season when he needed to be rebuilt. In that intense time, David had been able to look back and see that all that had happened to him—both good and bad—was actually working to shape him into the king he would soon become. With that perspective, David took all that churned inside his gut and turned it into either a song of praise or a heartfelt prayer.

When it came to receiving the Medal of Honor, Gary hoped he could turn the mix of feelings he was experiencing in a similar direction.

Breakfast finished, and Gary hiked back to the trailhead, drove into Lancaster, called his mother, and told her the news. She was excited for him—and all it meant—especially when Gary invited her, his little brother, and his aunt Jeanne to the ceremonies in Washington. His mom asked if he needed anything, and he mentioned he might need a sports coat. All he owned in addition to his boots, hiking jackets, and thermal pants were T-shirts, fatigues, and a pair of blue jeans. He also often wore a wide-brimmed felt hat to keep away black flies and mosquitoes when on the trail. She promised to mail him his old madras sports coat from high school.

The rest of that day, Gary kept quiet in classes. He borrowed a clip-on tie from one of the students and later bought a blue dress shirt and white corduroy Levi's. He was set.

Gary informed Clinton White, president of the school, that he needed to miss classes for a couple of days. President White had been in the air force during the Korean Conflict, so he was familiar with military medals and shocked to hear exactly what Gary was being awarded. President White didn't even know Gary had served in the military, although he'd heard of this unique student who went off to the mountains after classes. Gary didn't tell anyone else he was going to DC.

As the day of departure neared, Gary became more restless. He had no idea what to expect. What would the ceremony be like? What would it be like with all those eyes focused on him? Would there be questions from reporters—deep questions?

On the appointed day at 3:00 p.m., he showed up at the seminary to meet his escort officer and the military photographer who were accompanying him to DC. The escort officer, Captain Thornberry, took one look at Gary with his long hair and bushy mustache and hesitated. The captain was all military, and Gary wasn't sure exactly what the officer expected of a Green Beret, but Gary extended his hand, and the officer shook it and said it was an honor to meet Gary.

Honor. There was that word again. Gary didn't quite know what to do with it.

They drove to Burlington, Vermont, overnighted in a hotel, then caught an early flight to DC, where Captain Thornberry briefed Gary about the ceremony and events that would take place over the next few days. The ceremony would be held at the White House. Eight other military personnel were receiving the Medal of Honor—Gary Littrell, Michael Fitzmaurice, Leo Thorsness, Michael Thornton, Allan Kellogg, Kenneth Michael Kays, James Leroy Bondsteel, and Brian Thacker.

Following the ceremony, a reception would be held at the White House, and that evening the members of Gary's honor guard would take him out on the town to celebrate. They were given $1,500 to entertain him. The following day there would be a ceremony at the Pentagon, where recipients would be inducted into the Hall of Heroes. Afterward, each recipient's honor guard would take him out on the town again. The next few days were to be spent touring the city and visiting selected sites. Just hearing about it made Gary feel overwhelmed.

In DC Gary met a first lieutenant and three senior NCOs—two of whom had been to Vietnam—who were identified as his honor guard. He was escorted to a limousine and driven to the Madison Hotel, where he met his mother, brother, and aunt. After more than a year, they were excited to see him and surprised at how long his hair had grown.

Captain Thornberry introduced Gary to a Colonel Westmoreland (no relation to General Westmoreland, commander of US military operations in Vietnam), who said it was an honor to meet Gary. But the colonel did not react as subtly to Gary's appearance as the other officer had. Army regulations prohibited the wearing of a uniform with a hairstyle that did not conform to military standards, the colonel stated, so if Gary chose not to cut his hair, he would need to receive the medal in civilian clothes. Gary didn't hesitate. The Special Forces meant too much to him not to wear the uniform. He said he'd gladly cut his hair and trim his mustache. Every face around him relaxed in relief.

Gary went for a haircut; then his honor guard escorted him and his family up to their suites. Gary's was a large luxury suite with a huge cabinet filled with liquor. The three NCOs with him immediately broke out the bottles and glasses. Gary mentioned he didn't drink anymore but they were welcome to take the bottles for themselves. They put the bottles back, saying it wouldn't be right to party without him, and Gary could see they were disappointed. They mentioned the other recipients were ready to head out on the town and asked if Gary wanted to go to the local clubs. He thought, *Less than twenty-four hours ago, I was living in the woods. Now I find myself in this exquisite hotel in the middle of the capital, getting ready to meet the president of the United States. Do I want to party?* He took a deep breath. *What I really want to do is go back to the mountains.* But out loud he said only that he was tired and wanted to rest. They left him alone with his family.

Since it had been so long since his family had seen Gary, they asked him all kinds of questions about school and where he was living, how his visit with his father had gone. The questions flew rapid fire, and Gary tried to be respectful, sharing bits of information as he could. But his head swirled and he felt confined. He excused himself and went to his room for the night. His prayer was simply *God, tomorrow I'm going to receive the Medal of Honor. Help me understand. What do I need to know about honor?*

The next morning was a blur. Gary dressed in the new green wool class A uniform that had been given him. Soon he found himself in the White House among a sea of people—military personnel, politicians, and media. The recipients were arranged in a horseshoe pattern with their families and respective member of Congress beside them. Opening remarks were given by President Nixon; then citations were read describing the action taken by each recipient. The president draped the medal around each recipient's neck, shook his hand, and offered a few private cordial words.

As each of the other citations was read, Gary thought, *What am I doing here? These guys are the real heroes, not me. There's a Navy SEAL who ran through a hail of bullets to save his wounded senior officer. An air force officer on crutches who spent six years as a POW. Every man here is being recognized for unbelievable acts of bravery. What did I do? I just did what I was trained to do. Deo did the real work—he gave his life for me, but I'm still alive.*

Gary felt queasy, and images of the siege bombarded him while the ceremony was finishing. Explosions. Screams. He tried to stop the images but could not. The ceremony ended and Gary was escorted to the reception. He remembers meeting high-ranking officers and senior politicians, but he doesn't remember talking to them. The rest of the ceremonial events were a blur.

His honor guard returned him to the Madison and said if Gary wanted to get out of his uniform and change to something more casual, they'd love to take him out on the town. They still had $1,500 to spend. Gary said that he didn't have any clothes other than the Levi's and madras he'd worn on the plane. They offered to take him shopping. Gary didn't want to go, but he respected their efforts to entertain him, so he wrote down his sizes, and the honor guard went shopping on his behalf. They returned with a new sports coat and slacks, a shirt, a tie, and some fancy Italian shoes. They seemed genuinely pleased.

The next morning was a blur again as Gary was driven to the Pentagon to attend the second ceremony. Together the recipients were inducted into the Hall of Heroes. After the ceremony came a formal luncheon; then it was back to the hotel.

This time Gary's escorts told him they were taking him out and wouldn't hear no for an answer. Gary shrugged and put on his new clothes. He and his family and their escorts had dinner at the Watergate Hotel. He felt like a stuffed shirt. In October 1973, when Gary's Medal of Honor ceremony took place, the hotel was making big headlines. The president's men had broken into and bugged the Watergate a year earlier, although the bombshell of the president's impeachment and resignation would not occur until the following year.

After dinner Gary thanked his escorts and his family but said he didn't want to stay in DC any longer. He needed to get back to New Hampshire to attend classes. At least, that's what he said—in reality, he longed for the solitude of the woods. The next morning he was dropped at the airport and was finally on his way home. He felt more relaxed than at any time during the past few days.

When he reached the school, he got into his van and drove to the Appalachia parking area. He stuffed his new clothes and the Medal of Honor into his duffel bag. Although he wore his new clothes occasionally after that, he found he could not approach the medal. He wanted only to distance himself from its weight.

Seven years would pass before he ever touched the medal again.

———

The newspaper in Rochester ran his picture and an article. They paraphrased the portion of his citation that described how he "'ran through a hail of fire' to treat wounded soldiers and civilians during an attack on Camp Dak Seang." Then the article continued, "But that was three years ago, Beikirch gently said in a telephone interview . . . and he tries not to think about it. 'There's a lot I try to forget,' he said."

Other reporters came to Lancaster and contacted family members, and more stories were written. The *Coos County Democrat* printed a front-page article. But Gary did not return most of the calls from reporters. It was all too much to take.

Back in the cave, where he'd hoped to retreat to peace, the nightmares became more vivid and powerful. Receiving the medal only intensified the battle in his mind. Ghosts from the violent ground assault in Dak Seang sprang to life, and his days and nights were haunted. Civilians were dying all around him all over again. Gary fired into waves of enemy soldiers coming over the line. Again and again he stared at Thung, perfectly lifelike, who kept cradling the torso of his headless wife.

Gary found he didn't want to close his eyes, and it took a couple of days until he felt well enough to go back to class. Strangely the darkness of the outdoors at night didn't bother him. Gary wasn't afraid of darkness. The battle was within himself. It was the memories plaguing his interior landscape that prompted fear.

President White, a stocky man in his early forties with a barrel chest that shook whenever he laughed, called Gary into his office to talk. Gary mentioned he'd been having some trouble since receiving the award. White listened attentively and asked a few questions about the siege, which Gary answered. Then White said, "Gary, I see what you did as an act of perseverance, even more than an act of bravery. You went forward when plenty of others would have quit. You received it for your faithfulness and commitment. God has chosen each person for a purpose, and part of yours was to receive the medal. It's an honor, for sure, but the main reason isn't for your glory, so don't worry about feeling unworthy; the main reason is something God will show you in the future."

Gary thanked him, then returned to the cave. He felt some reassurance from the president's words, although he still felt uneasy. He recalled the plaque above the Green Berets' door in Dak Seang: "To really live, you must almost die. To those who fight for it, life has a meaning the protected will never know." Gary had almost died once. Maybe now he was learning how to really live—gradually, slowly—although the way forward remained unclear.

Oddly, a real-life storm would help clear his internal fog. Late one afternoon, a bad weather system was forecast throughout the north country, the first real storm of the winter. Gary finished classes, drove back to the trailhead, and hiked to his cave. The sky was overcast and ominous. Gary put on his down jacket and pants, set up his stove inside the cave, and fixed an early supper of chicken and rice. Then he simply switched on the flashlight that hung from his ceiling, grabbed a book to read, wrapped up in his sleeping bag, and settled in to wait.

The wind started to whip through the trees. He switched off the light, turned around, put his head near the cave's entrance, and studied what he could outside. Trees bent. Branches snapped and crashed to the ground. A massive cloud seemed to engulf the entire Dome area. The cloud was coming his way. Then Gary realized it was not a cloud but a huge orb of snow hurtling through the trees.

Instantly he weighed his options. The cave might be safer, but snow could bury the entrance. Anything could happen with the weight of the trees over the cave's roof. Gary snapped into action; he broke out his tent and assembled it outside the cave faster than ever before. He threw all his gear into the tent, jumped inside, and zipped it up.

The snow orb hit, and the wind howled through the trees—eighty miles per hour, maybe one hundred in gusts. The tent shivered. It was a high-altitude winter tent especially designed to withstand mountain storms, but Gary wondered if his stakes were driven deep enough. What if he was snowed in for several days? Even a week? Maybe all winter? Had he carried up enough supplies from the van?

A massive creaking was followed by a loud thunderclap and thud. He tried to imagine what had fallen in the dark. A tree? A boulder? Maybe the start of an avalanche? He reviewed everything he'd learned during survival training. He was growing colder, but he knew how to adapt and endure. He had a high tolerance for pain, for withstanding arduous situations.

Long ago, he'd learned not to complain, no matter what the circumstances. Complaining only increases a soldier's hardship, he knew. It erodes confidence, softens resolve, and creates a weak link in the chain, where an enemy can break through. He felt the temperature plummeting. Wind shrieked across the tent face. Gary began to lose the feeling in his fingers, toes, and face. An hour passed and then another. He tried to move around, tried to shake the blood to his extremities. But in the face of this blizzard, he knew he was losing the battle.

"God," he prayed with simple desperation. "I need you to help me get through this storm." That was the extent of his prayer, and just after he finished, one corner of Gary's mouth twitched into a smile. Warmth enveloped him, warmth much greater than his body heat could generate inside the down sleeping bag. Along with the warmth came an unmistakable feeling of care. He sensed the closeness of God, the fiery heat of the celestial realms. The wind gave one last mighty blast; then the storm tapered off. The snow stopped falling.

Gary slept that night without any nightmares, and in the morning he awoke and unzipped the tent. Everything looked fresh, new. There were no footprints around. As far as he could see in any direction, the landscape was white with snow.

———

Months passed. All winter Gary went to class during the day and spent nights in the cave. When the snow melted enough, he hiked other trails, sometimes overnighting in his tent.

One afternoon on a trail he met an elderly couple who looked as if they'd come straight from the Swiss Alps. They talked with Gary for some time and described how they'd explored mountains all over the world. The man said that other than the Alps, his favorite place to hike was the White Mountains. The couple seemed to possess the wisdom of years, the resolve of experience, and Gary couldn't help but notice a look they gave him, a look that encouraged him to keep going. In their eyes he was a seeker, and whatever he might be looking for, they were confident he'd find it. It made him newly confident too.

Slowly spring arrived. The weather turned warm, school let out for the year, and Gary was hired to do construction and yardwork at the seminary. A stonemason named Danny Wheeler was working on the jobsite of a new conference center on top of one of the hills. Danny sometimes talked about his kid sister, Lolly. Gary thought that sounded like a strange name, but he didn't inquire further. He helped clear the road to the jobsite, and each night he returned to his cave.

Summer ended, the second year of school started, and Gary sensed that he wouldn't be in his cave forever, although he still liked it. He started to make a friend or two around campus and found that he enjoyed seeing familiar faces at the school—and that they enjoyed seeing him. Occasionally he took his friends hiking. He started going to a small church in town.

Before the end of September, he hiked up the Valley Way Trail toward the summit of Mount Adams. The guidebook stated it was a four-and-a-half-hour trek, but the book must have been written in the summer, Gary concluded, because hours after that mark, he still hadn't reached his goal.

In certain places, he climbed boulders hand over hand. Remnants of snow chilled his gloved fingers. His back, stomach, and legs ached. He reached Madison Spring Hut, a stone bunkhouse on the Appalachian Trail, where he warmed himself for an hour, then kept hiking.

At last the summit came into view. He reached the top and looked out across miles and miles of mountains and trees. Exhilaration took hold of him, the age-old thrill known by those who reach summits.

Before the winter snows started to fall in earnest, he climbed Mount Adams several more times but not without a new awareness. He now saw the boulders not as hindrances but as rungs on a ladder that helped him get where he wanted to go. At first they'd been obstacles to his progress, but now he was glad the boulders were there.

The wilderness was doing its job of teaching him how to live.

One more incident during Gary's season in the cave would change his life irreversibly. He enrolled in a photography course, and one of the assignments was to do a photo shoot of a structure that held significance to the student. A tiny church sat in Lancaster, and Gary spent an afternoon taking pictures of the church. As he studied the building, shooting it from different perspectives, he had no idea that someone was across the street watching him.

A couple of days later, Gary hiked down from the cave and drove to the post office to get his VA check but found something resting on top of it—a folded piece of notebook paper. A twinge of apprehension shook him. The last time he'd opened a note, it had led to the phone call from the Pentagon. Taking a deep breath, he unfolded the note. As he read, his eyes widened . . .

Lolly's Rescue

The note in the mailbox blazed like a ray of sunshine. It read,

Hi. My name is Lolly and I've seen you around town. I was watching you take pictures of the church the other day and decided to write to you.

The young woman asked Gary questions and shared bits of information about herself. She'd been in her upstairs apartment across the street from the church when she saw Gary through her window. With his hair past his shoulders, Gary stuck out in the small, conservative New England town—much the same as if John Lennon had walked down Main Street.

At first, Gary didn't know how to answer her note or even how to get in touch with her. But he was intrigued. Buck and Jan had encouraged Gary to pray for a serious dating relationship, although while in the cave he was having a tough time relating to himself, much less another person. But Gary had begun to pray anyway. He folded up the note, put it in his pocket, and shook his head, puzzled.

A few days later, on a crisp December afternoon in 1974, Gary went back to the mailbox, more curious about further notes than about receiving any mail. Inside his box he found another piece of folded notebook paper.

Hi, Gary. I hope you don't mind me writing to you again.

He grinned. Lolly wrote about everyday happenings, things she was doing and planning to do. She explained she was the sister of Danny Wheeler, the stonemason whom Gary had worked with over the summer, so they already knew something about each other. She had asked a friend at the seminary about how to get in touch with Gary and had tracked down his post office box that way.

Gary was intensely curious about this young woman and looked forward to the notes, particularly when they started showing up in his box two to three times per week; he still felt reluctant to answer them, not knowing if he was ready for a relationship. He found out later that a girlfriend of Lolly's had encouraged her to keep writing, even if he didn't write back at first. One day when he opened his mailbox, an envelope was inside with her picture in it. She was blond and beautiful, holding a bouquet of flowers, wearing a patterned dress and a wide-brimmed sun hat. A note inside the envelope read,

Hi, this is me. Lolly.

"Wow!" Gary exclaimed out loud, then thought, *God's answered my prayer. I'm in love.* He gulped as he started second-guessing himself. *How could I ever have a relationship with her? Do I dare let her into those places of my life where I've hidden parts of me I can't accept?*

The next Sunday in church, Gary saw Lolly standing in the back of the sanctuary. He smiled. She smiled back. When the service ended, Gary tried to make his way through the crowd to see her, but she'd already slipped out the door. At least he knew now she was real.

A few days later while walking to class, Gary passed the laundromat and saw her again. Immediately, without time to develop anxiety, he went inside and said hello.

The conversation flowed, and they connected as friends right away. Her real name was Loreen, but her big brother hadn't been able to say her name when they were little. The nickname Lolly was easier to say and stuck.

Life in recent years hadn't been easy for her. She was nineteen and had a daughter of her own, Stephanie, almost two years old. Gary imagined what it would be like to raise a child as a teenage single mom in a town where everybody knew your business—what kind of chatter might occur behind a person's back and what kind of strength of spirit it would take to soldier on—and he admired Lolly even more.

Yet something held him back from asking her out. Within himself he sensed a strange hesitation, but he didn't know why.

Toward the end of December, Gary returned to Rochester to spend the holidays with his mother and family. In the new year he went back to Lancaster a few days before classes started, hoping to see Lolly. He played it cool, nonchalantly strolling by her apartment. His plan worked. She came running down the stairs to greet him. As soon as Gary saw her, he knew something was different. She was as beautiful as ever, yet there was something new within her smile, something relaxed and joyful. After the two caught up on small talk, Lolly filled Gary in on the change.

On New Year's Eve, friends had invited her to a big party in the next town, but she'd decided to take her daughter to an evening church service at the seminary chapel instead. Lolly seldom attended church. She went sometimes on holidays, and occasionally she stopped in at the town's Episcopal church to pray, although once a pine cone from a Christmas wreath had fallen on her head and she'd run out, believing God was mad at her. But that snowy New Year's evening in the seminary chapel, the minister had talked about the truest kind of hope for a new year, how a babe born in a manger had grown up to shoulder the world's weights on a Roman cross, how with God the old life can fade and a new life can begin.

That had sounded good to Lolly, so she'd bowed her head, decided to follow Jesus, and received the light that shines when all else fades. After the service finished, Lolly carried her little girl back to their apartment, and huge wet flakes began to sprinkle down from sky. Lolly looked up to heaven and felt as clean as the freshly falling snow.

In front of her apartment, Gary hugged her and she hugged him back. Any uneasiness Gary might have felt about her evaporated.

Soon he took her out to dinner, and after that, a movie, *The Towering Inferno* with Steve McQueen. Another day Gary went to Lolly's apartment for a meal and met Stephanie. The little girl looked up at him with huge blue eyes, and Gary was smitten.

Later, all three went for an afternoon drive and stopped at a store. Stephanie's eyes locked onto a huge lollipop in a display case, but Lolly said no—too much sugar. Stephanie started to cry. They got back in the car and headed toward the next town. Stephanie was still gulping, trying to control her tears, so at the next store the adults relented, and Gary bought her a huge lollipop.

On the drive the rest of the way home, Gary felt waves of blessing coursing through him. Not only had God brought him a potential companion in Lolly—he'd also brought him an immediate family.

A bold plan began to form in Gary's mind. He waited until they were all back in Lolly's apartment, a small two-room place without much furniture. A chair. A metal army cot that acted as a couch in the living room. A bookshelf. Gary noticed with a quiet grin that Lolly kept books by Thoreau and Emerson. They talked some more, and Stephanie was hugged and put to bed. When Gary left that night, he put his hand underneath Lolly's chin, gently lifted her face, kissed her softly on the forehead, and whispered, "Good night."

Lolly leaned forward, incredulous. The previous night she'd had a dream in which Gary was leaving her apartment. They were standing outside her door in the hallway. Gary gently lifted her head, bent, and kissed her forehead. As Gary kissed her, Jesus appeared over her and said, "Lolly, this is right." In less than twenty-four hours, the dream had become reality.

Lolly had befriended the wife of one of the seminary students and often went to her home to help out with housework and childcare. About a week after their first kiss, Gary went to the house where Lolly was overseeing the kids. He stood in the doorway and watched as she scrubbed the floor, searching for the perfect moment. The time had come to execute the bold plan, and he blurted, "So when are we going to get married?"

Surely it wasn't the world's most romantic proposal, yet Lolly jumped up anyway, ran to Gary, and gave him a long hug. "Yes, I'll marry you" was all she said.

They hardly knew each other. Their first official date had taken place only a few weeks earlier, near the start of January 1975. Neither of them believed in long engagements, so Gary and Lolly planned their wedding for two months later, March 30, 1975. Easter Sunday. They would marry in the early morning just as the sun rose—the perfect marker of their new life together.

Sure, a few challenges existed. For one, Gary was still living in the cave. Lolly had made it clear: she wouldn't live there with him. Gary talked to one of the school administrators, who helped him think through some of the more practical aspects of married life. The administrator was older and fatherly and had three grown daughters. He and his wife threw Gary and Lolly a shower, where gifts included a new camping stove. With the administrator's help, Gary rented a second-floor apartment above the flower shop in town.

The last day in the cave arrived. After a year and six months, Gary knew it was time to leave. As he hiked down the trail for the last time, he knew his time in the cave had been so important for him. In that place of quiet and solitude, he'd begun to heal and sense what the Medal of Honor was all about— something far greater than himself.

He loaded his few belongings into his van, drove to Lancaster, and moved into the apartment above the flower shop. The woods would always be there if he needed to get away and do some thinking, but he wasn't planning on return- ing anytime soon.

On Easter morning, standing hand in hand just outside town on a knoll called Cathedral Hill, Gary and Lolly promised to have and to hold each other from that day forward, to love each other in sickness and health, for better or worse, for richer or poorer, until parted by death. The bride wore a white dress she'd made and a ring of daisies in her hair. The groom wore slacks and a blue sports coat. President White officiated, and as he made the pronouncement that they were husband and wife and gave the benediction, snow began to fall like confetti from heaven.

Gary soon adopted Stephanie, and he found himself within his own family, loved, safe, and secure. A new season had arrived. Lolly's radiance and love had brought Gary out of the cave for good.

19

"Wear It for Us"

On April 30, 1975, one month after Gary and Lolly were married, South Vietnam fell to the Communists. The war was over, although its conclusion hadn't gone exactly as planned by the allies.

The news of the fall brought back memories of war for Gary—desperate feelings, ghosts of death and darkness. He thought of all the lives given to provide freedom for the people of South Vietnam. He thought of the Montagnards, the people he'd grown to love so dearly. The NVA had vowed to wipe them out. What would happen to the Montagnards now?

Gary had considered returning to the Montagnard tribes someday, perhaps as a medical missionary, but there was no way now he would be allowed back in the country. He knew he needed more schooling and began a program at the University of New Hampshire, majoring in sociology and psychology. It seemed the logical conclusion to his seminary studies. He was interested in what made people tick.

The president of the Medal of Honor Society, Charles "Mac" MacGillivary, asked Gary to become chaplain of the society. Gary's task would be to visit VA hospitals around New England to encourage the veterans and help with any spiritual needs. Gary took a deep breath. In many ways his life was still a mess, but he sensed that saying yes was part of God's larger plan.

To help with credentialing as a chaplain and at President White's urging, Gary became ordained through the United Baptist Fellowship of New England. In addition to his duties as chaplain of the society, Gary began another job of caring for the spiritual needs of prisoners throughout Massachusetts, New Hampshire, and Vermont.

Life seemed to be falling into place. Only a few months earlier, Gary had been living in a cave. Now he was married with a two-year-old daughter. He was a full-time college student again, an ordained minister, and a chaplain working in VA hospitals and prisons.

His days were full. Evenings were spent with Lolly and Stephanie. They rode bikes around Durham. They took car trips to the coast of southern Maine to tour lighthouses, explore beaches, and sit by the ocean. Gary loved taking little Stephanie by the hand and helping her look for starfish, crabs, and other marine life that inhabited the tide pools.

A son, Stephen, was soon born to Gary and Lolly. As the mountains had been, home life became Gary's new sanctuary.

But the way forward would not be easy.

———

Gary graduated magna cum laude from the University of New Hampshire and began looking into master's degree programs. He and Lolly and the children soon moved to Norway, Maine, to help with a pastoral ministry that Buck was beginning there. Money was tight, so Gary bought a twenty-acre hunting camp for $10,000 flat. A tumbledown shack stood on the property, but to reach it, you needed to ford a creek. Springtime runoff could sometimes make the creek impassible. The shack had no electricity, running water, or indoor plumbing. Heat came from a dilapidated woodburning stove.

"We're living here?" Lolly asked when Gary showed her the land, his chin held high. A slew of questions followed: "How do we get water? How will I do laundry out here? How can we cross the creek during spring runoff?"

Gary scratched behind his ear and thought, *Those are good questions*. He hadn't worked out all the details yet but was full of vision. They'd install insulation and dig a well. They'd get power out to the camp and install plumbing. Those were long-term projects. In the meantime they'd live like he'd lived with the Montagnards. Dig a latrine. Carry water from the creek. Boil it on the stove. They'd make things work. After all—they had twenty acres!

Lolly put on a brave face and tried to make the shack a home. She hung their lantern on a beam inside the shack and called it their "chandelier." She fixed Hamburger Helper on their tiny camping stove because the woodburning stove couldn't maintain a steady temperature. More than once she stood on the kitchen table with a broom to swing at mice that scampered along the rafters. Stephen dozed in his slatted crib, and Stephanie slept in a loft over the kitchen.

The Maine winter hit hard. During the day, water dripped through cracks in the roof, and when darkness fell, ice coated the inside of the cabin walls. One frigid January morning Gary watched as Lolly fixed some soup for Stephen and sat him by the stove to eat. He was still in his snowsuit, and his little hands shook so badly from cold he could hardly eat.

Gary realized the shack was no place to raise a family. They needed to move, but money was scarce, and how do you sell a shack in winter?

Complicating matters, the PTSD that had plagued Gary since the war now attacked with a vengeance. Some of Gary's behaviors could be explained. Others couldn't.

Once when Gary was repairing the chimney, he cut himself on a sharp edge of stovepipe and lost his temper. He beat the piping with a hammer until it ended up a crumpled mess on the floor.

Another time, Lolly bought Stephanie a Holly Hobbie lunchbox for school. Stephanie loved her lunchbox, but Gary ordered Lolly to take it back to the store. "You can use a paper bag," Gary told Stephanie. "The Montagnard kids played with empty bullet shells and scraps of metal." His voice was far too stern.

Without telling Lolly where he was going or why, Gary would often disappear into the woods for hours. One morning in early spring, Gary disappeared and Lolly felt a distinct urging to look for him. She hiked through the woods and spotted Gary in the distance, a glazed look on his face. He held a machete in one hand and a large snake in the other. Lolly knew Gary hated snakes. He was living through some sort of hallucination, and she considered approaching to ask what was wrong, but she felt another distinct urging not to do so but to keep her distance and pray for him.

When Gary came home, he had no memory of the incident.

In time, they moved to Rochester to care for Gary's mom. A third child, Sarah, was born. Gary enrolled in a master's program in counseling at nearby SUNY Brockport. A constant question, surprisingly, was how to handle the Medal of Honor—and all the gravitas it entailed. It felt like a blessing but also a burden.

Shortly after moving, Lolly was arranging furniture and hanging pictures. Gary scanned the room and saw she'd taken his framed medal citation and hung it on the wall. "No" was all he said. He took it down and placed it back in storage. He couldn't even broach the subject yet.

Coursework in the graduate program was designed to help students peer under the surface and find the honest truths of their inner lives. One professor encouraged his students to "discover the bear in your cave," an expression Gary found particularly ironic, although he wasn't encouraged by what he found. A whole pack of bears growled around in his cave—Angry Bear. Sullen Bear. Dismayed Bear.

Whenever the going got tough, Gary withdrew, keeping people at arm's length, deliberately separating himself from anybody around him—including his family, the people who loved him most. He knew he needed to confront his bears.

During class counseling sessions, every interaction, action, and reaction was open to examination. The professor, Dr. Jeremiah "Jerry" Donigian, encouraged the class to challenge simplistic answers, dig for honesty, develop real relationships, and confront if necessary. When it came time for Gary to be counseled by fellow students, he shared a bit about his life with the group, then waited for their responses. There were about fifteen students in the group. A student confronted Gary for not going deep enough. Another agreed, insisting Gary was sharing only safe information. They waited for him to share more.

A sheen of sweat broke on Gary's forehead. He tried digging deeper, but whatever he said sounded stilted. Phony. Another student charged him with trying to hide something, and still another accused Gary of not being a contributing member of the group.

Gary was agitated now, rubbing the back of his neck. He wanted to jump up and leave. "How can you ever expect to help anyone if you're not even able to help yourself?" a student asked, his voice demanding. "Come on, Gary. You've got to open up. We're here for you, but you won't trust us. What do you even want from us?"

"What do I want from you?" Gary asked, then exploded. Words spewed from his mouth, flowing from a place of deep hurt and rage. "I want you to hurt! That's what I want! I want you to hurt the same way I hurt. I want you to hold a friend in your arms and watch him die and not be able to do anything about it. I want you to hate so bad you chase an enemy through the forest—an enemy who's just killed your friends—and you hate him so much you wouldn't think twice about killing him if you caught him. I want you haunted by guilt and fear. I want you to see images so strong and lifelike you're afraid to close your eyes at night. I want you to have hallucinations of horror during the day. That's what I want! I want you to hurt like I hurt so I can see how you deal with it. I just want to feel normal so I can go on living. That's what I want!"

The group fell silent. It felt like hours before anybody moved. A side door opened, and the professor emerged from an adjoining room where he'd been watching the session with the other half of the class.

"Congratulations, Gary," the professor said. "You just reached the truth."

———

With the door to his inner life now unlocked, Gary began private counseling sessions with Dr. Donigian.

"Not long ago I was awarded the Medal of Honor," Gary said to him one afternoon during a session. He looked into his professor's eyes for a reaction. Gary had told a few people about the medal, but this telling felt different. Gary added, "It's a part of me that I don't know if I can accept. A part of me I don't understand. Can you help me?"

The professor nodded. "That must be a lot of pressure."

That one line communicated much. Gary knew he'd found someone who could help him understand why he still hurt, why his emotions were paralyzed. Why he couldn't forget. "Mostly I've just been trying to forget the war," Gary said. "But it isn't working too well."

"That's because forgetting isn't the answer," the professor said. "If you forget a hurt, that doesn't mean you've healed from it. To get better, you need to find a trusted friend to go with you into the depths of your hurt and grieve with you. You need someone who will endure the pain with you, who will stay with you so you don't have to go through it alone. You need someone to love you through the hurt, because with love you heal and with healing comes the ability to take those hurts and make them a part of you."

The professor paused. "You will never forget the hurts, Gary," he continued, "but you can draw strength from where you've been. With this strength you can comfort others. And as you comfort others, you will heal more."

Gary absorbed those words—and the force behind them. Over the next few months, as they continued to meet regularly, the professor became a trusted friend who listened to Gary and entered the world of hurt with him. Gary felt his stress lessening. His chest felt far less tight. His shoulders felt looser. The pain in the small of his back was gone. Lolly noticed Gary was more relaxed at home too.

One evening as Gary drove away from a session, he began thinking about Dak Seang. He wasn't forgetting the terrible times he'd experienced there, but he was also able to remember the joy he'd encountered in the village. He was able to think again of Deo and his sacrifice, and Gary's emotions weren't centered only on grief this time—he felt grateful too. Deo had given so much in order that Gary could live.

Gary felt fresh life welling up within him, a powerful flood, something he had not felt in years. His eyes grew blurry, but this time the blurriness wasn't from rage or dismay. Overwhelmed, he pulled his car over just in time. His insides erupted and he burst.

It took a moment for Gary to realize what was happening; this hadn't occurred in years. The last time was when Chom's daughter died.

He was crying.

—————

In another troubled country—Iran—fifty-two Americans had been taken hostage and held in the US embassy for 444 days. Their release occurred minutes after Ronald Reagan's inauguration as president on January 20, 1981.

As a Medal of Honor recipient, Gary had been invited to the inauguration. He was seated in the front of the crowd when he heard the news. Gary was happy for the hostages and noted the positive spirit of patriotism the release generated within the crowd.

Yet when he returned to Rochester, he started comparing notes with others at the Veterans Outreach Center (VOC). Some veterans wondered why the hostages were receiving such a hearty "Welcome home" from America when Vietnam veterans hadn't received anything close to the same. For these veterans, the hostages' warm welcome only incited painful memories.

Gary and Tom Gray, director of the VOC, decided to do something positive. They planned a welcome home rally for soldiers to be held at the focal point of Rochester, a downtown monument known as the Liberty Pole. Some twenty-seven thousand citizens of Rochester had served in Vietnam between 1965 and 1973, and more than 225 had died in the conflict. The Vietnam veterans and their family members were invited to the rally, along with politicians, community members and leaders, and the press.

Tom asked Gary to speak at the rally—and to wear his medal. Gary balked. He hadn't worn his medal since President Nixon had presented it to him seven years earlier. But Tom's eyes became like steel, and he said, "Don't wear it for you. Wear it for us—for all the veterans who served." His words carried much weight.

Early on the day of the rally, Gary took his medal out of storage, dusted it off, and hung it around his neck, although it still didn't feel as if it was fully a part of him. He affixed his Special Forces patch to his lapel; he felt better about that than the medal.

On a cold, windy morning, about three hundred people turned out for the rally. Some veterans came in their uniforms. Some came in wheelchairs. Gary took the microphone and spoke words of welcome, healing, and honor. The crowd cheered. Many veterans in the crowd said afterward that the rally helped. They felt at last as if they'd been welcomed home too.

For His Honor

In 1982, members of a group called Vietnam Veterans of America (VVA) made news by asking the Communist government of Vietnam to allow a group of American veterans to visit Hanoi. The VVA asked Gary to go along as the first Medal of Honor recipient to return to the country. Newsman Mike Wallace from *60 Minutes* and Associated Press reporter Denis Gray were set to go on the trip, along with six veterans, a lawyer, and a theater producer interested in a cultural exchange of ideas. Including travel time, the trip would last almost two weeks.

Gary talked with Lolly about him participating in the trip, and although she agreed in principle, she was still concerned. Gary was gone from home so much because of his work as an educator and his volunteer responsibilities with veterans. Money was tight. Their children were ages nine, five, and three and didn't see their father enough as it was.

Gary shook his head—he understood her concerns, but he felt he simply needed to go. Lolly wasn't as sure. They argued in their kitchen. At the height of their disagreement, Lolly walked to the wall-mounted phone, declared she was going to make plane reservations to take her and the children back to Lancaster, and picked up the receiver. Gary strode over to the phone, ripped it off the wall, and threw it across the room. Then he stormed out. He had to get quiet. Lolly, in tears, followed him out to the front lawn. Gary didn't know what to do.

He left for Vietnam without patching things up at home.

The delegation flew from the United States to Bangkok, where they received a stern warning from US government officials: The trip was potentially dangerous —America did not have formal diplomatic relations with Vietnam's government. The Vietnamese boat people crisis, during which thousands of refugees fled Vietnam's Communist regime after the war ended, was ongoing and was featured prominently in the news, much to the chagrin of the Vietnamese government. Tensions between the two countries ran high.

The group shook off the warning, boarded a small propeller plane, and took off for Hanoi. Group members' apprehensions rose along with the temperature, and sweat dripped from everyone aboard. As they flew over the Central Highlands, Gary looked down, saw the familiar triple-canopy jungle that had hidden the enemy, and retreated within himself, lost in images, sounds, and smells.

When the plane landed in Hanoi, a Vietnamese military officer and an interpreter welcomed the delegation, but the officer pointed at Gary and pulled him from line. The rest of the group looked alarmed, particularly when two soldiers escorted Gary and the officer to a small shed. Inside were two metal chairs positioned on opposite sides of an interrogation table. The soldiers motioned for Gary to sit and wait. They stood guard for what seemed like forever. The officer sat in the chair opposite Gary and stared straight at him but didn't say a word.

The heat grew unbearable. Gary wondered if they knew he was a Green Beret. Maybe they feared he was a CIA plant. No words were exchanged. No questions were asked. *I'm going to prison for sure,* Gary thought. Finally the door opened, and another soldier stepped in, whispered something to the officer, and left. The officer stood up, smiled, and held out his hand to shake. "Welcome to Vietnam," the man said. Gary shook his hand and was escorted back to the rest of the delegation.

No explanation was ever given for the strange encounter, and it created a deep uneasiness within Gary, still at the start of the trip.

The next ten days were a whirlwind of experiences, memories, feelings, and meetings. The delegation toured sites and met with Foreign Minister Nguyen Co Thach, who was seeking to normalize relations with the US. The foreign minister explained to Gary that some terrible things had happened to the Montagnards after the war. Gary was able to piece together information from other sources too.

When American and South Vietnamese forces left the highlands, the Montagnards' war didn't end. Some Montagnards escaped to Cambodia and Thailand, where they received a mixed response—some were welcomed, some were sent back to Vietnam, and others were thrown into prison. Other Montagnards were eventually evacuated to America, where some three thousand settled in North Carolina, not far from Fort Bragg where Green Berets were trained. But other Montagnards who remained in the highlands were assaulted, arrested, harassed, brutalized, and killed by the Communists. Montagnard land was seized. Some Montagnards were forcibly taken to "reeducation" camps. Cultural rights, education, religious freedom, and employment opportunities were severely restricted.

Gary was deeply troubled at the news, although he didn't know what to do except further the dialogue. The foreign minister didn't know what to do either. The two men shook hands, then walked away, both visibly distressed.

—————

During the rest of the trip, the delegation met with Asian American street children who'd been fathered by American GIs and heard heartbreaking stories of abandonment. They met with political committees and asked questions about the 2,494 American soldiers still listed as missing in action but were unable to get any firm answers about their whereabouts or release, if they were still being held in prison camps. They toured Tay Ninh Province, an area devastated by the spraying of Agent Orange, and were aghast.

At a roadside beach one hot afternoon, Gary talked with a former officer who'd fought with the NVA. Respectfully Gary and the officer talked for some time about the war, the duties they'd discharged, and the wounds they had suffered. The officer described how he had lost many friends and family members in the battles and then had been seriously wounded himself but had "healed well."

The man seemed so genuine, so self-collected and restful, that Gary asked him to explain what he meant by the last phrase. The officer said, "Vietnam has been at war for many years with many different countries. War is terrible. Nobody really wins. Everybody loses and everybody suffers. But I have learned that if I am to heal and rebuild my life, I cannot hate. This is the secret of my healing—to go forward, I must forgive."

Amazed, Gary nodded and shook hands with the man . . . once an enemy.

———

On one of their final days, while touring a youth center, the delegation watched as a group of children performed a concert on traditional Vietnamese instruments, many of which Gary had never seen. A group of grade-school-aged girls performed a ballet afterward; then the instructor asked if the former soldiers in the delegation would like to join them. Gary and some of the others hesitated, then nodded.

The girls came over, took them by their hands, and led them out to the center of the room. The music began, the dance started, and Gary felt as if he was on a strange and mystifying journey. He was rising to a cloud, and as he danced, he left behind so many of the burdens and memories that weighed him down. He knew the Vietnam War and its immediate aftermath had been staggering in their desolation and complications. So many people had suffered, including his beloved Montagnards, and so much still felt difficult and undone.

Yet just as Gary had deliberately carved out a place of restoration for himself in the cave, he felt a new sense of peace emerging from this trip back to Vietnam. Within the dance he felt a bit of personal closure. He knew he'd done serious work on his own life since returning home, and his healing was gradually expanding and settling.

From the sidelines, the hardened newsman Mike Wallace watched. He saw the former soldiers dance with the children of the enemy and, like so many in the room that day, he couldn't help but weep.

———

Lolly was not there to meet Gary when he and the delegation returned from Vietnam. Newspaper reporters were there. Politicians were there. TV crews were there. But when Gary scanned the crowd at the airport, he didn't see his wife and children.

A press conference began. Gary answered questions about the trip and had pictures taken with the other delegates. Then he drove home, weak and jet lagged, his stomach in knots. He had contracted dysentery in Vietnam and lost ten pounds. But that wasn't the only tension he felt. He knew he needed to patch things up with Lolly because of their argument before he left. But when he got home, no one was there either.

A knock sounded on the door—a neighbor was there to say that Lolly had left a few days earlier. She'd taken the children and gone.

Gary jumped in the car and headed for Lancaster. On the drive he battled himself. He knew he loved his family, but he also knew he hadn't loved them enough—not in the way they needed. Somehow he'd missed that they'd been hurting too, right along with him. They needed him to be an openhearted husband and father, and Gary knew he was lacking there. He was aloof too often. He was overly stern. He hadn't opened his heart to let them in.

Gary arrived in Lancaster, and the children ran up and hugged him. Lolly said she was willing to talk, and Gary listened with new ears. Lolly explained that she was not upset about Gary returning to Vietnam and that she truly did not want to leave Gary. But she was upset because she needed him to be present—and she meant more than physically present. The kids needed him on a deeper level too. Lolly hadn't left Gary because she was angry. She'd left him because she needed to get away from the way they were living.

Lolly and Gary prayed together, and Lolly and the children went home with him to Rochester.

In days, weeks, months, and years to come, Gary made great strides in his personal life. He changed jobs and cut back on his volunteer responsibilities so he could be home more often. With Lolly's help Gary found the support, love, and guidance needed to enter the caves of his life, to explore, to hurt, to heal, and once again to live. The change didn't happen overnight, but it definitely did happen. As a gesture of his genuine healing, Gary bought a brand-new Holly Hobbie lunchbox for Stephanie and gave it to her on her sixteenth birthday. They both knew she was too old for Holly Hobbie by then, but Stephanie understood the symbolism behind the gift and gave him a warm hug in return.

Today, Gary clarifies that although he grew during his season in the cave, his healing did not arrive fully until he felt deeply the unconditional love of Lolly, his family, and his friends. The wilderness experience taught him much, but the wilderness wasn't a destination. Lolly brought him out of the cave and kept him from returning, and then she entered many more emotional caves with Gary over the years and helped him emerge again.

With Lolly's love, as Gary invested in the lives of his family and in the lives of the students he eventually worked with, he found significance. He rebuilt his life by giving back to others. The people closest to him gave insight, comfort, and encouragement along the way.

———

It took quite a while before Gary felt fully comfortable wearing the Medal of Honor. After the rally at the Liberty Pole, Gary put the medal away for several more years. Thousands of vets had returned from the war, and Gary felt it was wrong for him to be singled out for special recognition. Yet as he continued to work with more and more vets, he saw himself simply as one of them—nothing more, nothing less—and he understood that his mission with the medal was to gain acceptance and recognition for all who serve honorably.

It wasn't until Gary began working as a guidance counselor with students at Arcadia Middle School in Greece, New York, that he realized it was time to take the medal out of storage for good. He saw how each new generation needed to see and learn what true honor is all about.

One morning in class, Gary was telling his students about Deo, about how the fifteen-year-old soldier had laid down his life to save Gary, and he quoted the motto he'd repeated to himself so many times over the years: "To really live, you must almost die. To those who fight for it, life has a meaning the protected will never know."

A student raised his hand and said, "Wait a minute, Mr. B. You're telling me I need to die in order to live? I don't get it."

"Well, in a sense, yes," Gary answered. "You need to die to yourself. If you're only interested in getting things for yourself, in getting ahead so you can get more, then you'll never learn to truly live. That's what that saying means. When you realize there's more to life than 'me,' when you begin to invest in others, that's when you discover what life is truly all about."

"I still don't get it completely," the student said. "Especially the fighting part. Are you telling me to go pick a fight with somebody in the hallway after class?"

Gary chuckled and shook his head. "No, that's not the fighting I'm talking about. The battles are fought in our hearts and minds. The weapons are the values of love, sacrifice, integrity, and service. Whenever we fight battles with those weapons, life takes on a meaning that others will never know. That's what it truly means to live with honor."

The class nodded. They were getting it. Gary was getting it too.

Not long afterward, Gary was asked to speak at a church a few states away. The minister was a former Special Forces officer who had heard about Gary, and he was particularly interested in Gary's story in the context of his faith. Gary hesitated about saying yes; then with Lolly's encouragement he felt a change come over him, a new peace. In his house he went to where the medal was held, lifted the lid, and took the medal out of storage. He knew it was time to step forward in confidence. The past was behind him. The best was yet to come.

"My story is God's story," Gary told the people at the church a few weeks later. "This medal is not about me. This medal is about him. Without God's grace, I wouldn't have been able to survive Vietnam. Without his forgiveness in my life, I wouldn't have been able to live with myself. Without his love, I wouldn't have healed from my wounds. This medal is ultimately about him, and I wear it for his honor."

Epilogue

In 2013, Gary Beikirch retired after a thirty-three-year career in education. At his retirement ceremony, student after student described how they loved and respected him. He was affectionately known as "Mr. B.," the soft-spoken guidance counselor who cared for everyone he interacted with.

Today, Gary travels and speaks extensively. He is still active as chaplain of the Medal of Honor Society, visiting the hurting and wounded, ministering to their needs.

During each holiday season, the Beikirch home is filled with their three children and their spouses, plus fourteen wondrous grandchildren.

In 1999, Lolly was encouraged to steer in a new career direction—counseling—although she'd already informally been providing people with insight, wisdom, and love for years. She graduated from a university program and became certified through the American Association of Christian Counselors. Her specialty became trauma counseling. Gary became certified as well, and over the years he and Lolly have often counseled individuals and couples together.

When Lolly is asked why she stayed with Gary during their most difficult seasons, during the bouts with PTSD and life in the shack, she answers, "Because he was my gift from God." In recent years, both she and Gary have fought and won battles against cancer. They are quick to point out that their story has not ended, but they can face the future in part because of what they have learned from the past.

Gary describes how the wholeness found through his faith and through hard inner work over the years has developed into a lasting peace. Through the years of education, marriage, parenting, service work with veterans, and care and concern for his students, the peace ebbed and flowed, yet it's grown constant at last.

Gary has long since given up trying to forget. He knows the scars of the Vietnam War will always remain. Yet Gary has used his scars to develop a passion for helping people heal and thrive. He describes how he will always treasure his time with the Montagnards, knowing they helped provide him with a foundation of love and acceptance. He will always treasure his time in the cave, mostly because he learned there to look beyond the cave. And he has grown to love his wife and family in the deepest ways possible, being present in mind, body, and spirit. He's become the husband and father he's always wanted to be.

In a recent newsletter article for the Medal of Honor Society, Gary wrote,

Pain is not something to be hidden deep inside us or covered with a façade of bravado. Just as joy is to be shared with those we love, it's equally important to share our pain with those we love, for in doing so we acknowledge the closeness of our relationships. We acknowledge that we are important to one another. We acknowledge the care that makes our relationships grow deeper.

We acknowledge we are not alone.

Official Medal of Honor Citation

For conspicuous gallantry and intrepidity in action at the risk of his life above and beyond the call of duty. Sgt. Beikirch, medical aidman, Detachment B-24, Company B, distinguished himself during the defense of Camp Dak Seang.

The allied defenders suffered a number of casualties as a result of an intense, devastating attack launched by the enemy from well-concealed positions surrounding the camp. Sgt. Beikirch, with complete disregard for his personal safety, moved unhesitatingly through the withering enemy fire to his fallen comrades, applied first aid to their wounds and assisted them to the medical aid station.

When informed that a seriously injured American officer was lying in an exposed position, Sgt. Beikirch ran immediately through the hail of fire. Although he was wounded seriously by fragments from an exploding enemy mortar shell, Sgt. Beikirch carried the officer to a medical aid station.

Ignoring his own serious injuries, Sgt. Beikirch left the relative safety of the medical bunker to search for and evacuate other men who had been injured. He was again wounded as he dragged a critically injured Vietnamese soldier to the medical bunker while simultaneously applying mouth-to-mouth resuscitation to sustain his life. Sgt. Beikirch again refused treatment and continued his search for other casualties until he collapsed. Only then did he permit himself to be treated.

Sgt. Beikirch's complete devotion to the welfare of his comrades, at the risk of his life, is in keeping with the highest traditions of the military service and reflects great credit on him, his unit, and the U.S. Army.

With Gratitude

Danny Moore. Rick Richter and the team at Aevitas Creative Management. Madeleine Morel at 2M Communications. H. C. Jones and D. L. Brotherton. Pamela Fogle for your mapmaking skills. Andrew Stoddard, Bruce Nygren, and the team at Penguin Random House, WaterBrook & Multnomah. Thanks to all our readers, always.

Notes

The majority of information in this book comes directly from Gary and Lolly Beikirch via a series of extensive interviews conducted with the author, Marcus Brotherton, from January 2018 to April 2019. Additionally, Gary supplied the author with copious first-person written accounts of his experiences and recollections, including specific wording he recalled for dialogue and prayers. Due to the volume of interviews and materials provided by the Beikirchs, this information is not cited or dated in text, except where noted.

To prepare for this project, the author read an abundance of helpful books, articles, website content, and documents, and also viewed many photographs and videos. Without providing an exhaustive list of works and organizations consulted, the author wishes to note in particular the Medal of Honor Society; the Congressional Medal of Honor Foundation and their Character Development Program; the National Archives; the Pritzker Military Museum and Library; the Army Medical Department of the US Army (AMEDD); the AMEDD Regiment and its oral history program; the Disabled American Veterans organization; the *New York Times; Stars and Stripes;* the Associated Press; the Rochester *Democrat and Chronicle;* the *Greece Post;* the *DROP* (Special Forces Association magazine); the *Coos County Democrat;* the *Corry Journal;* Greece Central School District; the American Association of Christian Counselors for their educational video featuring Gary and Lolly Beikirch (*Care and Counsel for Combat Trauma*); the *Washington Post;* the Military Assistance Command, Vietnam—Studies and Observation Group; photographer John Beard and his work in Dak Seang; photographer Christopher J. Childs and Fold3.com; the Veterans Outreach Center tapes and the late Stirlin Harris (who conducted lengthy interviews with Gary and Lolly Beikirch in 1993 and 1999); Stanley Karnow for his book *Vietnam: A History* (Viking, 1983); the thirteen-part PBS documentary series *Vietnam: A Television History* (1983); Lieutenant General Harold G. Moore and Joseph L. Galloway for their book *We Were Soldiers Once . . . and Young* (Random House, 1992); the book *Marine Sniper* by Charles Henderson (Stein and Day, 1986); Captain Allen Brady and Dawn Quarles for their book *Witnessing the American Century* (Kent State University Press, 2019); Brigadier General Robin Olds and his daughter Christina Olds and Ed Rasimus for their book *Fighter Pilot* (St. Martin's Press, 2010); Colonel Jimmie Dean Coy for his book *Valor: A Gathering of Eagles* (Evergreen Press, 2003); Tim O'Brien and his breathtaking work of fiction about Vietnam *The Things They Carried* (Houghton Mifflin, 1990); Ken Burns, Lynn Novick, Geoffrey C. Ward, and their controversial though informative ten-part documentary film series, *The Vietnam War;* and the Vietnam Center and Archive at Texas Tech University for gathering, maintaining, and making available many research materials, letters, photographs, and military after-action reports regarding the siege of Dak Seang.

Prologue

3 **"first day of the siege."** The exact amount of time Gary spent on the battlefield after being wounded remains unclear. Most soldiers who were there, including Sergeant Bob Hill, who was instrumental in Gary's evacuation (see note 13 of chapter 9), say that Gary was evacuated on the evening of the first day. Yet other soldiers believe Gary was there for at least two days, perhaps longer. Because of the chaos of circumstances during the siege, the soldiers don't debate the topic heavily among themselves. In reference to the siege, Dizzy notes, "It was a madhouse" and "The whole month I was there seemed like *one long day.*" Interestingly, Dizzy was the last of the original team of Green Berets to be evacuated from the camp. He was ordered to leave by officers in Kontum but did not want to leave. His Montagnard bodyguard, Brer, was still alive at that time and was with Dizzy when he got on the chopper.

They hugged, and Dizzy gave his watch to Brer. Dizzy then asked the chopper pilot whether they could circle the camp as they left so he could get one final look at home. The camp had been virtually destroyed.

3 **"medical assistant named Tot."** Dizzy recalls Brer as well as Tot being present in the bunker, although Gary does not remember Brer being there. Gary knows that after Deo was killed, Tot picked up where Deo left off and carried him around and eventually to the bunker. Again, the topic is not heavily debated because of the chaos of the siege, and it makes sense that Tot and Brer may have come and gone from the bunker during Gary's bouts of unconsciousness.

5 **"medevac helicopter."** Many helicopter units responded to the siege. According to the Vietnam Helicopter Pilots Association, for April 1, 1970, the first day of the siege, "an estimated force of three regiments had encircled Dak Seang. The 189th AHC did most of the support for the 2d ARVN Rangers, the MIKE Strike Force, and the CIDG; but concentrations of automatic 37mm and .51 cal fire brought ships down one after another. *Air strike after air strike, the enemy continued to bring down helicopters*" (emphasis added). "Siege of Dak Seang Information," Vietnam Helicopter Pilots Association, May 26, 2019, www.vhpa .org/KIA/panel/battle/70040120.HTM.

Chapter 1: Heart of a Warrior

8 **"*Democrat and Chronicle*."** "2-Story Fall Injures Baby," *Democrat and Chronicle* (Rochester, NY), May 5, 1949.

8 **"cousin Janet."** Regarding young cousin Janet's extensive prayer for the hospitalized toddler. At San Francisco General Hospital a researcher tested the practice of prayer and found it to have a positive medical effect on people. Several hundred hospital patients were split into two groups—those who were prayed for and those who weren't. Over a period of ten months, follow-up showed that the group that had been

prayed for had a significantly lower severity score. The other group "required ventilatory assistance, antibiotics, and diuretics more frequently than patients in the IP [intercessory prayer] group." Randolph C. Byrd, "Positive Therapeutic Effects of Intercessory Prayer in a Coronary Care Unit Population," *Southern Medical Journal* 81, no. 7 (July 1988): 826–29, www.ncbi.nlm.nih.gov/pubmed/3393937.

11 **"rides at Seabreeze."** "History," Seabreeze Amusement Park, https://seabreeze.com/about/history. Note that Seabreeze was technically renamed Dreamland in the forties, and the name wasn't officially changed back to Seabreeze until c. 1970, but Gary has always referred to the park as Seabreeze.

13 **"God loved."** Regarding Mrs. Koch's message to the group of boys. See John 3:16–17, NLT.

17 **"his letters home."** For copies of the letters of Don Jacques, see *Dear America: Letters Home from Vietnam,* ed. Bernard Edelman (New York: W. W. Norton, 2002).

Chapter 2: Death or a Better Man

21 **"committed its resources."** Neil Sheehan, "Vietnam Archive: Pentagon Study Traces 3 Decades of Growing U. S. Involvement," *New York Times,* June 13, 1971, www.nytimes.com/1971/06/13/archives/vietnam -archive-pentagon-study-traces-3-decades-of-growing-u-s.html.

21 ***De oppresso liber.*** Stewart Smith, "Creed and Mottos of Special Operations Command (SOCOM)," Balance Careers, January 6, 2019, www.thebalancecareers.com/creed-and-mottos-of-the-special-operations -command-socom-4108507.

22 **"the following oath."** Lucas Harper, "Swearing In: The Oath of Enlistment and the Oath of Office," Military Authority, February 3, 2018, www.militaryauthority.com/wiki/swearing-in-the-oath-of-enlistment -and-the-oath-of-office.html.

Chapter 3: The Thousand-Yard Stare

37 **"remembered the hardships."** Larry Getlen, "Could You Be a Green Beret?," *New York Post,* January 6, 2013, https://nypost.com/2013/01/06 /could-you-be-a-green-beret.

43 **"Joe Houle."** Regarding the thousand-yard stare. Arthur L. Stone, "Retired Sgt. Maj. Joe Houle Recounts Vietnam Tour," Marines, May 2, 2002, www.lejeune.marines.mil/News/Article/511426/retired-sgt-maj -joe-houle-recounts-vietnam-tour.

Chapter 4: In-Country Chaos

47 **"free-fire area."** *FM 6-20-20: Tactics, Techniques and Procedures for Fire Support at Battalion Task Force and Below* (Washington, DC: Department of the Army Headquarters, 1991), 1-19, https://usacac.army .mil/sites/default/files/misc/doctrine/CDG/cdg_resources/manuals/fm /fm6_20_20.pdf.

47 **"Civilian Irregular Defense Group."** For more information about the Civilian Irregular Defense Group (CIDG) program, see Francis J. Kelly, *U.S. Army Special Forces: 1961–1971* (1973, repr., Washington, DC: Department of the Army, 2004), 19–20, https://history.army.mil/html /books/090/90-23-1/CMH_Pub_90-23-1.pdf.

48 **"walk on the moon."** Eric Linkenhoker, "What Effect Did the First Moon Landing Have on the World?," Sciencing, April 21, 2018, https://sciencing.com/effect-first-moon-landing-world-8789492 .html.

49 **"Montagnard people."** *Encyclopaedia Britannica Online,* s.v. "Montagnard," www.britannica.com/topic/Montagnard-people.

49 **"Dan 'Mac' McGinley."** See Master Sergeant Dan McGinley's three-volume memoir: T. Daniel McGinley, *A Walk with Giants* (self-pub., 2005), www.pritzkermilitary.org/explore/library/online-catalog/view /oclc/849513509.

51 **"Saigon."** "Population Growth of Ho Chi Minh City (HCMC)," ICLEI, 2004, http://resilient-cities.iclei.org/fileadmin/sites/resilient-cities /files/Resilient_Cities_2011/Presentations/A/A6.B6.__Storch_2.pdf.

51 **"corps areas."** Vietnam was divided into four corps areas: I Corps was the northernmost area, II Corps was the Central Highlands, III Corps was lowland areas, and IV Corps was in the delta area.

Chapter 5: Jungle Shangri-La

57 **"To really live."** The quote above the team house in Dak Seang is usually attributed to Henri René Albert Guy De Maupassant, (1850–1893) a French writer. His original quote, translated, is close to this: "You've never lived until you've almost died. For those who have fought for it, life has a flavor the protected shall never know." Various translations exist. See *The Short Stories of Guy de Maupassant,* vol. xi (Miniature Masterpieces, 2017), Kindle.

64 **"Dr. Patricia Smith."** Christine Clarridge, "Dr. Smith Provided Care, Compassion to Vietnam," *Seattle Times,* January 1, 2005, www.seattle times.com/seattle-news/dr-smith-provided-care-compassion-to-vietnam.

65 **"Tet Offensive."** "Doc Grandma Plots Return to Highlands," *Stars and Stripes,* Pacific ed., May 3, 1972, www.thebattleofkontum.com/stars/22 .html.

66 **"military importance of the Central Highlands."** J. F. Loye Jr. and L. J. Johnson, *Project CHECO Report: The Defense of Dak Seang* (Hickam Air Force Base, Hawaii: Department of the Air Force, February 15, 1971), 4, https://apps.dtic.mil/dtic/tr/fulltext/u2/a486861.pdf.

Chapter 7: Hours of Darkness

85 **"troops were congregating."** J. F. Loye Jr. and L. J. Johnson, *Project CHECO Report: The Defense of Dak Seang* (Hickam Air Force Base, Hawaii: Department of the Air Force, February 15, 1971), 3, https://apps .dtic.mil/dtic/tr/fulltext/u2/a486861.pdf.

86 **"falciparum malaria."** Regarding the illness contracted by Chom's daughter. Farlex Partner Medical Dictionary, s.v. "falciparum malaria," https://medical-dictionary.thefreedictionary.com/falciparum+malaria.

91 **"four o'clock."** Gary believes dawn broke about 4:00 a.m. The CHECO report places the time of heavy incoming attacks at approximately 6:45 (page 1). Gary notes that the attacks came just as the funeral was ending.

91 **"He and Dizzy."** Dizzy and Gary both recall being at the funeral, yet Dizzy is fairly certain he was at the team house by the time the first rockets came, although Gary believes he and Dizzy were both still at the funeral. Gary knows he was at the funeral when the attack began, and it may be that Dizzy had left the funeral by that point.

Chapter 8: Siege of Dak Seang

96 **"Gary's spirit."** Regarding Gary's out-of-body experience after being hit. Intense emotion or pain can prompt unique responses, even including out-of-body experiences, during which "the center of awareness appears to the experient to occupy temporarily a position which is spatially remote from his or her body." Henry J. Irwin and Caroline A. Watt, *An Introduction to Parapsychology,* 5th ed. (Jefferson, NC: McFarland, 2007), 179. Psychologists have studied these experiences for more than a century and remain puzzled by what actually occurs. British researchers David Wilde and Craig D. Murray note, "That an out-of-body experience does occur is without doubt. Whether or not the event is a literal separation of something from the physical body or an elaborate hallucination is a matter for further investigation." "Interpreting the Anomalous: Finding Meaning in Out-of-Body and Near-Death Experiences," *Qualitative Research in Psychology* 7, no. 1 (2010): 57–72.

Chapter 9: True Soldier

102 **"First Lieutenant Ed Christensen."** Several eyewitness statements regarding the rescue of Lieutenant Christensen were placed in Gary's

case file in 1970 for his Medal of Honor recommendation. All eyewitnesses attest to Gary's rescue of Christensen, yet variants exist as to when exactly Gary was paralyzed. Gary believes that he was already paralyzed prior to Christensen's wounding and that upon Gary's directive, Deo quickly dragged him to Christensen; then Deo helped take them both back to the medical bunker, which is when Gary was hit again. Other eyewitnesses hold that Gary ran to Christensen under his own power and was wounded either immediately prior to reaching Christensen or as Gary dragged Christensen back to safety or perhaps later. Today, the veterans don't debate the sequence among themselves, and one theory for the variants is that Deo was so often near Gary's side that the eyewitnesses might have overlooked Deo's presence.

Here are excerpts of the statements:

Captain Paul Landers wrote, "Hearing that . . . Lieutenant [Christensen] . . . lay exposed to a volume of fire so murderous that no one was able to reach him, Sergeant Beikirch immediately raced into the open in search of his wounded comrade. As soon as this gallant individual approached his fallen team member the enemy redoubled their fire. Under this deadly onslaught Sergeant Beikirch was felled by mortar fragments in the back. Disregarding his painful wounds and the withering enemy fire, he heroically crawled to his injured friend and began administering first aid."

Operations sergeant Thomas Drake similarly wrote that Gary was hit as he approached Christensen.

Medic Dan Noonan wrote that Gary "immediately raced . . . through intense enemy artillery and small arms fire, in search of [Christensen]. A short time later Sergeant Beikirch returned carrying Lieutenant [Christensen]."

Medal of Honor Award Case File: Gary Beikirch, 12, 14, 17, box 1, folder 15, Tim Frank Collection, Vietnam Center and Archive, Texas Tech University, Lubbock, TX, www.vietnam.ttu.edu/reports/images .php?img=/images/1870/18700115001.pdf.

102 **"Thomas Drake."** Gary, although paralyzed, continued to give medical aid on the battlefield. All eyewitnesses agree to this. See in particular the testimony of operations sergeant Thomas Drake, *Medal of Honor Award Case File: Gary Beikirch,* 14.

103 **"tactic similar."** Douglas Porch, "Battle of Dien Bien Phu," in *The Reader's Companion to Military History,* ed. Robert Cowley and Geoffrey Parker (Boston: Houghton Mifflin, 1996), 131–33.

105 **"true soldier."** (Sometimes written as "real soldier.") G. K. Chesterton, "Christmas and Disarmament," *Illustrated London News,* January 14, 1911, in *The Collected Works of G. K. Chesterton,* ed. George J. Marlin, Richard P. Rabatin, and John L. Swan, vol. 29, *The Illustrated London News: 1911–1913,* ed. Lawrence J. Clipper (San Francisco: Ignatius, 1988), 22.

106 **"sitting duck."** The CHECO report describes this sitting-duck strategy. Note that high numbers of enemy casualties were indeed reported afterward, and although the camp was virtually reduced to nothing, Dak Seang technically did not fall. J. F. Loye Jr. and L. J. Johnson, *Project CHECO Report: The Defense of Dak Seang* (Hickam Air Force Base, Hawaii: Department of the Air Force, February 15, 1971), 4, 31, https://apps.dtic.mil/dtic/tr/fulltext/u2/a486861.pdf.

106 **"enemy body count."** As marine Lieutenant Philip Caputo states in his memoir *A Rumor of War,* "[The] mission was . . . to kill. . . . Victory was a high body-count, defeat a low kill-ratio, war a matter of arithmetic. The pressure on unit commanders to produce enemy corpses was intense." *A Rumor of War,* 40th anniversary ed. (New York: Picador, 2017), xxvii.

106 **"hold Dak Seang."** Regarding no retreat possible for the defenders. Loye and Johnson, *Project CHECO Report,* 4.

106 **"couldn't flee to safety."** Loye and Johnson, *Project CHECO Report,* 4.

106 **"*New York Times.*"** James P. Sterba, "Truce Is Called at Besieged Camp," *New York Times,* April 30, 1970, www.nytimes.com/1970/04 /30/archives/truce-is-called-at-besieged-camp-foe-at-dakseang-proposes -return-of.html.

106 **"*Stars and Stripes.*"** "Allies Kill 496 near Besieged Dak Seang," *Stars and Stripes,* Pacific ed., April 9, 1970.

106 **"after-action reports."** Regarding the number of enemies attacking. The Twenty-Eighth NVA Regiment was found to be three kilometers north of the camp. Other enemy infantry was seen close to the camp perimeter. A few days after the siege began, still "with no let up in the intensity of the attacks," another NVA regiment was discovered south of the camp. Loye and Johnson, *Project CHECO Report,* 1–2. It's believed today that the Sixty-Sixth NVA Regiment and the K30 and K33 Battalions of the Fortieth NVA Artillery Regiment, as well as the K37 Battalion, "probably participated" in the campaign. The D-2 Transportation Battalion was also "positively identified." It's considered "possible" that the K20 Sapper Battalion participated. USAAG, II Corps Tactical Zone, *The Dak Seang Campaign: 1 April–8 May 1970,* 3, Records of the Military Assistance Command, Part 1: The War in Vietnam, 1954–1973, box 44, folder 7, Sam Johnson Vietnam Archive Collection, Vietnam Center and Archive, Texas Tech University, Lubbock, TX, www.vietnam.ttu.edu/reports/images.php?img=/images/F0158/F0158 00440007a.pdf.

106 **"four hundred Montagnard fighters."** Some reports place the number of Montagnard defenders anywhere from 450 to 550 fighters. But Gary holds that the number was closer to 400. Some Cambodian troops had been staying in Dak Seang earlier and got mixed in with the count, but they were gone by the time of the siege.

111 **"Sergeant Bob Hill."** Bob Hill, conversation with Gary Beikirch, as related to the author. See also Alex Topor, "Vietnam War Veterans Reunite After 48 Years," *Corry Journal* (Corry, PA), November 10, 2018, www.thecorryjournal.com/news/article_aa5762b0-e6b0-11e8-b183-7fa957a1a95e.html.

Chapter 10: Wounded

123 **"controlled the runway."** Jack Fuller, "NVA Forced to Ease Siege on Dak Seang," *Stars and Stripes,* Pacific ed., April 10, 1970.

123 **"Australian-led cadre."** "Red Grip Broken at Viet Camp," *Stars and Stripes,* Pacific ed., April 12, 1970.

123 **"Corpses littered."** "Allies Kill 496 near Besieged Dak Seang," *Stars and Stripes,* Pacific ed., April 9, 1970.

Chapter 11: Seeking

132 **"thirty-eight days."** Regarding the length of the entire siege. J. F. Loye Jr. and L. J. Johnson, *Project CHECO Report: The Defense of Dak Seang* (Hickam Air Force Base, Hawaii: Department of the Air Force, February 15, 1971), 31, https://apps.dtic.mil/dtic/tr/fulltext/u2/a486861.pdf.

132 **"mid-June."** John Wilcox, "Dak Seang Still Lives," *Typhoon,* July–August 1970, 2.

132 **"allied ground troops."** Another American soldier, Sergeant First Class Gary L. Littrell, would receive the Medal of Honor for his actions taken outside the camp during the siege. Littrell was an adviser to the ARVN Twenty-Third Battalion, Second Ranger Group. His citation reads in part,

> After establishing a defensive perimeter on a hill on April 4, the battalion was subjected to an intense enemy mortar attack which killed the Vietnamese commander, 1 advisor, and seriously wounded all the advisors except Sfc. Littrell. During

the ensuing 4 days, Sfc. Littrell exhibited near superhuman
endurance as he single-handedly bolstered the besieged
battalion. Repeatedly abandoning positions of relative safety,
he directed artillery and air support by day and marked the
unit's location by night, despite the heavy, concentrated enemy
fire. "Medal of Honor Recipients: Vietnam War," US Army
Center of Military History, https://history.army.mil/html/moh
/vietnam-a-l.html#LITTRELL.

132 **"American and allied forces flew."** Regarding air support key to Dak
Seang. Loye and Johnson, *Project CHECO Report,* 31.

132 **"eyewitness described."** Wilcox, "Dak Seang Still Lives," 2.

132 **"2,922 enemy dead."** Loye and Johnson, *Project CHECO Report,* 31.
When it was all over, an after-action report stated, "[The siege of Dak
Seang] caused senior commanders to take a hard look at the camp to
determine whether its worth as a border surveillance base justified the
tremendous cost of lives and resources expended in its defense."
USAAG, II Corps Tactical Zone, *The Dak Seang Campaign: 1 April–8
May 1970,* 96, Records of the Military Assistance Command, Part 1:
The War in Vietnam, 1954–1973, box 44, folder 7, Sam Johnson
Vietnam Archive Collection, Vietnam Center and Archive, Texas Tech
University, Lubbock, TX, www.vietnam.ttu.edu/reports/images.php
?img=/images/F0158/F015800440007b.pdf.

138 **"pigs running."** Beatles, "I Am the Walrus," by John Lennon, *Magical
Mystery Tour,* copyright © November 27, 1967, Capitol Records.

Chapter 13: The Breaking Point

153 **"Kent State University."** Noah Adams, "Shots Still Reverberate for
Survivors of Kent State," NPR, May 3, 2010, www.npr.org/templates
/story/story.php?storyId=126423778.

153 **"students across the country."** Zoe Altaras, "The May 1970 Student Strike at UW," University of Washington, http://depts.washington.edu /antiwar/may1970strike.shtml.

158 **"jazz festival."** "Newport Jazz Festival: 1971," Rhode Island Rocks, http://rirocks.net/Band%20Articles/Newport%20Jazz%20Festival%20 1971.htm.

161 **"one entry."** Gary Beikirch, journal entry, used by permission.

Chapter 14: Blaze of Light

168 **"Children of God."** "Children of God/The Family," Cult Education Institute, www.culteducation.com/group/918-children-of-god-the-family .html.

168 **"L. Ron Hubbard."** John Weldon, "Scientology," CRI, June 10, 2009, www.equip.org/article/scientology.

172 **"quiet desperation."** Henry David Thoreau, *Walden* (London: George Routledge & Sons, 1904), 30.

173 **"described a man."** Jesus overturned tables (Matthew 21:12), gave nicknames (Mark 3:16–17), and insulted the dinner host (Luke 11:37–52).

174 **"words of the book."** John 14:1, 5–6.

174 **"reading the next."** John 15:13–14, 16.

Chapter 15: Trailhead

177 **"Trailhead."** Specific thanks to poet and fisherman Roger Chamberlin for conversations surrounding the imagery of a trailhead as an invitation into an adventure of the heart, the trail less traveled.

179 **"road patrol team."** "Millie and George: They Believe in Togetherness— Even in a Patrol Car," *Sheriff's Star* 13, no. 11 (January 1970): 6–7, www.flsheriffs.org/uploads/star/THE_SHERIFFS_STAR_VOL_13, _NO_11,_JANUARY_1970.pdf.

187 **"warning signs."** Gary recalled snippets of these two signs from when he lived in the cave. See Philip Werner, "Trail Signs," SectionHiker, https://sectionhiker.com/trail-signs; Nestor Ramos, "The Young Woman and the Mountain," *Boston Globe,* February 22, 2015, www.bostonglobe.com/metro/2015/02/21/the-young-woman-and-mountain/SEBPuca GpA1Fun4R5uoj7K/story.html.

188 **"heard something."** See Ezekiel 1:22–28.

188 **"I know the plans."** Jeremiah 29:11, 13.

188 *"Come and see."* Psalm 66:5; Isaiah 66:18; John 1:46.

Chapter 16: The Cave

196 **"within nature."** See Romans 1:20.

196 **"still small voice."** See 1 Kings 19:11–13, KJV.

199 **"number of recipients."** As of June 25, 2019, during this book's creation, there are 3,524 US service members who have been awarded the Medal of Honor. As of July 2019 there are seventy-one living Medal of Honor recipients. "Medal of Honor," Medal of Honor Historical Society of the United States, www.mohhsus.com/medal-of-honor.

200 **"service personnel from Vietnam."** Only 262 Medals of Honor were awarded for service during the Vietnam War. By comparison, 472 were awarded during World War II, and 1,523 were awarded during the Civil War. "Medal of Honor," Medal of Honor Historical Society of the United States, www.mohhsus.com/medal-of-honor.

Chapter 17: The Medal

201 **"When anxiety."** Psalm 94:19.

203 **"Eight other military personnel."** "Medal of Honor Recipients: Vietnam War," US Army Center of Military History, https://history.army.mil/html/moh/vietnam-a-l.html.

    Gary Littrell: see note 3 of chapter 11.

Michael Fitzmaurice: During a firefight on March 23, 1971, in Khe Sanh, Fitzmaurice smothered the blast of an enemy-thrown explosive charge with his flak vest and body to protect other soldiers. Seriously wounded and partially blinded by the blast, he then continued to fight. After his rifle was damaged by a second explosive blast, Fitzmaurice acquired another rifle from an enemy sapper—defeating him with his bare hands—and continued to fight, refusing medical evacuation. https://history.army.mil/html/moh/vietnam-a-l.html#FITZ MAURICE.

Leo Thorsness: During a mission on April 19, 1967, as pilot of an F-105 aircraft and despite being low on fuel, he returned alone through hostile airspace to defend a downed crew. https://history.army.mil/html /moh/vietnam-m-z.html#THORSNESS.

Michael Thornton: On October 31, 1972, Thornton and his patrol came under heavy fire and engaged the enemy in a fierce firefight. The senior adviser was hit and believed to be dead. Thornton ran through the bullets to the lieutenant's last position, quickly disposed of two enemy soldiers, and carried the seriously wounded and unconscious officer to the water's edge. He inflated the lieutenant's life jacket and towed him out to sea. They were picked up two hours later by support craft. https:// history.army.mil/html/moh/vietnam-m-z.html#THORNTON.

Allan Kellogg: On March 11, 1970, under Kellogg's leadership, a small unit was evacuating a fallen comrade when they came under heavy fire in the jungle. During the ensuing firefight, an enemy soldier crept through the dense foliage and hurled a hand grenade into the marines' midst, which glanced off Kellogg's chest. He stomped the grenade into the mud, threw himself on top, and absorbed the blast. He suffered multiple wounds to his chest, right shoulder, and arm, yet he continued to direct the efforts of his men until all could reach safety. https:// history.army.mil/html/moh/vietnam-a-l.html#KELLOGG.

Kenneth Michael Kays: Kays was a medical aidman. On May 7, 1970, a heavily armed enemy force attacked at nighttime, wounding and killing a number of American soldiers. Under fire, Kays moved to assist his fallen comrades but was targeted, and an explosive charge severed the lower portion of his left leg. He applied a tourniquet to himself, then kept helping other wounded soldiers, administering aid and helping move them to safety. https://history.army.mil/html/moh/vietnam-a-l .html#KAYS.

James Leroy Bondsteel: On May 24, 1969, near the village of Lang Sau, platoon sergeant Bondsteel organized his men into combat teams and spearheaded an attack by destroying four enemy-occupied bunkers. He then raced under heavy enemy fire to reach an adjoining platoon that had begun to falter. After rallying this unit and assisting their wounded, he returned to his own sector with critically needed munitions. He moved to the forefront and destroyed four enemy-occupied bunkers and a machine gun that had threatened his advancing platoon. Although wounded by an enemy grenade, Bondsteel refused medical attention and continued his assault by neutralizing two more enemy bunkers. Shortly thereafter, he ran to the aid of a severely wounded officer and struck down an enemy soldier who threatened the officer's life. Bondsteel then continued to rally his men and led them through the entrenched enemy until his company was relieved. All told, he destroyed ten enemy bunkers and accounted for a large toll of the enemy, including two key enemy commanders. https://history.army .mil/html/moh/vietnam-a-l.html#BONDSTEEL.

Brian Thacker: On March 31, 1971, he was serving as a first lieutenant in Battery A of the First Battalion, Ninety-Second Field Artillery Regiment. On that day Thacker's base in Kontum Province was attacked by North Vietnamese Army forces. He assisted in the defense of the base, and when evacuation became necessary, he stayed behind to cover the retreat. Trapped behind enemy lines, Thacker was able to evade capture until being rescued by friendly forces eight days later. https://history.army.mil/html/moh/vietnam-m-z.html#THACKER.

205 **"Watergate Hotel."** "Watergate Scandal," United Press International, 1973, www.upi.com/Archives/Audio/Events-of-1973/Watergate-Scandal.

205 **"president's impeachment."** "In 1974, President Richard Nixon resigned in the wake of a scandal when it was obvious that public opinion no longer supported him." Steffen W. Schmidt et al., *American Government and Politics Today* (Boston: Wadsworth, 2014), 181.

206 **"newspaper in Rochester."** Bob Minzesheimer, "From Medic to Medal to Missionary," *Democrat and Chronicle* (Rochester, NY), October 15, 1973.

210 **"Madison Spring Hut."** "Madison Springs Hut—4,800'," Hike the Whites, http://hikethewhites.com/mad_hut.html.

Chapter 18: Lolly's Rescue

215 **"Episcopal church."** St. Paul's Episcopal Church of Lancaster, New Hampshire, has maintained their open-door policy. See "Home," St. Paul's Episcopal Church, www.stpaulslancaster.org.

215 **"old life."** See 2 Corinthians 5:17.

Chapter 19: "Wear It for Us"

219 **"Charles 'Mac' MacGillivary."** "Charles A. MacGillivary; Medal of Honor Winner," *Los Angeles Times,* July 3, 2000, http://articles.latimes.com/2000/jul/03/local/me-47333.

221 **"Lolly put on a brave face."** See 1 Corinthians 13:4.

221 **"PTSD."** Gary notes that during the 1970s and early '80s, veterans such as himself who were dealing with the trauma of war had fewer resources to help than are available today. Evident among the veteran community were increased suicide and divorce rates, alcohol and drug

use, encounters with the law, depression, paranoia, schizophrenia, and loss of impulse control. Dr. John Wilson from Cleveland State University and Dr. Jack Smith from Duke University believe that there is something inherent in war that affects individuals physically, psychologically, emotionally, behaviorally, and interpersonally. These effects are natural and not attributable to mental illness. Dr. Wilson was commissioned by the Disabled American Veterans organization to conduct a study to examine his beliefs. It was entitled *Forgotten Warrior Project* and resulted in a new understanding of what used to be called "shell shock" (World War I) or "combat fatigue" (World War II). It also gives veterans encouragement and hope that there is a way to heal.

222 **"Dr. Jeremiah 'Jerry' Donigian."** See a summary of Dr. Donigian's philosophy of therapy at Jeremiah Donigian, "Group Process," 1996, World of Education Library, www.library.educationworld.net/a3/a3-35.html.

225 **"fifty-two Americans."** "Iran Hostage Crisis Ends," History.com, A&E Television Networks, November 24, 2009, www.history.com/this-day-in-history/iran-hostage-crisis-ends.

225 **"citizens of Rochester."** Jim Redmond, "Vietnam Veterans Honored at Rally," *Democrat and Chronicle* (Rochester, NY), January 1981.

226 **"three hundred people."** Also in the crowd that day were members of a group called Young Vietnamese for Freedom, who still wanted to see their homeland freed from the Communists. Redmond, "Vietnam Veterans."

Chapter 20: For His Honor

227 **"first Medal of Honor Recipient."** Denis Gray, "First Medal of Honor Winner Returns to Vietnam," Associated Press, June 1982.

228 **"boat people crisis."** Some seven hundred thousand to eight hundred thousand Vietnamese fled their country by boat between 1975 and 1997. W. Courtland Robinson, *Terms of Refuge: The Indochinese Exodus and*

the International Response (London: Zed Books, 1998), 193. See also appendixes 1–2.

229 **"settled in North Carolina."** Rebecca Onion, "The Snake-Eaters and the Yards," *Slate,* November 27, 2013, https://slate.com/news-and -politics/2013/11/the-green-berets-and-the-montagnards-how-an -indigenous-tribe-won-the-admiration-of-green-berets-and-lost -everything.html.

229 **"Montagnards who remained."** Dan Southerland, "An Update on the Montagnards of Vietnam's Central Highlands," Radio Free Asia, October 23, 2018, www.rfa.org/english/commentaries/vietnam -montagnards-10232018155849.html. See the organization Save the Montagnard People, Inc., a North Carolina–based nonprofit that seeks to help the Montagnards today, www.montagnards.org. See also the Council of Indigenous Peoples in Today's Vietnam for initiatives that seek to preserve the rights of indigenous people in Vietnam, http:// ciptvn.org. See also the Montagnard Human Rights Organization (MHRO), which seeks to defend human rights in the Central High- lands of Vietnam, www.mhro.org. For concise yet detailed information on atrocities that happened to the Montagnards after the war, see Rong Nay, "Summary of Montagnard History," MHRO, www.mhro.org /montangards-history.

229 **"missing in action."** Jack Jones, "Vietnam Vet, Back from Hanoi, Says Trip 'Definitely Meaningful,'" *Democrat and Chronicle* (Rochester, NY), June 6, 1982.

230 **"dance started."** Denis Gray, "'I Have to Forgive, Even If It Is Hard,'" *Democrat and Chronicle,* June 20, 1982.

231 **"Mike Wallace watched."** Observed by Gary Beikirch.

About the Author

Marcus Brotherton is a *New York Times* best-selling author and collaborative writer known for his books with high-profile public figures, humanitarians, inspirational leaders, and military personnel. Among his honors is the Christopher Award, given for literature that "affirms the highest values of the human spirit."

His books include the widely acclaimed *Shifty's War, We Who Are Alive and Remain, A Company of Heroes,* and *Feast for Thieves,* which received the Christy Award for writing excellence.

Coauthored and collaborative works include books with the elite World War II paratroopers featured in HBO's *Band of Brothers* miniseries, the elite World War II marines featured in HBO's *The Pacific,* and Oscar®-nominated actor turned advocate Gary "Lieutenant Dan" Sinise.

Born in British Columbia, Marcus earned a bachelor's degree from Multnomah University in Portland, Oregon, and a master's degree from Biola University in Los Angeles, where he graduated with high honors. He lives with his wife and their three children in Bellingham, Washington.

———

MarcusBrotherton.com